Essential Strategy & Enterprise Architecture

Strategy and Enterprise Architecture for business-aligned, SOA-based IT solution developed through different phases of Preliminaries & Foundation, Business Architecture, Information System Architecture, Application & Data Architecture, Platform & Technology Architecture

- **Haloedscape Haves**
- **(Haloedscape Publication - HBS)**

Colophon

Title: Essential Strategy and Enterprise Architecture

Description: The book presents the strategy, enterprise architecture, business architecture, application architecture and platform architecture to acquire business-aligned, agile, SOA-based IT solution in order to enable business services, illustrated with investment banking business domain.

Author: Neeraj Singh

Technical Coordinator: Rashmi Singh

Series: Haloedscape Series

Host: Haves Group, Haloedscape Business Services (HBS), Harappanet

Book Presenter: Author, host, publisher and other entities involved in preparing and publishing this book

Copyright: Author

Website: www.harappanet.com

No liability is assumed for incidental or consequential damages arising out of use of the concepts or information contained herein.

Dedicated to dignity of Sun; & his grace Saurya;

For any further enquiries about the book and content, contact HAVES services group of HBS at: haves<A~T>harappanet.com

Contents

Preface

This is a unique publication of its kind about imperative, focused enterprise architecture aligned with strategy.

In this book, architectural design is modeled as SOA in an integrated holistic manner for each phase of architecture, wherein services are improved with optimal capabilities to increase the ability and business value of functional services.

The book presents strategy, business architecture, information system, application architecture, platform architecture and technology architecture to be applied to any business domain function.

First chapter starts with Strategy, which acts as tool to overcome the increasing challenges faced by business and IT. Strategy is governed across every layer of architecture to accomplish SOA based service possessing strategic capabilities.

Business Strategy plans the business to achieve strategic alignment, desired growth, synergy realization and competitive advantage under all circumstances at minimal cost.

Based on business strategy, IT Strategy evolves which leads to IT Foundation composed of IT Capability Model and IT Operating Model.

Enterprise architecture vision and approach to solution are also presented for each phase of enterprise architecture development.

Second chapter presents development of Business Architecture, which elaborates the business illustrated with Frameworks, Business Motivation Model, Organizational Structure, Value-added Chain, Key Performance Indicators, Key Risk Indicators,

Strategy and Tactics, Business Scenarios, Business Process Model, Business Services, Use Cases, Capability Models and Business Services.

Capability based planning approach supported with alignment framework applies SOA to transform business functionalities into business services supported with capabilities.

Business architecture includes the domain functionalities modeled as SOA based service aligned with strategy. The business architecture built as SOA based consolidated business services are directly mapped into IT services for business-aligned, agile and effective IT solution.

Third chapter deals with development of Information System, Data and Application Architecture. Information system consolidates the core functional and data services, which acts as development and execution environment for enterprise wide applications.

Applications architecture is elaborated with service inventory, use-cases, classes, activity and components diagrams. Data management, workflow automation, security and availability, real-time events based computation are elaborated.

The business driven IT supported with framework achieves business aligned IT where business services and capabilities are transformed into IT services.

Fourth chapter presents the Platform and Technology Architecture. Platform empowered with required technology executing applications are elaborated with respect to distributed computing, service platform, workflow automation, session and transaction services, enterprise integration, service bus, data management, security & availability etc.

Applications are supported by distributed computing platform possessing events based object/message oriented middleware. Overall system architecture is illustrated for consolidated view of system components like client, server, protocols, data and services.

Information system and applications are supported with right platform possessing required technology, so that IT solution acquires the enterprise characteristics and strategic capabilities.

Key advantages of enterprise architecture and high-end standard automation presented in this book are as follows:

- Strategy based architecture-design leading to enterprise architecture possessing strategic capabilities.
- Enterprise architecture based business-aligned IT to maximize ROI while reducing the costs and overall risks.
- SOA based agile IT which easily adapts the changes of market conditions and customer requirements with fast Time-to-Market (TTM). SOA applied to each phase of architecture development.
- Business services and capabilities transformed into IT services leading to business aligned IT.
- Capability based planning approach where change activities can be sequenced and grouped in order to provide continuous and incremental business value.
- IT capability and operating model plans enterprise architecture development, service management and governance.
- Effective and efficient solution helps achieve competitive advantage with standardization, optimization and integration. Getting rid of non-standard practice, like using Excel for analysis and valuations.
- Information system consolidates data and functional services fulfilling strategic requirements and delivers these

services to each business-unit application. In our approach, information system automates governance in applications.

- Automated STP workflow integrates the crucial event like deal execution with remote modules like performance, risks and post-execution functionalities.
- Innovative and sophisticated platform enabling the business objectives with event based object/message oriented middleware.
- Integration of functionalities at various levels like data integration, process integration, service integration and application integration.
- and many others ...

To illustrate the enterprise architecture & strategy with examples, we use investment banking business functions, like Private Equity, Venture Capital, Mergers and Acquisitions (M&A) etc, wherever examples of business functions are required.

The technical and functional professionals will benefit a great lot about enterprise architecture based automation that fulfills the enterprise need and possesses the strategic capabilities.

Chapter 1: Strategy and Foundation of Enterprise Architecture

Acronyms & Definitions used in this chapter:

Acquisitions: The purchase of one firm by another firm, where voting shares of the target firm's stock is acquired, without negotiation necessarily taking place.

Artifacts: The Artifacts are high level logical diagram for a module/case-study etc. used in order to conceptualize the Enterprise Architecture (EA) planning. It is similar to core diagram except not being so intensive and comprehensive.

Architecture: It is a framework and set of guidelines to build systems which includes the overall design of a computing system and the logical and physical interrelationships between its components. The architecture specifies the hardware, software, access-methods and protocols used throughout the system.

Business Capability: An effective ability to execute a specified course of action to achieve specific strategic goals and objectives.

Business Function: Represents the business behavior associated with an organization unit.

Business Service: Represents an external view of the services, an organization provides or sells to its customers to achieve business objective. Technically, business service encompasses and uses business capabilities to enable business functionality; and is transformed into and realized by IT service.

CBP – Capability based Planning: It is referred as a methodology of enterprise architecture to accomplish structured operating model for mission critical business services to improve the ability and business values effectively under any adverse circumstances.

Core diagrams: High level logical diagram for a model/process etc. used in order to conceptualize the Strategy and EA. Core diagram acts as a guide to decide upon Strategy and IT Foundation.

Enterprise: The highest level of description of an organization that typically covers all of its missions and functions.

EA - Enterprise Architecture: The organizing logic of key business process with tightly aligned, consolidated IT for whole enterprise to execute strategy. EA, as per Gartner's definition, is the process of translating business vision and strategy into effective enterprise change by creating, communicating and improving the key requirements, principles and models that describe the enterprise's future state and enable its evolution

Framework: A tool that models and simplifies the specific process of interest.

IT-OM - IT Operating Model: Abstract representation of how business functions, IT process, IT platform and architecture combine together to deliver predefined business results.

Service: A logical representation of a repeatable business activity that has a specified outcome. A service is self-contained logical unit, may be composed of other services, and is generally a "black box" to its consumers.

SOA: Service Oriented Architecture- Most sophisticated, advanced modular concept of components designed with service oriented principles in order to achieve optimal, business-aligned, agile and effective IT for the sake of reusability, flexibility, high-quality and costs-saving.

H_EA: Enterprise Architecture (IT) wing of Haloedscape.

One of the supporting & enabling functions of an imaginary investment bank "Haloedscape" is Enterprise Architecture of IT. Haloedscape has a separate wing denoted as H_EA for providing enterprise-architecture based automation aligned with strategy.

Sophisticated strategy and enterprise-architecture strives to deliver high quality, enterprise-wide, agile automation for long term. In this chapter, we will develop "Strategy & Solution Approach" in such a way that leads to foundation of Enterprise Architecture.

1.1   Executive Summary

The "Executive Summary" mentioned here is specific to H_EA of our imaginary bank Haloedscape developing strategy and enterprise architecture in order to:

1) Improving business plans and actions to outsmart competition, increasing business profit and sustaining business growth on medium and long term, and

2) Acquiring high performance, effective automation of business functions, which maximizes the ROI and enables the strategic business objectives.

Haloedscape's (H_EA) Vision & Mission:

Strategic Vision:** **To deliver the excellent IT services to clients with optimized and sophisticated solutions executed on world-leading platforms & technology which outsmarts competition and helps us provide most competitive & innovative investment banking services in the world.

Objective statements of IT Strategy: ***Assuring an open-standard, capable, efficient, secured and business-driven IT Architecture leading to effective IT which helps maximize the ROI.***

Business Strategy is most important specification of corporate strategy which deals with long term business planning to achieve the desired profit, growth and competitive advantage under all circumstances at minimal cost.

Abilities and values of business services are enhanced with capability based planning. Business capability is an effective ability possessed by business-units to execute a specified course of action to achieve specific strategic objectives and goals. Business capability model is capability based planning which generally measures the objectives and maturity level of business and is therefore bound directly to business enablement and strategy.

Business function delivers business capabilities closely aligned to an organization. Business service encompasses business capabilities to realize business function and support business objectives. Business services and capabilities are transformed into and realized by IT service.

Business strategy and corresponding tactics specify the rules and guidelines which gives direction for business planning, operation and development.

There is a need of developing the IT Strategy so that business could be executed in a world-class advanced environment with maximum success keeping the costs and risks under control.

The strategy we undertake at startup is focused-strategy so that most of strategic benefits could be achieved at minimal costs. The focused strategy directs us to consider and apply the strategic steps only to core business processes to keep it practical, accountable, focused and result-oriented.

IT Strategy is an actionable plan to achieve an agile, business-aligned, effective, automated solution which enables business objectives with maximum ROI on medium and long run. Approach and principles of IT strategy are guide to design the business solution which encompasses the business strategy and strategic IT foundation composed of IT capability and operating model.

IT Capabilities specify how H_EA delivers IT services and value to the business so that capability based planning of business strategy could be realized. IT Capabilities Model includes Structured Operating Model (SOM), Service Oriented Architecture (SOA) and Service Oriented Infrastructure (SOI).

The goals of IT Operating Model (IT-OM) are to focus on core capabilities, derive the architecture & infrastructure, guide the business process and corresponding information system, select the appropriate IT systems and justify IT investment decision. IT-Operating model is developed and managed under an integrated collection of frameworks – Enterprise Architecture Development; IT-Service Management; and Governance; which guides and directs the development of strategic enterprise architecture enabling our business objectives with highest ROI.

IT governance process enforces a direct link of IT resources & process to enterprise goals in line of strategy. There is a strong correlation between maturity curve of IT governance and overall effectiveness of IT. The IT Control's framework for governance by COBIT is integrated with enterprise architecture.

Enterprise Architecture is an optimal IT Architecture for whole enterprise where strategic requirements and principles are fulfilled to acquire business driven capabilities and enable the business objective.

Our Enterprise Architecture developed in the book is an innovation based extended instance of TOGAF, COBIT and ITIL. We primarily use "The Open Group" product, TOGAF 9 framework to develop Enterprise Architecture. TOGAF allows other standard frameworks like COBIT and ITIL to be adopted, integrated or extended with it. COBIT as IT Management and Governance framework is used to control the IT alignment with business and performance of IT solution. As IT service Management (ITSM) tool, we use ITIL v3 that focusses on service management and aligning IT services with business functions.

Key Initiatives to achieve effective IT:
- Develop right business strategy which is adapted into IT strategy.

- Identify and specify the core capabilities incorporated into capabilities model.
- Improve and structure functionalities, process, data & platform to specify operating model.
- Develop IT foundation consisting of core IT capabilities and operating model, which could execute strategy.
- Build capability based information system with SOA approach which could fulfill strategic requirements and realize its objectives.
- Information system should govern strategy to applications through governance framework.

Key challenges in realizing IT Strategy:
- Delay in initiating strategy and growing on maturity curve
- Diversified / Isolated business units without enterprise-architectural concerns
- Lack of strategic governance at each business unit
- Lack of direction and skilled workforce for understanding and realization of strategy

The objective of IT Strategy is to ensure that IT provides an open and secure exchange of information, consistent with technical architecture and standards, reduces risks & costs and directly contributes to mission success.

Right business strategy is all about improving the plans, actions and directions to gain competitive advantage and sustainability of business growth on medium and long run.

Right IT strategy ensures high performance, sophisticated IT solution which enables business objective on medium and long run ensuring maximum ROI keeping risks and costs under control.

By stating all these, we will conceptualize, formulate and develop strategy which leads to improved business plan and enterprise architecture to acquire business-aligned, agile, effective IT solution to overcome the challenges of business and IT.

1.2 Overview and Approach of Enterprise Architecture

An architecture framework is a foundation structure which helps develop enterprise architecture of IT solution for broad range of different business domains.

IT is made aligned to enterprise-wide business requirements and processes with the help of SOA based enterprise architecture. TOGAF Frameworks help us achieve this.

The Architecture Development Method (ADM) is core of TOGAF which describes a method for developing and managing the lifecycle of enterprise architecture. The first phase of ADM is preliminary phase which provides the foundation to develop target enterprise structure.

Preliminary Phase

Preliminary Phase (PP) is about defining "where, what, why, who, and how we do architecture" in the enterprise. PP is to analyze and determine the architecture capability.

In this phase, we analyze the high level business requirements, strategic requirements of automation, approach of solution, and initial vision of architecture.

Business strategy and IT strategy are used as essential inputs for enterprise architecture.

Business strategy, tactics, rules, plans, business capabilities, principles are finalized. IT strategy containing capability model, operating model, SOA adoption, governance and approach to solutions are elaborated.

At last, an initial artifact for selection of methods, tools, frameworks are made, vision of architecture is modeled, and roadmap for strategic enterprise architecture is initialized.

Management Framework

There are four key management frameworks taken under considerations.

- **Business Capability Management** - what business capabilities are required to deliver business value
- **Portfolio/Project Management Methods** - how a company manages its change initiatives.
- **Operations Management Methods** - how a company runs its day-to-day operations
- **Solution Development Methods** - how business systems are delivered in accordance IT

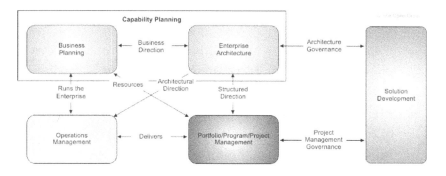

Figure 1.1: Copyright © The Open Group, TOGAF® 9.1, Management Frameworks

The management frameworks of TOGAF complement each other.

- Business planning provides initial direction to EA.

- Solution development (*develops the components*) is used within the Portfolio Management Framework to create the architectural component specified.
- Project management (*delivers the components*) receives the direction to build required.
- Operation management (*incorporates the components*) receives the deliverable and integrates them with the corporate infrastructure.

Capability Planning

Capability is matured, value-added, process-based abilities to achieve specific target in efficient and effective manner. Capability is driven from business requirements where core business service is modeled as capability in order to acquire the maturity and improved values. Capability-based planning helps acquire strategic business capabilities.

IT capabilities are matured IT services supported by sophisticated platform to enable the business service. *Refer IT Capability in later section.* Capabilities help ensure following:

- Capability-based planning focuses on planning, engineering, and delivery of strategic business capabilities to the enterprise.
- Frames all phase of architecture development in business outcomes context. It links IT vision, architectures, and implementation & migration plans with corporate business plans
- Ensures business plan drives the enterprise from a top-down approach, while adaptable to leverage bottom-up innovations.

Architecture Vision

The preliminary phase of TOGAF leads to vision of architecture. Architecture vision describes how the new capability will meet the business goals and strategic objectives.

Objectives of architecture vision are to:

- Develop a high-level aspirational vision of capabilities and business value to be delivered by the EA
- Ensure proper endorsement from corporate, and support from line management
- Obtain approval from stakeholders for building the further phases of enterprise architecture.

TOGAF and SOA

Enterprise architecture is overall construction of the enterprise, whereas SOA is a particular construction technique that can be used to build enterprise IT.

SOA delivers enterprise agility. With SOA, the IT systems perform services that are defined and described in the context of the enterprise's business activities. SOA is implemented as modular services having interface definition and contracts, achieving enterprise agility and interoperability.

The starting point for SOA development with TOGAF is that the enterprise adopts service-orientation as an architecture principle, and is in position to acquire in future the required resources and infrastructure to deliver SOA based services.

1.3 SOA Approach

A Service-Oriented Architecture (SOA) facilitates the creation of flexible, re-usable assets for enabling end-to-end business solutions. With SOA, the automation of enterprise architecture is realized as a set of software services facilitated by service platform.

Essence of SOA guides that the enterprise level data and functionalities are made available as service to be used across whole enterprise. Individual department of an enterprise accesses these enterprise services and use choreography/orchestration to develop the application (business process) for their need. Services orchestration/choreography shows how a business process can be implemented using discrete services. Orchestration refers to the central control of the behavior of a distributed system, while choreography refers to a distributed system which operates according to rules but without centralized control. The primary difference between orchestration and choreography is executability and control. An orchestration specifies an executable process that involves message exchanges with other systems, such that the message exchange sequences are controlled by the orchestration designer. Choreography specifies a protocol for peer-to-peer interactions, wherein protocol is not directly executable, as it allows many different realizations. Choreography can be realized by writing an orchestration for each peer involved in it.

SOA solution as proposed by OMG, for an enterprise business is depicted as a meta-model in form of a set of logical layers. OMG based SOA layer architecture has five separated horizontal layers for business computation; and four vertical layers for transforming the system into strategic enterprise system. The vertical layers are embedded into each of horizontal layers to transform our computational system into enterprise based strategic system.

SOA modeling is holistic modeling approach where business processes are represented by data/functions services enabled by IT services, wherein each service features the requirements of governance, information, QoS & Integration; improves abilities in terms of business and technical capabilities; and consolidates the whole enterprise supported with SOA horizontal layers to form enterprise architecture aligned with strategy.

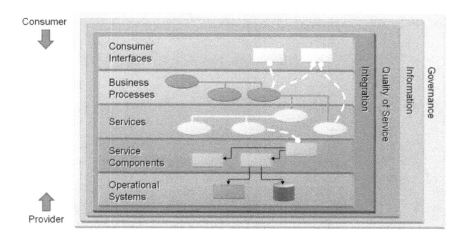

Figure 1.2: © OMG, SOA Logical Layers Architecture

Vertical Layers: Governance, Information, QoS, Integration

Governance Layer

IT governance process enforces a direct link of IT resources and processes to enterprise goals in line of strategy. Strong IT governance with clear delineation of decision rights across business leads to high performance and effective IT. IT Governance includes process governance, computational governance and technology governance. *Refer IT Governance in later section.*

SOA governance ensures that the services and SOA solutions within an organization are adhering to the defined policies, guidelines, and standards that are defined as a function of the objectives, strategies, and regulations applied in the organization and that the SOA solutions are providing the desired business value. The Governance Layer includes both SOA governance (governance of processes for policy definition, management, and enforcement) as well as service governance (service lifecycle).

The value of this layer is to ensure that the mechanisms are in place to organize, define, monitor, and implement governance from an enterprise architecture and solution architecture view.

Governance layer ideally governs the business and IT strategy across each layer of SOA solution. Governance includes-

- SOA governance which ensures business/IT policy management and enforcement

- Service governance which ensures the fulfillment of service design principles and service life-cycles.

- SLAs, OLAs, capabilities, performance, security and monitoring are also covered as strategic principles which are enforced with governance.

In our approach, the enterprise governance must be transited into each elements of operating model. The decisions taken for functionalities and processes must be available at information system, which are automatically transited into individual applications. All services of Information System fulfill the requirements of business principles, tactics, rules and IT strategy. Applications of enterprise are built only with information system services, which is the only gateway for application to enterprise resources like data, functions, platforms, servers etc. The data and functional services are governed with strategic principles and policies.

Information Layer

The Information Layer provides ability to integrate information across the enterprise in order to enable information services capability. A shared, common and consistent expression of data and functionalities across enterprise makes the services interoperable and natively integrated.

The Information Layer is responsible for manifesting a unified representation of the information aspect of an organization as provided by its IT services, applications, and systems enabling business needs and processes. It also supports the ability for an information services capability, enabling a virtualized information data layer capability. This enables the SOA to support data consistency and high data quality.

Information maturity is accomplished with following:

- Information System
- Data Models
- Information Management

Information system is constituted of enterprise service inventory. Data-models are evolved from SOA modeling, and are business driven. Information management is achieved with logical unification, singularity and centralization supported by enterprise repository fulfilling the data principles.

In particular, an information virtualization and information service capability typically involves the ability to retrieve data from different sources, transform it into a common format, and expose it to consumers using different protocols and formats.

QoS Layer

QoS layer features the capabilities that include command and control management, security management, IT system management, SOA management, business activity management, event management, policy enforcement, configuration and change management. The key responsibilities of the Quality of Service Layer include:

- Managing at the business level in terms of Key Performance Indicators (KPIs), events, and business activities in the business processes, and at the IT systems level for the security, health, and well-being of IT systems, services, applications, networks, storage, and compute servers

- Monitoring and enforcement of a multitude of policies and corresponding business rules including business-level policies, security policies, access privileges, data-access policies, etc.

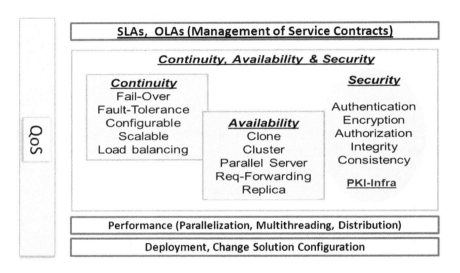

Figure 1.3: © HBS, Applied SOA - QoS

QoS layer provides solution for various issues like efficiency, availability, reliability, security, performance, recovery etc. QoS management is mechanisms to support, track, monitor and manage QoS control.

- QoS manages and monitors the security of IT systems. It manages the roles and identities, access rights and privileges, data protection, encrypted communications,
- QoS provides monitoring and management of services and applications.
- Event management is required under SOA which provides the ability to manage events and associated processing in real-time to keep the service agile.

- QoS ensures policy monitoring and enforcement to upkeep business-level policies, security policies, access privileges, and data access policies.
- QoS provides a framework of change solution configuration.

In SOA Solution, every service has its policy which is configured to provide required service level agreements. QoS are supported as service level policy at the enterprise system level, and department specific applications.

Integration Layer

The Integration Layer addresses the issues and provides the capabilities to integrate the protocols, financial product, data-models, services, business process and application. The Integration Layer is a key enabler for an SOA as it provides the capability to mediate which includes transformation, routing, and protocol conversion to transport service requests from the service requester to the correct service provider.

The integration layer provides a level of indirection between the consumer of functionality and its provider. A service consumer interacts with the service provider via the Integration Layer. Service integration across systems is achieved with Enterprise Service Bus (ESB). ESB mediates between service provider and consumer to avoid the point-to-point integration. Consumers and providers are decoupled; this decoupling allows integration of disparate systems into new solutions. This means, each service is exposed via ESB to be invoked by consumer. ESB acts as broker to provide central point of service access. It also decouples the provider and consumer handling the service request and service response. Technically, ESB supports variety of protocols to serve any type of service. ESB is bundled together with message queue to support the messaging methods of one-way, pubs/subs, request-response etc. To accomplish ESB, one needs unification of protocol formats like RMI/IIOP, SOAP/HTTP, SOAP/Queues, SOAP/JMS so that it could strategically be able to mediate & support services of any systems.

To access the remote distributed objects of one system, one needs the support of required protocol and object reference service. Data models of integrable systems should be interoperable so that optimal and effective computation can be guaranteed.

The business application in form of choreographed service could directly be accessed and integrated between different systems.

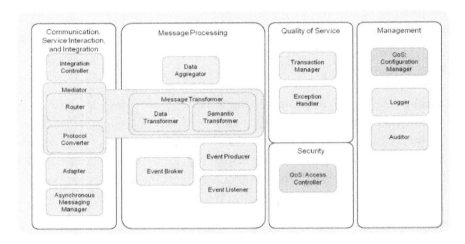

Figure 1.4: © OMG, Structural Architecture of Integration Layer

There are multiple set of categories of capabilities that the Integration Layer supports. These categories are:

- Communication, Service Interaction, and Integration: This category of capabilities provides the ability to route requests to correct the provider after necessary message transformation and protocol conversion and to connect the service requestor to the service provider and its underlying solutions platforms realizing the requested service. It also provides the ability to discover services and, at runtime, to support the virtualization of services so that changes to the end-points (or locations from where the services are called and where the services are provided) can occur without impact to service consumers and service providers.

- Message Processing: This category of capabilities provides the ability to perform the necessary message transformation to connect the service requestor to the service provider and to publish and subscribe messages and events asynchronously.
- Quality of Service: This category of capabilities supports handling of transactions and exceptions and other NFRs.
- Security: This category of capabilities helps in enforcement of access privileges and other security policies.
- Management: This category of capabilities provides the ability to maintain service invocation history and monitor and track the service invocations.

The Integration Layer relies on other cross-cutting layers of the architecture to fulfill its responsibilities. The integration layer interacts with Governance layer to access service registry, service repository, event manager and business rules manager. It relies on the Quality of Service Layer to authenticate/authorize for service invocation and messages.

Horizontal Layers: Operational Systems, Service Components, Service, Business Process, Consumer

Operational Systems Layer

This layer contains and consolidates the runtime and deployment infrastructure like technologies, application servers, runtime environment like virtual machines etc.

The Operational Systems Layer includes –
- All software and hardware necessary to support the SOA components at runtime and design time.
- All operational and runtime hosting of underlying physical system components in form of cloud, cluster, clones etc.

The services for all assets required to support the functionality of services in the SOA.

There are multiple categories of capabilities that the Operational Systems Layer needs to support. Different categories of capabilities are:

- **Service Delivery**: This is required for delivery of the functional elements of services. This includes the finding of the components implementing the services, the wrapping and the composition/ decomposition of the underlying services, and the implementation of the services.

- **Runtime Environment**: This is required for providing a runtime environment representing runtime infrastructure for SOA. This includes capabilities to support both the components required to support service functionality and those required to actually run the components and building blocks of the SOA itself. This includes hardware, operating system components and the solution building blocks, which are the runtime instances or realizations of all layers in the SOA.

- **Virtualization and Infrastructure Services**: This provides underlying infrastructure such as computing power, network, storage, etc. in native or a virtualized manner.

Thus this layer provides the building blocks supporting the operational systems which implement the functional capabilities of the other horizontal layers and the supporting/cross-cutting layers. This layer represents the intersection point between the actual runtime infrastructure and the rest of the SOA which runs on that infrastructure.

Software platform like message and object oriented middleware provides technical services to upper layers. Technical services are provided by the technological platform physically residing at this layer.

At bottom of this layer is the infrastructure layer which is optimally and effectively used with services like cloud, cluster, cloning etc.

This layer possesses all the basic platforms to compute the SOA based application. It includes events framework, messaging platform, service platform, object & message oriented middleware, application servers and cloud based virtualized infrastructure for secured, optimal, and effective computing.

Service Components Layer

Services components layer contains the functional/technical libraries, utilities, components, platform services needed to implement the services of upper layer.

Key business and technical components required to deliver the upper layer services are as follows:
- Library: Math & financial library etc., Utilities
- SOA platform services like SDL, Clint stubs, Service skeletons etc.,
- Events and Messaging services: Provides service agility. Events based notification.
- Message Oriented Middleware Components
- Object oriented Middleware Components
- Data Model & Management

The service components layer is comprised of libraries, data, utilities, messaging/event service components etc required to realize the service of upper layer. Data models evolve from SOA modeling of business services. Data management process ensures high quality data fulfilling the data principles – consistency, integrity, persistency, non-redundancy, accessibility and security.

There are multiple categories of capabilities that Service Component Layer need to support in the SOA based solution. These capabilities include both design-time and runtime capabilities. These capability categories are:
- **Service Implementation**: This category of capabilities supports the realization of the services.
- **Service Publication and Exposure**: This category of capabilities supports service exposure and service contract publication.

- **Service Deployment**: This category of capabilities supports service deployment.
- **Service Invocation**: This category of capabilities supports service invocation.
- **Service Binding:** This category of capabilities supports service binding.

The Service Component Layer manifests the IT conformance with each service contract/description/specification defined in the Service Layer; it guarantees the alignment of IT implementation with service description.

Service Layer

The Services Layer consists of all the services defined within the SOA. This layer can be thought of as containing the service descriptions for business capabilities and services as well as their IT manifestation during design time, as well as service contract and descriptions that will be used at runtime.

The Services Layer describes functional capabilities of the services in the SOA introducing the notion of services which are well-defined interfaces for a capability into the architecture with the advent of SOA. Service specifications provide consumers with sufficient detail to locate and invoke the business functions exposed by a provider of the service

The service layers are categorized into two different types: business services and technical services. Business services are of types functional or data services. These are basic business services which are required to fulfill the requirements of applications.

Business services as Information System: Collection of core business services of enterprise to fulfill the use-cases of business constitutes information system. Service layer acts as information system which provides all the required services to build application (choreographed services) at business process layer.

Service layer possesses the service of SOA platform to accomplish:

- Service Definition – Contracts based Service description
- Service Runtime Enablement – Service versioning, Loosely coupled Implementation, Provision Services,
- Service Policy Management – Manage and enforce governance and QoS policies associated with services.
- Access Control – Security access control description for services to realize secured service access.
- Service Clustering – Enhances the service performance and reliability. Distributed service computation enhances the computational optimization and service efficiency.

An ideal SOA platform implements the services fulfilling the SOA key design principles, which are as follows:-

- Standardized Service Contract – Communication Agreement
- Service loose Coupling – Minimizes dependency for high agility
- Service Abstraction –   Hidden implementation logic
- Service reusability -   Promotes reuse
- Service Autonomy –   Services control the object
- Service Statelessness – Delegate the state to extended entity for performance
- Service discoverability – Services are effectively discovered & Invoked
- Service composability – Effective composition
- Service granularity -   Optimal & right granular level of functionality.
- Service relevance –   Service must be relevant to user.
- Service encapsulation - Service encapsulated under SOA principles.
- Service location transparency - Service location is irrelevant

Besides support of service platform, Service Layer also needs the technological services delivered by middleware. To build functional services, one needs the technical services like naming and directory services, security services, transaction services, availability services etc.

The Services Layer can be thought of as supporting categories of capabilities of the business and IT:

- Functional capabilities services that enable business capabilities that business performs to achieve a business outcome or a milestone
- Supporting capabilities to define and specify the "services" in terms of service interface/contract/description, message specification, and policy descriptions
- Supporting capabilities to enable the runtime execution of the service and the support of service virtualization

Integration with upper layer: The interfaces of services are made available to business process layer which access the service through ESB.

Integration with lower layer: To build services, one needs the libraries, components, utilities, platform etc. which are external functions used inside the service implementation.

Business Process Layer

Business processes represent the backbone of the flow of a business. The Business Process Layer covers process representation and composition, and provides building blocks for aggregating loosely-coupled services as a sequencing process aligned with business goals. Data flow and control flow are used to enable interactions between services and business processes. The interaction may exist within an enterprise or across multiple enterprises. The layer is called the Business Process Layer and allows externalization of the business process flow in a separate layer in the architecture and thus has a better chance to rapidly change as the market condition changes.

Compositions of services exposed in the Services Layer are defined in this layer: atomic services are composed into a set of composite services using a service composition engine. Note that composition can be implemented as choreography of services, or orchestration of the underlying service elements.

The interfaces of functional and data services are made available at this layer.

The combination of functional services fulfills the business use-cases. Business process layer also needs to access the IT services which include session management, transaction services, security services, availability services etc.

Integration with lower layer: The choreographed service accesses the functional and technical services through Enterprise Service Bus (ESB), which acts as a single point broker to mediate with all available services.

Integration with upper layer: The choreographed services are accessed in B2B mode like from Summit, in B2C mode from explorer and from standard thick clients. Service Choreography, Collaboration and Orchestration should be facilitated by system.

Access Integration: The services enabling business process should be accessible from process of any platform so that B2C or B2B integration can be achieved.

This layer supports and manages business processes and enables the SOA to choreograph or orchestrate services to realize business processes. Business Process Management (BPM) is to be found to start in this layer. There are multiple categories of capabilities that the Business Process Layer needs to support. These categories of capabilities are:
- **Process Definition**: This category of capabilities is required for defining the business processes/operational flow of the business.
- **Event Handling**: This category of capabilities handles business events in the context of a business process such as emitting/publishing events and subscribing/listening to business events.
- **Process Runtime Enablement**: This category of capabilities enables BPM and helps to realize the business processes in the runtime environment using standards such as BPEL, SCA, etc.
- **Process Information Management**: This category of capabilities manages the information needs of a business process

such as managing its state, transforming data in the process flow, and maintaining a repository of assets.

- **Decision Management**: This category of capabilities defines and manages the decision points and associated rules within a business process.
- **Process Integration**: This category of capabilities facilitates integration with others layer of the SOA and helps to expose business process as a choreographed service.
- **Security and Policy Compliance**: This category of capabilities enables access control and policy enforcement in the business processes.
- **Process Monitoring and Management**: This category of capabilities monitors and manages business processes, identifies bottlenecks in the business processes, and optimizes workload assignment.

Business Process Layer in the SOA plays a central coordinating role in connecting business-level requirements and IT-level solution components through collaboration with the Integration Layer, Quality of Service Layer, as well as the Information Layer, the Services Layer, and the Service Component Layer.

SOA modeling is holistic modeling approach where business processes are represented by data/functions services supported with technical services wherein services add values in terms of business and technical capabilities in form of enterprise architecture aligned with strategy.

Consumer Layer

The interfaces of business services are made available at this layer to be accessed by consumer. The Consumer Layer is the entry point where all external consumers interact with the SOA. External consumer could be other systems, other SOAs, cloud service consumers, human users, etc. providing access for Business-to-Business (B2B) or Business-to-Customer (B2C).

Key responsibilities of consumer layer are as follows:

a) Usage - Consumer interaction and integration; i.e., the ability to capture the input from the user (consumer) of the SOA and provide the response to the consumer.

b) Presentation - It includes a presentation, composite view and presentation control, and the consumer-centric configuration of views.

c) Configuration – End users should be able to configure the services as per need and manage to supply the required inputs.

d) Navigation - The usage of business process in terms of choreographed business services should be navigated through user-interface. It provide navigation logic and flow for the processing of consumer interactions

e) Business Process Display – Business process is modeled in graphical form to supply the inputs and display the outputs or use the outputs as inputs for other services.

f) Accessibility - User interface should be able to generate the display the meta-data for current business processes and provide accessibility to business services.

g) Caching and Streaming Content: It addresses the support of information buffering and performance, and supports the operation of the Consumer Layer.

h) Security - It supplies the user data for QoS, information protection, and security.

SOA decouples the user interface (channel), and thus the consumer, from the components and the implementation of the functionality

This decoupling between the consumer and the rest of the underlying SOA provides organizations with the ability to support agility, enhanced re-use, and improve quality and consistency.

The Consumer Layer is that part of the SOA which enables platform independent access to business processes and services supported by various applications and platforms. This is important for the effective use and adoption of the SOA. The Consumer Layer provides the ability to integrate services from within the SOA, and the ability to transform, integrate, and personalize information into the content and mediate with the consumer channels (both for user and non-user interfaces).

1.4 Overview of Strategy

Strategy is a means to achieve business targets with reduced cost, risk and time to market. Using a specification of strategy, one provides vision and leadership to ensure that:

a) H_EA is improving the plans, actions and directions to gain competitive advantage and sustainability of business growth on long run.

b) IT investments are managed in such a way as to ensure the company achieves maximum ROI besides acquiring high performance effective automation.

Strategy is comprised of two interrelated domains – business and IT.

Business Strategy

Business Strategy is a long term business planning to achieve the desired profit, growth and competitive advantage.

Strategic business objectives are deemed most important to the current and future health of a business. Six of the most common areas to focus strategic business goals are in the areas of market share, financial resources, physical resources, productivity, innovation and action planning.

In our scope, we will develop the business plan, analyze and identify the business tactics and rules which will help us delivering matured business services.

IT Strategy

IT Strategy strives to achieve an open, standardized, integrated, scalable and secure IT environment at low costs and risks.

IT Strategy gets the input from business-strategy and specifies the IT Foundation which constitutes IT Capabilities and IT Operating Model (IT-OM). IT Foundation specified by IT strategy provides the guidelines and direction for enterprise architecture in order to achieve enterprise wide effective IT with highest ROI.

IT Strategy improves the IT process of business functionalities as it strives to achieve:

- Business-aligned, agile IT services
- SOA based advanced architecture
- standardized, optimized and integrable process

Strategic Enterprise Architecture

Enterprise Architecture is a framework and set of guidelines to build systems which includes the overall design of a computing system and the logical and physical interrelationships between its components of whole company in holistic manner. The architecture specifies the hardware, software, access methods and protocols used throughout the system.

The input to Enterprise Architecture (EA) comes from business and IT Strategy. Business Architecture, Information & Application Architecture, Platform & Technology Architecture developed in this book are focused to achieve business driven sophisticated IT which delivers effective automation of business functions.

Enterprise Architecture concerns enterprise wide complete functionalities to be considered in holistic way to achieve effective IT which ensures maximum ROI on medium and long run. In this book, we will develop "Focused Enterprise Architecture" where we consider only the core functionalities of business. Focused enterprise architecture derived from IT strategy is a key to acquire business driven, high performance IT in form of enterprise solution at low costs & risks besides attaining highest ROI.

There are four IT architecture domains that are commonly accepted as subsets of enterprise architecture: 1- Business Architecture, 2- Information System Architecture (Data Architecture & Service Architecture), 3- Application Architecture and 4- Platform & Technology Architecture. In subsequent chapters, we would go through each of these subsets to cover the details.

Challenge driven Strategy

Strategy has been increasingly important because of increasing challenges faced by business and IT.

Challenges faced by business are:

- Tough Competition
- Changing customer and market requirements
- Rapid innovations
- Strict regulatory compliance
- Increasing cost
- Continual requirements of increasing efficiency

Challenges for IT supporting business:

- High maintenance costs – operation, extension, integration needs costly investment
- Slow delivery for changed/new functionality
- Monolithic silo based solutions with little or no integration and reusability
- Redundant development across business units
- Redundant computations causing misuse of costly resources and delay in output
- No business driven solutions – IT not aligned with business
- Costly investment with multiple redundant solutions due to missing enterprise architecture
- No state of art - SOA based enterprise architecture

Right strategy achieves better result in overcoming the challenges of business and IT. Strategy leads to business architecture which is crucial to acquire effective IT solution because in our approach, IT is a business-enabler rather than driver – essentially business is driver of IT.

For thorough understanding of focused enterprise architecture, we will develop the architecture for business of Haloedscape from scratch. In this chapter, we will discuss strategy, frameworks and one of the phases of Architecture Development Method - "Preliminaries and Architecture-Vision" to develop Enterprise Architecture.

1.5 Business Strategy

Business strategy is a core management function specifying an action plan for a long term designed to achieve business goals under all circumstances at minimal cost.

Business strategy is developed for core business tasks only at start up so that benefits of profit and growth could be maximized at low cost. The core business tasks are the ones which are mission critical and mandatory for company's survival. Business strategy accounts for improvement of business functionalities so that IT strategy could adapt these changes to enable the improved business objectives. Corporates and business strategy set a series of strategic objectives which is achieved efficiently with business capabilities, as it acts as a powerful tool for strategy alignment.

1.5.1 Capability Based Planning (CBP)

Business Capability is value-added ability that business-unit possesses for its core competencies. It is directly bound to business strategy and objectives.

Business capability is supported, delivered and made aligned to organization by business functions. Capability built with private business services is invoked by public business services to serve the customers better.

Business service encompasses and uses business capability to deliver an improved service to customer to achieve and support business objectives.

Business capability is matured ability possessed by company which helps deliver business-focused outcome efficiently and effectively and is measured in terms of value addition to the enterprise. Capability model is a capability-based planning approach where change activities can be sequenced and grouped in order to provide continuous and incremental business value.

Core business capabilities required for each business domain is identified. Specific business services which are of utmost importance for success of business should be treated as capabilities. Under CBP approach, capability is a set of associated services whose main objective is to improve the ability and values of a business service. A business service categorized as business capability should use some capability-based services to be executed efficiently and effectively under any adverse circumstances addressed under CBP.

1.5.2   Generic Business Principles

Business principles act as direction and guidelines to plan the business for maximizing its success.

Generic Business Principles are:
- Maximize benefit to enterprise
- Business continuity
- Business ownership
- Compliant with legislation
- Principles governance

1.5.3 Business Strategy

Developing business strategy is a think tank assignment which analyses every detail of business function to generate the planning and guidelines for business with the aim of achieving medium and short term business objectives at lowest costs. Development of business strategy is essential because it provides direction, guidance and action-plan to achieve benefits of business on medium and long term.

Significant benefit from business is achieved if it is used to increase firm and financial values that lead to strategic competitiveness and better returns.

H_EA acquires the planning for business function aligned to business strategy. Each motivational factors and rationale for business function is analyzed to plan the activities aligned to strategy. Corporates and business strategy lie at heart of developing the business function strategy.

H_EA acquires and uses an enhanced knowledgebase that helps in strategic analysis, planning and decision making for business function. Strategic directions and guidelines are prepared after proper analysis and evaluation.

Business functions must be enabled by automated solutions delivering the crucial analysis and decision-support supported by strong knowledgebase. The sub-functions of business should be integrated together with collaboration and automated workflow in real-time for consistency and holistic approach to complete business transaction. Core business requirements and technical requirements for automations are analyzed and specified.

Business high-end automation tracks and manages all assumptions, synergies, documents, activities, risks, issues, and measurements and achievement related to transaction besides generating additional values for business.

1.5.4 Strategic Rules and Tactics for Business

Strategic rules and tactics specify the guidelines which give direction and control for business planning, development and realization.

Strategic Tactics for Improving Financial Values

The market control in terms of outsmarting the competition and commanding the market dominance must be improved.

Rising prices and recession are controlled with cost cutting and capacity reduction which should not reduce the current financial returns or market control.

Restructuring is done to change the business of financial structure to reduce the ineffective resources.

Performances are quantified in terms of KPIs to measure the success and correct the course of actions if required.

Risk mitigation is handled with automated solution providing project management, analytics and decision support modules.

Legal factors affecting the business functions are also taken as input for defining rules and tactics.

Strategic Requirements of Business Automation

Business high-end automation tracks and manages all assumptions, planning, synergies, activities, risks, issues and performances related to transaction besides generating additional values for business.

Value generation with business high-end automation should be as follows:

- Project management for visualizing, controlling and managing each path of business process in holistic approach
- Methods to create driver and its measure for business performance and success
- Identification and resolution of cross functional issues
- Business services enabling functions
- Task assignment, tracking and reporting
- Automated data collection, usage and maintenance
- Strategic governance
- Real-time automated workflow with deal execution

- Decision support functions
- Consolidated system for holistic approach to whole business process
- System possessing security, availability, integrity, scalability, transparency, auditing and configurability
- Enabling business capabilities
- Service based delivery

Strategic Modules - Knowledgebase, Analytics and Decision Support
Strategy controls the accountability of managers where success rate is quantified. Corresponding tactics suggest that the measures and decision taken by managers must be validated by decision support system. The high automation level of business is also suggested by strategy. The business decisions must be supported and analyzed with stress test, scenario analysis, sensitivity analysis etc.

Decision support is required to take optimal decision at different lifecycles of business and devising an action plan.

Analytic modules for complete lifecycle of business process should be automated to analyze the specific execution path. Analytics module is core of automation and most of functions are dependent on analytics.

Domain-knowledgebase in form of comprehensive information repository should be acquired which helps automate different life cycles of business process.

> *Strategic business rules and tactics protect company from general and specific issues which cause failure to business and helps achieve strategic objectives in medium and long term. Proper handling of business process aligned with business strategy, rules and tactics help succeed in achieving business objectives.*

1.6 IT Strategy

IT strategy is actionable plan to achieve an agile automated solution which helps achieve business objectives at low cost, risk and time to market. Strategy acts as a capability owned by firms to achieve effective IT at low cost which maximizes the ROI on medium and long term.

1.6.1 IT Strategy Process

IT strategy process is an actionable IT planning process that identifies, creates and supports an agile IT foundation intended to automate the business functions fulfilling business strategy. Accomplishments of strategy are:

- IT Strategy provides strategic direction for architectural vision, approach and methodology of IT Solutions.
- IT Strategy leads to IT-Foundation comprised of IT Capabilities and IT Operating Model.

IT strategy gets it input from business strategy. Based on changes to business strategy, IT strategy adjusts itself to be aligned with business strategy in order to enable the business objectives. In our approach, the business strategy which cannot be adapted into IT strategy is invalid and needs to be rectified.

IT Strategy is so formulated that its four basic characteristics to improve the IT solutions are retained. The strategy directs and guides that:

- IT services should be aligned with business services so that IT delivers effective and optimal solution.
- Service should be agile so that the solution could easily adapt the changes of customer's requirements and market conditions.
- Service should be standardized and optimized so that it could be extended, integrated, operated and maintained at low cost.

- Service should be integrable and interoperable so that the functionalities could be integrated together without investing extra resources.

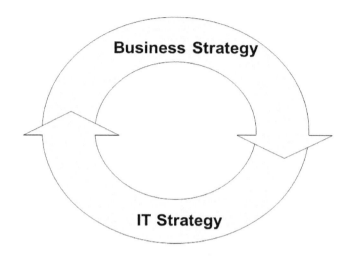

Figure 1.5: © HBS, Iteration of Business and IT Strategy

1.6.2   IT Strategy Principles

IT Strategy principles are guide to design the business solution which encompasses the business strategy and strategic IT foundation.   IT solution must fulfill these principles so that enterprise architecture could be achieved which possesses the strategic capabilities. IT solution should fulfill following consolidated principles:-

Business Principles
  – Maximize benefit to enterprise
  – Business continuity
  – Business ownership
  – Compliant with legislation
  – Principles governance

Information System, Application & Computational Principles

- Business driven architecture tightly coupled with strategy
- Process improvement (Service Optimization, Standardization & Integration)
- Service Oriented Architecture (SOA)
- Shared Application Components
- Computational efficiency & effectiveness
- Non redundant computation

Data Principles
- Non-redundant, Shared, Securely persisted, Accessible and Consistent Data
- Active Data-Management to maintain high quality data

Technology and Platform Principles
- Technology Independence
- Highly available and secured resources
- Efficient use of resources
- Sophisticated technology to support efficient computation and business fulfillment

> *We will elaborate these strategic principles in subsequent chapters while developing the business, information system, data, application and platform architecture.*

1.6.3   IT Strategy Objectives

The objective of IT Strategy is to ensure that IT provides an open and secure exchange of information, consistent with technical architecture and standards, reduces risks & costs and directly contributes to mission success.

The strategic objectives are as follows:

- Enhanced, agile and business-aligned IT services across enterprise for each of the business-unit application.

- Strong focus on supporting the core business needs with an appropriate level of information, communication and integration technology capability.
- Service collaboration and orchestration for application-unit and workflow automation.
- Standardization, optimization and integration of IT services.
- Secured and responsible information system in accordance with strategic principles and requirements.
- Sophisticated technology support for IT Services
- Strategic investment in IT with maximum business returns with low costs and risks.
- Governance of IT-Strategy to acquire, operate and maintain IT solution.

Potential candidates identified for transformation are follows:-

- Transform the process having poor alignment with business and IT strategy.
- Transform the process which is non-sustainable in terms of risks and maintenance costs.
- Transform the monolithic, silo based, aging, poorly integrated system.

1.7   IT Capability

IT Capabilities specify how H_EA delivers value-added, matured IT services to enable the business services so that capability based planning of business strategy could be realized.

1.7.1   IT Capability Model

The IT Capabilities are categorized into three IT domains - SOM, SOA and SOI.

1- Structured Operating Model (SOM)

A model of firm associating the business capabilities, processes, functions automated with advanced technology required for business success. SOM helps achieve enterprise wide IT architecture resulting in flexible processing resiliency with effectiveness. IT–SOM serves as an important management tool for aligning IT with business.

Refer the detail of "IT Operating Model" in later section.

2- Service Oriented Architecture (SOA) Model

Service oriented Architecture (SOA) in IT context is defined as architecture of IT software based on service oriented design principles, that transforms business functionalities and deliver them as services.

IT service designed with SOA principles is self-contained autonomous software that alone or in combined form gives logical representation of enterprise business function.

Service Oriented Architecture (SOA) ensures business aligned effective IT. SOA also leads to business agility due to optimized, simplified, loosely-coupled and reusable services. SOA gives the core foundation of Enterprise-Architecture. Important SOA Principles are:
- Standardized Service Contract
- Loose Coupling
- Abstraction
- Reusability
- Autonomy
- Statelessness
- Discoverability
- Compositional

The alignment of IT with business, loosely coupled component based agile design, simplified and optimal process are achieved with SOA.

In our approach, business is seen as system and we apply the service orientation right from business architecture to lead a business aligned IT and improve the business capabilities. In the context of IT, SOA provides architecture of software based on service oriented design principles that transforms business functionalities and deliver them as IT services.

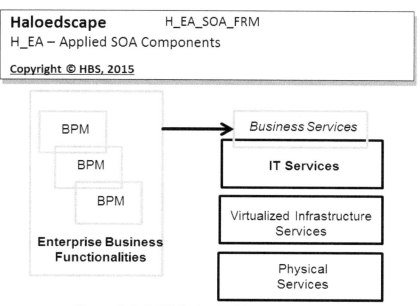

Figure 1.6: © HBS, Applied SOA Components

Our information system must be completely SOA based supported with innovative platform empowered with required technology. SOA based IT solution achieves strategic objective of business aligned, agile and effective IT which maximize the ROI while reducing overall risks and costs.

3- Service Oriented Infrastructure (SOI) Model

Service oriented Infrastructure (SOI) is architectural design for describing IT infrastructure in terms of service. Infrastructure services typically use and/or provide a virtualized pool of shared resources (Servers, Network, Storage, Infrastructure software) which are deployed and managed in a highly automated way. SOI provides foundational support for service-oriented information system architecture and application architecture.

Infrastructure Service Characteristics are following:

- Scalable : quantum of service used can be scaled up or down
- Independent and modular: should be possible to be used stand alone.
- Discoverable: easily traced in a network
- Configurable: should be possible to attach to an application service in real time
- Dynamic : should be possible to switch from one user to another in real time
- Measurable : service level and service availability should be measurable
- Secure : should be possible to set levels of access based on definitions
- Location transparency: logical names should identify network resources
- Contingencies : what is to be done when the service is not available
- Cost: cost of using the service in terms of resources and operational expenses
- Service: should be exposed using standard interfaces

1.7.2 IT Capability Statement

IT Capabilities Statements specify the IT abilities, rules, methods, guidelines and directions for strategic IT services so that value added business-capabilities are realized. IT capabilities are foundation on which IT-OM is decided and designed.

The key capabilities statements are as follows:

Core Strategic Capabilities:

1- Establish think tank with vast outstanding experience, knowledge and skills to conduct continual research on: improving current business/IT process, deriving future business process, improving intelligence and dynamics of platforms in order to deliver perfect solutions.

   The prime tasks of think tank are:

   a) Improve the business process specifying an action plan designed to achieve business objectives and goals under all circumstances ensuring desired profit, growth and competitive advantage.

   b) Study the company's business and IT strategy and map out enterprise-architecture for world leading IT solutions.

   c) Develop quantification methods for IT-investment. There should be subsequent decrease in investment and increased levels of IT maturity with time.

   d) Assure that the information architecture is designed and periodically updated to support the strategic requirements.

2- Switch from business-unit aligned to enterprise aligned IT, leading to shared service model.

3- Strive for sophisticated technology. To be successful and competitive, the company must carefully track new and emerging technologies.

4- Achieve an open standard, scalable and secure IT Environment. An enterprise wide, open standards-based, common operating environment, SOA-based under information system architecture should be established.

5- Improve the business process with standardization, modularity and integration.

6- Achieve the process automation without violating the business, computational, data and technology principles.

7- IT system should satisfy capability based planning approach as specified in business architecture.

Capabilities for SOA:

8- Acquire IT system built with SOA approach.

9- Build the information architecture with enterprise services which achieve strategic capabilities.

10- The information system architecture must fulfill service-oriented design principles. Automate governance with information system.

11- Build service inventory to consolidate the services of whole enterprise.

12- IT service should be business driven. Business services are transformed into IT services.

13- The services should be so designed that it fulfills the service oriented design principle.

Capabilities for Process Improvement:

14- Achieve process standardization, optimization, modularity and integration to reduce the risks and costs in every phase of software engineering.

15- Achieve high performance in computing process through distributed computing, parallelization, clustering, cloning and work-load management.

Capabilities for Secured Computation:

16- Achieve proper security for process. Secure the process with authentication. The users under a group need to be authorized with access control list.

17- The data in transmission should be encrypted with SSL.

18- The certificates and digital signature should be managed with PKI infrastructure in the company.

Capabilities for Strategic business:

19- Achieve real time platforms for decision support system.

20- Achieve the service oriented solution to avoid the monolithic computation

21- Avoid proprietary deadlock and prefer the platform compliant to open standards.

22- Achieve Business Intelligence (BI) for strategic improvements. The methods to quantify the strategic decision should be supported with decision support.

23- Build the knowledge base and skills in the company to operate, maintain and develop the sophisticated system delivering the mission-critical solutions.

Capabilities for Technology and Infrastructure:

24- Achieve cloud facility and virtualization for resources to be used as services. The resources should be scalable to optimize its usage.

25- Use clones with work load management which support the distributed computing with fail-over to achieve 100% availability.

26- The data should be persisted in secured, recoverable, fault-tolerant devices.

27- Acquire cluster, parallel servers to deliver reliable, high performance IT.

1.8 IT Operating Model

IT-Operating Model (IT-OM) specifies how an organization operates across process, functionality and technology domain. IT-OM is a model associating the business capabilities, processes, functions and technology required for business success with the IT resource that enables them.

1.8.1 IT-OM Process

IT-OM is represented as logical integrated collection of frameworks to design, manage and interface IT with business. It provides the foundation and flexibility required to execute the firm's initiatives.

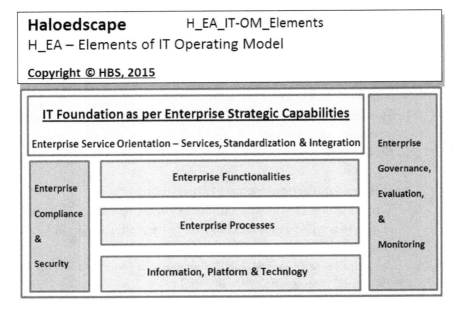

Figure 1.7: © HBS, Elements of IT-OM

The elements of IT-OM are: -

- Enterprise Service Orientation – In our IT-OM, service orientation is used across all phases of enterprise architecture development.
- Enterprise Business Functionalities – Enterprise unified modeling (EUM) is used to specify the dynamic design of enterprise wide business services and capabilities.
- Enterprise Processes – The consolidated view of steps of execution that deliver business functionalities are categorized into IT-services, workflows, data and applications.
- Enterprise Information, Platform & Technology – Foundation of enterprise-wide Information System (IS) delivering the business services are supported on required platform and technology.

- Enterprise Compliance and Security – The business functionalities and processes of enterprise must be complaint to principles and laws. The information system, platform and technology must deliver the required security services for securing the information system services and applications.
- Enterprise Governance – The enterprise governance must be transited into each elements of operating model. The decisions taken for functionalities and processes must be available at information system, which are automatically transited into individual applications.

IT-OM process specifies the relationships between enterprise wide business functionalities, automated process, process structure, computations, information flow and applications of different business-units supported on required platform and technology. It associates organization's business and technology domain.

1.8.2   IT-OM Framework

The goals of IT-OM are to focus on core capabilities, derive the architecture and infrastructure, guide the business process and corresponding information system, select the appropriate IT systems and justify IT investment decision.

The target IT-OM aligns all components to effectively evaluate the opportunities to maximize the customer value. It represents the high level requirements that drives the future business and IT development.

IT strategy model leads to IT foundation which executes strategy. Enterprise Architecture is created with architecture development framework, managed with strategic service management framework and governed with controlling framework.

The strategic enterprise architecture is evolved in following way:

- IT Strategy provides requirements for architecture core diagram.
- IT foundation is optimized based on capability model and IT-OM.
- Strategic principles, guidelines and direction are governed into every individual projects which leads to enterprise architecture.

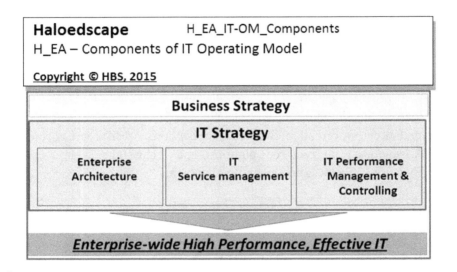

Figure 1.8: © HBS, Components of IT-OM

IT-Operating model, a part of IT strategy is developed and managed under an integrated collection of frameworks, which guides and directs the development of enterprise architecture, management of IT services and IT governance.

IT-OM: Service Management
The IT Infrastructure Library- ITIL, a framework for IT Service management (ITSM) to align IT services with business was developed by UK Governments' Central Computer and Telecommunications Agency. For details, refer: < http://www.itil-officialsite.com/ >

For optimized and professional approach to ITSM, strategic framework like ITIL 3 should be followed to achieve perfection.

Service Strategy and Design

There should be a standardized approach of Service Strategy and Service Design.

Service Strategy Process comprises- Demand Generation, Strategy Generation, Service Portfolio Management and IT Financial Management.

Service Design Process comprises- Service Catalogue Management, Service Level Management, Capacity Management, Availability Management, Service Continuity Management, Information Security Management.

Portfolio Management

The complete portfolio of key IT projects should be available in enterprise landscape to be optimized in a holistic approach with a framework. The enterprise architecture development needs a portfolio of IT-projects for consolidation of services in information system.

Quality Management

- IT services must be business driven which leads to business aligned effective IT.
- IT solution must be agile to adapt the changes of business.
- The process should be optimized, standardized and integrated.
- IT solution must secure the business execution and continuity.
- Information system must fulfill the strategic requirement and possess the enterprise capabilities.
- Applications should get access to enterprise function and data only through information system, enforcing quality governance for enterprise data/functions to department specific applications.
- Information system should be designed as SOA.

- Capability based planning approach should be applied for each business service wherein business service is modeled as matured capability.

Risk management

The risk should be assessed in project portfolio. The project failure factors should be evaluated to eliminate or minimize the risk. Risk impact assessment and residual risk reports should be a part of risk management activities.

IT-OM: Performance Management and Controlling

IT Performance Management and Controlling (ITPC) is an enterprise. end-to-end consolidated approach to enhance the performance and controlling to achieve effective IT. A holistic approach is required for all functionalities and derived processes to refine the efficiency and effectiveness.

ITPC includes the following:

- Governance models: Organize IT governance objectives and good practices by IT domains and processes, and links them to business requirements.
- Control objectives: Provide a complete set of high-level requirements to be considered by management for effective control of each IT process.
- Management guidelines: Help assign responsibility, agree on objectives, measure performance, and illustrate interrelationship with other processes
- Maturity models: Assess maturity and capability per process which helps address gaps. The organization must achieve a capability maturity as specified by CMM-3.

Strong IT governance with clear delineation of decision rights across business leads to high performance IT. Due to its importance, IT governance has become integral part of corporate governance.

IT-OM: Enterprise Architecture

Refer "Enterprise Architecture" described later.

1.8.3   IT-OM Governance

IT governance process enforces a direct link of IT resources and processes to enterprise goals in line of strategy. Strong IT governance with clear delineation of decision rights across business leads to high performance and effective IT.

The objectives of IT-Governance are:
- IT value and alignment
- Accountability
- Performance measurement
- Risk management.

IT-OM Governance Framework

The governance process is simplified with the help of framework like COBIT. There is a strong correlation between maturity curve of IT governance and overall effectiveness of IT. The IT control's framework for governance is integrated with enterprise architecture.

The business orientation of COBIT consists of linking business goals to IT goals, providing metrics and maturity models to measure their achievement, and identifying the associated responsibilities of business and IT process owners.

COBIT components include:
- Framework: Organizes IT governance objectives and good practices by IT domains and processes; and links them to business requirements
- Process descriptions: A reference process model and common language for everyone in an organization. The processes map to responsibility areas of plan, build, run and monitor.
- Control objectives: Provide a complete set of high-level requirements to be considered by management for effective control of each IT process.

- Management guidelines: Help assign responsibility, agree on objectives, measure performance, and illustrate interrelationship with other processes
- Maturity models: Assess maturity and capability per process which helps address gaps

COBIT 5 principles are enterprise specific that are used into enterprise context, allowing value to be derived from the supporting guidance effectively. COBIT supports IT governance by providing a framework to ensure that:

- IT is aligned with the business
- IT enables the business and maximizes benefits
- IT resources are used responsibly
- IT risk is managed appropriately

In our context, IT Governance includes Process Governance, Computational Governance and Technology Governance. For business function in our focus, we will govern following in our enterprise architecture.

SOA based Process Governance:
- Business driven IT Services: The business services are transformed into IT services.
- Strategic Information System: Information system fulfills all the strategic requirements and possesses the enterprise capabilities.
- Information System as Service Provider: Information system contains consolidated IT service inventory corresponding to each of the business service and capability. These IT services of information system are accessed by business-unit application to execute their business function.
- Standardized, Optimized and Integrable Process: The process must be improved to be standardized, optimized and integrable.

SOA based Computational Governance:

- Delta Computation: Redundancy of computation must be avoided. Only those process should be computed, which causes change in results due to occurrence of events.
  Refer Information System and Platform Architecture for details.

- Automated Workflow: Distributed interactive activities of isolated modules are part of workflow which should be automated.
- Highest Grade of Computation: Functionalities should be automated to highest level.
- Automated Decision Support: Decision of business functions must be analyzed, aided and validated with decision support.
- Events based Processing: Computation should be driven by events to process in real-time leading to computational non-redundancy and efficiency.

SOA based Technology Governance:
- Service Oriented Platform – Service oriented platform must be provided to information system and applications.
- Information System: Sophisticated and complex requirements of service based information system to be accessed from enterprise wide applications.
- Appropriate Technology: Events based Object/Message based middleware is an innovative distributed computing environment which should be acquired to fulfill the requirements of IT solution.
- Optimal Resource Selection: The process should be automatically allocated to execute at most healthy infrastructure dynamically in distributed computing.
- Infrastructure as Cloud: The infrastructure should be used as services and scaled based on demand.

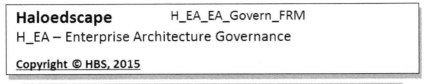

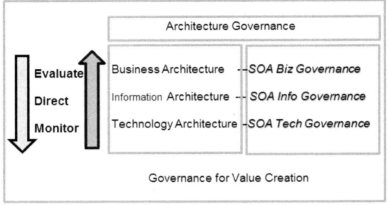

Figure 1.9: © HBS, Enterprise Architecture Governance

Service orientation starts at business architecture where business functionalities and capabilities are delivered in form of services. The alignment of IT with business, loosely coupled component based agile design, simplified and optimal process are achieved with SOA.

> *IT governance is a framework and structure that links IT resources and information to enterprise goals and strategies. The architecture development of business function is done in such a way that requirements of governance mentioned above are fulfilled. The Information System, Application and Platform architecture discussed in later chapters incorporate the fulfillment of governance.*

In the context of IT, Service oriented Architecture (SOA) is defined as architecture of software based on service oriented design principles, that transforms business functionalities and deliver them as IT services.

Information system services make interfaces available to enterprise wide application to access the enterprise services and capabilities. SOA based information system achieves strategic objective of business aligned agile IT, which automates the governance to enterprise wide applications. We will elaborate the details of automated governance in later chapter.

Our approach towards governance is to include the strategic values inside each phase of architecture so that the IT foundation is capable of executing strategy. In this book, the architecture is developed in such way that strategic directions, guidelines and control are embedded into each phase of development so that governance process could be automated through SOA based information system to achieve the enterprise architecture.

1.9   Enterprise Architecture

IT Architecture is a framework and set of guidelines to build IT systems. It is an overall design of a computing system and the logical & physical interrelationships between its components. The architecture specifies the hardware, software, access methods and protocols used throughout the system.

Enterprise Architecture is an organizing logic of key business process with tightly aligned IT to execute strategy. It is an optimal IT Architecture for whole enterprise where strategic requirements and principles are fulfilled to acquire business driven capabilities and achieve the business objective

Our Enterprise Architecture for investment banking developed in the book is an innovation based extended instance of TOGAF, COBIT and ITIL.

We use primarily "The Open Group" product, TOGAF 9 framework to develop Enterprise Architecture. TOGAF allows other standard frameworks like COBIT and ITIL to be adopted, integrated or extended with it.

COBIT as IT Management and Governance Framework is used for governance process.

As ITSM (IT service Management) tool, we use ITIL v3 that focusses on aligning IT with business.

We have used several innovative, extended, derived frameworks beyond TOGAF, ITIL and COBIT in this book to achieve better architecture that leads to high performance solution.

1.9.1   Enterprise Architecture Framework

An architecture framework is a foundation structure which helps develop enterprise architecture of IT solution for broad range of different business domains.

IT practices is made aligned to business requirements and processes. Frameworks help us achieve this. We use primarily "TOGAF 9.1", an architecture framework published by "The Open Group" to develop Enterprise Architecture for Investment Bank. In our case study, other frameworks like COBIT and ITIL are adopted in TOGAF to address governance and service issues more precisely.

TOGAF

The Architecture Development Method (ADM) is core of TOGAF which describes a method for developing and managing the lifecycle of enterprise architecture. There are 8 different phases (A to H) in which first 4 phases (A to D) are sufficient to achieve our initial Enterprise Architecture.

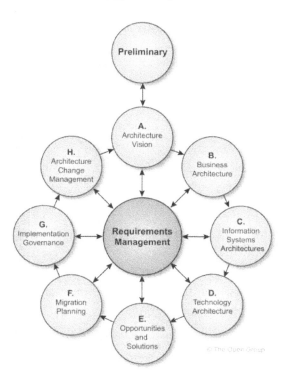

Figure 1.10: Copyright © The Open Group, TOGAF® 9.1, Architecture Development Cycle

Preliminary phase is about defining where, what why, who and how we do architecture in the enterprise. It should determine the desired and reasonable approach to enterprise architecture. Key outputs of this phase are to generate initial artifacts/docs regarding following:

- Specify the requirements of architecture work
- Specify the frameworks to be used and their relationship
- Specify initial principles, policies that should act as guidelines and constraints for architecture
- Evaluate enterprise's maturity
- Analyze and identify architecture repository, governance frameworks

Architecture Vision phase leads to an official high-level aspirational vision of capabilities and business values to be delivered by enterprise architecture.

Creating the Architecture Vision requires the following tasks:

- Describes how the new capability will meet the business goals and strategic objectives
- To verify and understand the documented business strategy and goals, and may integrate enterprise strategy and goals with current architecture

The outputs of this phase are to generate following artifacts/docs:

- Architecture vision overview, project plan, scope
- Problem description, Objective, Summary views, Refined key stakeholders agreements
- Strategic Principles and Capability Assessment

In this chapter, we elaborate the preliminary and architecture vision phases, which act as input to business architecture discussed in next chapter.

Business architecture phase deals with developing the target business architecture that describes how the enterprise needs to operate to achieve the business goals, and respond to the strategic drivers set out in the Architecture Vision, and addresses the Request for Architecture Work and stakeholder concerns

Business Architecture describes the product strategy and the organizational, functional, process information, and geographic aspects of the business environment.

Knowledge of Business Architecture is a prerequisite for architecture in Data, Application, and Technology. Therefore it is the most important key architecture activity to achieve appropriate enterprise architecture.

The artifacts of business architecture include the business modeling techniques like value chain, organizational diagram, KPIs allocation, activity models, service and capabilities diagram, use-case models, class models, business scenarios etc.

A business scenario represents a business need, and enables vendor to understand the value of developed solution. Business scenario describes:

- A business process, application or set of applications enabled by the architecture
- Business and technology environment,
- People and the computing components
- Desired outcome of proper execution

Refer Business Architecture in chapter 2.

Information Systems Architecture phase deals with developing the target Data & Application Architecture that enables the Business Architecture and Architecture Vision, while addressing the request for architecture work and stakeholder concerns.

Key considerations of Data Architecture are data management, data migration and data governance. Outputs of Data Architecture are data models, application-data matrix, logical data, data dissemination, data security, data migration etc.

Application Architecture deals with SOA based choreographed service that enables the business services, and focusses on application-level components, services, service collaboration, data entities etc to provide an integrated information infrastructure.

Refer Information Systems Architecture in chapter 3.

Technology Architecture phase deals with developing the target Technology Architecture that enables the logical and physical application and data components and Architecture Vision, addressing request of architecture work & stakeholder concerns.

The outputs of Technology Architecture are following:

- Technology components and their relationship to information systems
- Platform anatomy and requirements fulfillment
- Technology platforms and their decomposition
- Environments and locations
- Hardware and network specification

Refer Technology Architecture in chapter 4.

Architecture Content Framework (ACF)

ACF provides a structural model for architecture content that allows major work products to be consistently defined, structured and presented

Each Architecture development phase results in deliverable, which are outputs contractually specified and reviewed, and are archived in Architecture Repository as reference model.

One of essential contents produced are Artifacts, which are aspects of the architecture, specified as catalogs, matrices and diagrams like use-cases, class diagram. Artifacts form content of Architecture Repository, supports enterprise continuum by storing different classes of ADM architecture outputs.

Content Metamodel is definition of a set of entities that allow architecture concepts to be captured and represented. Core metamodel entities are:

- Actor, Application Component, Business Services, Data Entity, Function, Information System Service, organization unit, Platform Service, Role, Technology Component

- Process: used to describe flow of interactions between services and functions
- Functions: units of business capability
- Business Services: support organizational objectives and defined at a level consistent with level of governance, are deployed onto application components
- Application components: deployed onto technology components

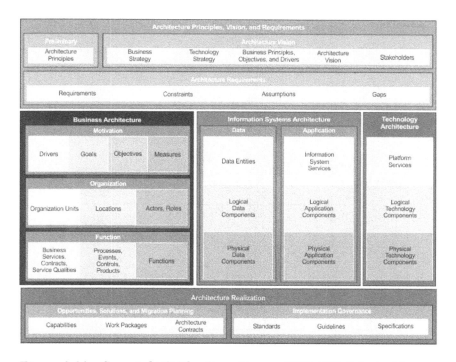

Figure 1.11: Copyright © The Open Group, TOGAF® 9.1, Architecture Content Framework

TOGAF Content Framework provides an underlying structure for the ADM, i.e. how the architecture should look like. It defines inputs and outputs in more details.

High level Content Framework contains:

- Architecture Principles, Vision, and Requirements artifacts: capture context of architecture models, typically collected in Preliminary and Architecture Vision phases
- Business Architecture artifacts: capture architecture models of business operation
- Information System Architecture artifacts: looking at applications and data in line with TOGAF ADM phases
- Technology Architecture artifacts: capture procured technology assets
- Architecture Realization artifacts: capture change roadmaps showing transition between states

Following matrix relates the content of enterprise repository for each of Architecture Development Method phase.

ADM Phase	Artifacts
Preliminary	Principles Catalog
Architecture Vision	Stakeholder Map Matrix
	Value Chain Diagram
	Solution Concept Diagram
Business Architecture	Organization/Actor Catalog
	Role Catalog
	Business Service/Function Catalog
	Business Interaction Matrix
	Actor/Role Matrix
	Business Footprint Diagram

	Business Service/Information Diagram
	Functional Decomposition Diagram
	Product Lifecycle Diagram
Information Systems	Data Entity/Data Component Catalog
(Data Architecture)	Data Entity/Business Function Matrix
	Application/Data Matrix
	Conceptual Data Diagram
	Logical Data Diagram
	Data Dissemination Diagram
Information Systems	Application Portfolio Catalog
(Application Architecture)	Interface Catalog
	Application/Organization Matrix
	Role/Application Matrix
	Application/Function Matrix
	Application Interaction Matrix
	Application Communication Diagram
	Application and User Location Diagram
	Application Use-Case Diagram
Technology Architecture	Technology Standards Catalog
	Technology Portfolio Catalog
	Application/Technology Matrix

	Environments and Locations Diagram
	Platform Decomposition Diagram

COBIT

An acronym for Control Objectives for Information and related Technology, created by the Information Systems Audit and Control Association (ISACA) and the IT Governance Institute (ITGI), which provides a set of recommended best practices for governance and control process of information systems and technology.

COBIT 5 consolidates COBIT4.1, Val IT and Risk IT into a single framework acting as an enterprise framework aligned and interoperable with TOGAF and ITIL.

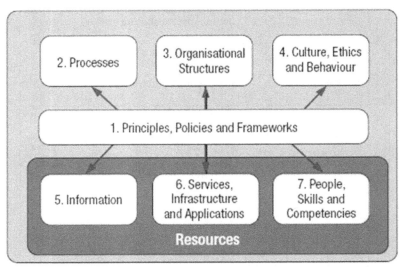

Copyright COBIT® 5 © 2012 ISACA® All rights reserved.

Figure 1.12: Copyright © 2012 ISACA, COBIT® 5, COBIT Framework

The business orientation of COBIT consists of linking business goals to IT goals, providing metrics and maturity models to measure their achievement, and identifying the associated responsibilities of business and IT process owners.

COBIT 5 Principles

COBIT 5 principles are enterprise specific that are used into enterprise context, allowing value to be derived from the supporting guidance effectively.

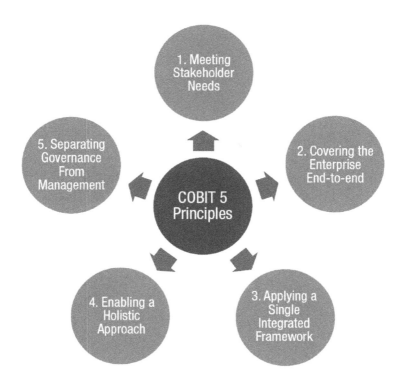

Figure 1.13: Copyright © 2012 ISACA, COBIT® 5, COBIT 5 Principles

ITIL

The IT Infrastructure Library- ITIL, a framework for IT Service management (ITSM) to align IT services with business was developed by UK Governments' Central Computer and Telecommunications Agency. For details, kindly refer: < http://www.itil-officialsite.com/ >

ITIL v3 (published in May, 2007) is enterprise oriented holistic approach to full life cycle of services covering the entire IT organization.

Service Lifecycle:

ITIL v3 presents following five volumes for services.

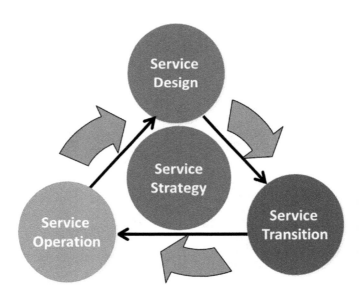

Figure 1.14: Copyright © 2007 ITSM, ITIL® CCTA®, ITIL Framework

These service volumes interlinked with each other are as follows:

- ITIL Service Strategy
- ITIL Service Design
- ITIL Service Transition
- ITIL Service Operation
- ITIL Continual Service Improvement

Our focus regarding ITIL:

We will focus mainly on ITIL Service Strategy and Service Design to achieve initial enterprise architecture.

Service Strategy provides the direction and vision of establishing IT services. It influences the organizational attitudes and culture towards creation of values.

Service Strategy process comprises:
- Demand Generation
- Strategy Generation
- Service Portfolio Management
- IT Financial Management

Service Design concerns with design of services, ensures design are consistent and capable in line of strategy, evaluates the alignment of services with business.

Service Design process comprises:
- Service Catalogue Management – Business/Technical service catalogue
- Service Level Management – SLAs and success measure with KPIs
- Capacity Management
- Availability Management
- Service Continuity Management
- Information Security Management

Important Frameworks and Standards for Architecture and Management

In the book, TOGAF, COBIT and ITIL are primarily used for architecture development, IT governance and service management respectively. Additionally, following frameworks are referred and used wherever applicable in suitable contexts.

- TOGAF® (Enterprise Architecture)
- COBIT® (IT Controls Framework)
- ITIL® (ITSM)
- CMMI (Maturity Models)
- ISO 20000 (ITSM)
- PRINCE2®, PMBOK® (Project Management)
- ISO 27000 (InfoSec)

1.10 Enterprise Architecture Guidelines and Solution Approach

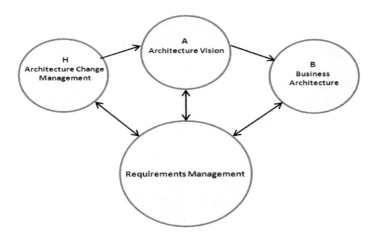

Figure 1.15: Copyright © The Open Group, TOGAF® 9.1, Arch Vision-Architecture Development Cycle

In the first phase of ADM - Architectural Vision, we outline the business requirements, IT aspirational vision, concepts, approach, action plan and guidelines so that our path ahead of developing enterprise architecture becomes clear and focused.

The framework of TOGAF for "Architecture Development Method" guides that Business Architecture gets its input from Architecture Vision- which is essentially our Strategy discussed in this chapter. All of these phases of Architecture (Architecture Vision/Strategy, Business) interact in bidirectional way with Requirements Management so that each phase of architecture development keeps its essence of fulfilling the requirements as its top objective.

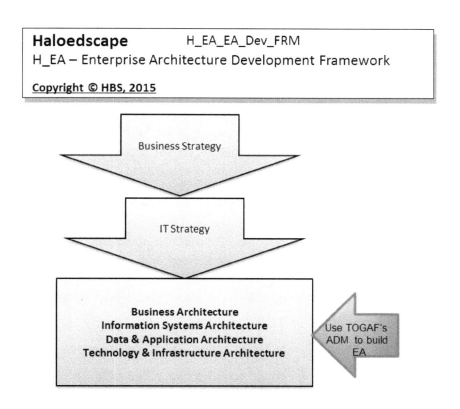

Figure 1.16: © HBS, Architecture Development Framework

As described in this chapter, Preliminaries and Architecture Vision, the initial phases of Architecture Development Method phase includes our high level artifacts, capabilities, strategy, goals, principles, architecture and solution approach which direct and guide the subsequent phases of architecture development.

Guidelines, Action plan and Approach for Business Architecture Development

Develop the business architecture which fulfills the strategic requirements, improves business process, optimizes the business models with capabilities and services and specifies the requirements to develop information system architecture.

Develop a framework of business architecture where strategy is accepted as input and business models are generated as output to be supplied further as input to information system and application architecture.

Business Motivation Model (BMM) should be used to structure, communicate and organize the business plans. The elements of BMM like End, Vision, Mission, Goals and Objectives should be consolidated and interrelated together.

Apply the strategy, tactics and business rules to create the architecture for business functionalities and process. The architecture of business domain should include elaboration of business motives, lifecycle, values addition, transition, transactions and service realization. The business function should be depicted with lifecycle, business descriptions, key performance indicators, business scenarios and value added chain diagram etc.

The strategic objectives of business function should be quantified with key performance indicators.

Detailed business process should be described with Business Process Model (BPM) to make it more precise and less subjective.

Describe the deal transaction and dependent functionalities. Achieve the integration of isolated modules like risk & performance management and integration with events like deal execution.

Develop the capability model to fulfill the capability based planning approach where change activities can be sequenced and grouped in order to provide continuous and incremental business value.

Develop an effective framework to formulate the interrelation of business objectives, business functions, business services and business capabilities so that they remain absolutely aligned with each other and fulfill their target to achieve strategic enterprise architecture.

Apply SOA to business architecture so that business capabilities and business functionalities are all service oriented which can be directly transformed into IT-services to achieve services-oriented IT solutions

Guidelines, Action plan and Approach for Information System, Data and Application Architecture

Information System should be completely SOA based supported with innovative platform with required technology.

Develop the automated governance through information system which ensures strategic governance across enterprise wide applications. Consolidated enterprise data services and functional services should be part of information system which fulfills all strategic requirements. Enterprise data service and functional services are accessed by applications only through information system governing the fulfillment of strategic requirements in the applications to achieve enterprise capabilities in automated way.

Information system and application architecture should include the design and architecture of business functionalities like Strategic Governance, Business Tactics, Due Diligence, Pricing, Financing, Deal Structure, Deal Execution, Accounting & Taxation, Compliance,

Performance & Risk Management, Integration, Domain Knowledgebase, Analysis and Decision Support.

Data management is crucial for enterprise where data unification, centralization, access, non-redundancy, sharing, security and consistency are managed to maintain high quality data.

Application should be able to compute in real time besides being able to efficiently compute for the changes by subscribing to receive notification at occurrence of events for specific topic/content.

The services should be implemented on distributed computing platform supported with object oriented and message oriented middleware. Business Application should be equipped with advanced capabilities to provide innovative and sophisticated solution.

Applications should be designed to be secured with encryption, authentication and authorization. Some of the sequential tasks which needs manual intervention should be automated with workflow using parallel split and synchronize patterns.

Workflow automation should be achieved with STP where remote modules of risk and performance management (middle/back office) are integrated together with deal implementation (front office function).

Business function delivers business capabilities closely aligned to an organization. Business service encompasses business capabilities to realize business function and support business objectives. Business service and capabilities are transformed directly into and realized by IT services.

Develop an effective framework to interrelate the business service, business capability, information system services and applications. Application architecture should align the application, business services and business capabilities to ensure IT alignment with business.

Guidelines, Action plan and Approach for Platform and Technology Architecture

To acquire IT solution with enterprise characteristics and strategic capabilities, information system and applications should be supported with right platform possessing required technology.

The SOA based platform delivers IT service which fulfills the strategic requirements, lowers down the risks & costs and maximizes the ROI.

Many components of business functions like pricing engine, simulations, stress test and scenario analysis require high performance distributed computing environment delivered by object oriented middleware.

The platform needs to support the applications with session and transaction management so that application could maintain its state and also the critical operations are guaranteed maintaining the state of consistent data and synchronized process.

Platform should provide security service so that applications could configure, extend and enable encryption, authentication and authorization.

Platform supported workflow service is required to automate workflow and execute the heavy computation in parallel split & synchronize pattern.

The services are implemented on distributed computing platform supported with events based object and message oriented middleware.

Platform should deliver distributed computing environment, ESB, EAI, STP and service oriented capabilities to applications.

The infrastructure services like scheduling, pooling, clustering, cloning and cloud services should be available to applications.

> *Our target in this and following chapters is to develop an Enterprise Architecture for generic & standardized business function.*

The requirements for enterprise architecture come from business and IT strategy. In our approach, there are four architecture domains that are subsets of enterprise architecture: Business Architecture, Information System Architecture (Services & Data Architecture), Application Architecture and Platform & Technology Architecture. In subsequent chapters, we would go through each of these subsets to cover the details.

For better & complete understanding of focused enterprise architecture, we develop the Enterprise Architecture from scratch. In this chapter, we discuss the strategy, frameworks and first phase of Architecture Development Method - "Preliminaries & Architecture-Vision" to develop Enterprise Architecture.

1.11 Roadmap for Achieving Strategic Enterprise Architecture

In this section, roadmap for acquiring strategy & enterprise architecture is presented with rough estimates of activities and timeline.

Timeline is kept generic so that company can decide upon the timeline for each stage of architecture development based on number of professionals employed in task, their experience and skills level, IT maturity level of organization, infrastructure and budget allocations. Timescale is somewhat factual but that also depends on the competence and resource availability for specific stage of enterprise architecture development. The roadmap depicted in figure could be considered as an instance for specific company, which varies for different companies.

First of all, discussion about strategy and vision of enterprise architecture are initiated. In parallel the landscape of all core functionalities are consolidated and analyzed.

Next phase starts with development of working version of business and IT strategy. Business & IT capability model for capability based planning and IT operating model for effective acquisition and management of IT solutions are analyzed and prepared. In parallel EA vision is discussed and conceptualized where effective frameworks for alignment, architecture development, management and governance are finalized.

Next phase starts with developing business architecture where motivation alignment, process improvement, business agility, and service orientation of capabilities and functionalities are elaborated. In parallel, the business services and capabilities are identified and consolidated to be transformed into IT services.

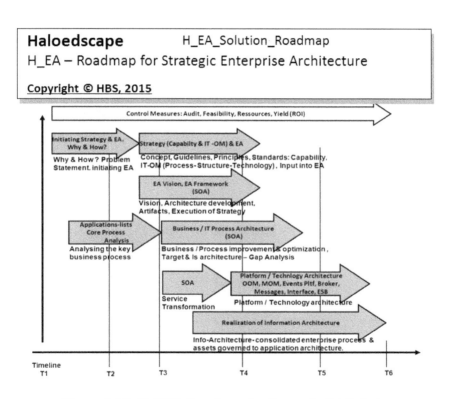

Figure 1.17: © HBS, Roadmap for Strategic EA Solution

Next phase is the development of information system architecture, data and application architecture where all enterprise services are consolidated in information system which acts as IT development environment for enterprise-wide applications.

In parallel, right platform empowered with required technology is identified which can support our sophisticated IT information system and applications. We develop the architecture of platform with technology and plan for its acquisition to support our required IT solution aligned with business.

Finally, realization of information system takes place, which acts as development environment for applications. Applications access information-system, collaborate and configure them and is finally deployed to be used as enterprise application. Normally a small prototype of information system with some set of data and tiny application is developed as proof of concept in big corporates to analyze the benefits of enterprise architecture in terms of costs, risks, business-alignment, agility, effectiveness and ROI.

1.12 Conclusion - Strategy and Foundation of Enterprise Architecture

We start our chapter with elaborating strategy, which acts as a tool to overcome the increasing challenges faced by business and IT. Strategy is a means to achieve business targets at reduced costs, risks and time to market.

Business strategy plans the business for long term in such a way that desired profit, growth and competitive advantage are achieved under all circumstances at minimal cost.

As next, business capability was elaborated which is an effective ability possessed by business-units to execute a specified course of action to achieve specific strategic goals and objectives.

Strategy leads to business architecture which is crucial to acquire effective IT solution. IT Strategy gets input from business strategy and adapts to align itself with business strategy. IT Strategy is an actionable plan to achieve an agile, effective automated solution which helps achieve business objectives with highest ROI.

IT Strategy leads to IT foundation which is composed of IT Capability and IT Operating Model.

In next section of this chapter, IT Capabilities Model was elaborated with framework which includes Structured Operating Model (SOM), Service Oriented Architecture (SOA) and Service Oriented Infrastructure (SOI). SOM is model of firm associating the business capabilities, processes, functions automated with advanced technology. SOA is defined as architecture of IT software based on service oriented design principles that transforms business functionalities and delivers them as services. SOI is architectural design for describing IT infrastructure in terms of service.

In our approach, SOA is applied to each phase of enterprise architecture development. Business is seen as system and we apply the service orientation right from business architecture to lead a business aligned IT and improve the business capabilities. Our information system must be SOA based, supported with sophisticated platform with required technology. SOA based IT solution achieves strategic objective of business aligned agile IT which maximize the ROI while reducing overall risks and costs.

We specify the IT Capabilities Statements which are IT abilities, rules, methods, guidelines and directions for strategic IT services so that value added business-capabilities are realized.

IT-OM is elaborated with frameworks of elements and components. IT-OM is a model associating the business capabilities, processes, functions and technology required for business success with the IT resource that enables them.

We present IT-Operating model with innovative framework, which guides IT architecture to be developed, managed and governed under an integrated collection of frameworks, leading to optimal enterprise architecture. Components of IT-OM are IT- Service Management framework, Enterprise Architecture Development framework and IT Governance framework.

As next, we simplified the governance process with the help of governance framework. There is a strong correlation between maturity curve of IT governance and overall effectiveness of IT. The IT control's framework for governance by COBIT is integrated with enterprise architecture. Our approach towards governance is to include the strategic values inside each phase of architecture so that the IT foundation is capable of executing strategy.

Our enterprise architecture developed in the book for generic business domain is a derived and extended instance of TOGAF, COBIT & ITIL. Our vision is to build an optimal IT architecture for whole enterprise where strategic requirements and principles are fulfilled to acquire business driven capabilities and enable the business objectives.

The required architecture design, solution approach and vision are elaborated for each phase of enterprise architecture development.

At last, roadmap for strategic enterprise architecture was described which gives the generic timeline for sequential and parallel activities.

Strategy and foundation of enterprise architecture elaborated in this chapter will be used in each phase of architecture development in subsequent chapters of this book.

2 Chapter 2: Business Architecture

Acronyms & Definitions used in this chapter:

BA: Business Architecture – Business architecture is a description of business function and processes in context of strategic requirements of organization which, drives the business design choices and leads to application and technology architecture delivering required business solution.

Business Capability: An effective ability to execute a specified course of action to achieve specific strategic goals and objectives.

Business Function: Represents the business behavior associated with an organization unit. Business function is an organizational perspective on business behavior.

Business Process: It is a flow of activities that describes how the organization executes business capability.

Business Service: Represents an external view of the services, an organization provides or sells to its customers to achieve business objective. Technically, business service encompasses and uses business capabilities to enable a business sub-function; is transformed into and realized by IT service.

CBP – Capability based Planning: It is referred as a methodology of enterprise architecture to accomplish structured operating model for mission critical business services to improve the ability and business values effectively under any adverse circumstances.

Service: A logical representation of a repeatable business activity that has a specified outcome. A service is self-contained logical unit, may be composed of other services, and is generally a "black box" to its consumers.

H_EA: Enterprise Architecture IT wing of Haloedscape.

One of the supporting & enabling functions of an imaginary investment bank "Haloedscape" is Enterprise Architecture of IT. Haloedscape has a separate wing denoted as H_EA for achieving enterprise-architecture based automation, aligned with strategy.

In this chapter, our goal is to develop the target business architecture of generic business function. Some examples of investment banking functions like Private Equity, Venture Capital, M&A, are presented to illustrate the concept.

2.1 Executive Summary

Essential objectives of any business are to create a value for shareholders and for the company's growth. As new economies gain strength, market and needs shift, and aggressive new competitors emerge, staying ahead of the curve becomes more complicated and important, and thus requires consolidated service-based, agile automation for excellent performance.

In this chapter, we develop the sophisticated metamodel of Business Architecture (BA) that are applied to business functions for enterprise-wide automation. Business Architecture is a tool for business transformation to meet the agility and responsiveness, which are biggest challenge of business today. BA articulates the structure of an enterprise in terms of its capabilities, governance structure, business processes, and business information.

Business Architecture elaborates the business functionalities illustrated with Business Motivation Model, Organizational Structure, Value-added Chain, Key Performance Indicators, Strategy & Tactics, Business Scenarios, Business Process Model, Business Services, Use Cases, Capability Models and Business Services.

Business planning is based on understanding of various business scenarios and the company's resources & capabilities. It is required to ensure that business projects are consistently well-managed. There are several keys to doing so, including the creation of end-to-end business guidelines and process descriptions that also define roles, responsibilities, key milestones and deliverables throughout the entire lifecycle.

End-to-end domain and project documentation and all other business assets should be archived in an easily accessible knowledge repository so they can be used in analysis and decision making.

Business models change more rapidly today than ever before. Time-to-value for businesses seeking competitive differentiation, new business models or revenue growth, is often pursued through initiatives in strategy, transformation for business process improvements and appropriate IT solution.

BA meta-models, BA methods and tools and BA models constitute together business architecture. BA models contain a set of elements and their relationship that visualize the business activities to achieve its objectives.

We present the vision, goal and objectives, as startup activities of Business Motivation Model (BMM). BMM in enterprise architecture provides a scheme and structure for developing, communicating, and managing business plans in an organized manner.

Business principles are presented which provides the directions and guidelines for improving and planning the business and presenting the business architecture in a way which helps acquire sophisticated information system and application.

Business strategy and corresponding tactics specifies the directions, rules and guidelines for operation, planning control and development of business.

Business strategy guides to make the pricing and valuation process highly automated, more precise and less subjective.

Important events of business execution are most important factors that need active participation of most of business modules.

Business capability is supported, delivered and made aligned to organization by business functions. Capabilities are values-adding service attached to business services to enhance the values and ability of business service.

Business function realizes, possesses and delivers the business services governed by strategy to provide specific services to customer. Business service encompasses and uses business capability to deliver an improved service to customer to achieve and support business objectives.

Business capabilities are matured ability possessed by company which helps deliver business-focused outcome efficiently and effectively and are measured in terms of values addition to the enterprise. We present capability model which is a capability-based planning approach where change activities can be sequenced and grouped in order to provide continuous and incremental business value.

The interrelations of business objectives, business functions, business services and business capabilities are formulated so that they remain absolutely aligned and fulfill their target to achieve business-aligned agile architecture for automation.

Approach to business architecture is based on strategy alignment, capabilities enhancement, excellent agility to market, high performance, and service based deliveries.

In our approach, business is seen as system and we apply the service orientation right from business architecture to lead a business aligned IT and improve the business capabilities.

Our approach towards governance is to include the strategic values inside each phase of architecture so that the IT foundation is capable of executing strategy. In this book, the business architecture is developed in such way that strategic directions, guidelines and control are embedded into the architecture so that governance process could be automated to achieve the enterprise architecture.

In our context, ideal business architecture adapts to technological innovations and is used in Business Architecture.

We present innovative extended frameworks to interrelate and align business functions, services, capabilities and objectives.

To illustrate the business architecture with examples, we use investment banking business functions like Private Equity, Venture Capital, Mergers and Acquisitions etc.

2.2   Strategic Requirements of Business Architecture

Business architecture is a description of business function and processes in context of strategic requirements of organization which drives the business design choices and leads to application and technology architecture delivering required business solution.

In short, Business Architecture is defined as the formal representation and active management of business design.

Business architecture acts as crucial link between business-strategy and enterprise- architecture.

a) It deals directly with business strategy, realizing it with organizational structure, functions, process roles and responsibilities.

b) It also drives the acquisition, deployment and integration and maintenance of business solutions running on technical platforms for information management.

Right business architecture is most crucial pillar of enterprise architecture which leads to effective IT for whole enterprise. Precise and clear business architecture leads to better business design and business aligned IT. Strategy treats IT as business-enabler and business as driver of IT.

Impact of Business Architecture (BA):

Business architecture is most significant phase in achieving enterprise architecture. BA possesses the strategic input, improves business process, optimizes the business models with capabilities and services, and specifies the requirements to develop information system architecture.

Business Architecture achieves the business functions improvement in following ways:

- Improved value added business process to achieve profit, growth and competitive advantage
- Process optimization, control, improvement and simplification
- Business impact and continuity
- Enhanced business intelligence and decision support for business
- Interoperable business process
- Business processes fulfilling business strategy
- Capabilities based planning approach to deliver improved business services
- SOA applied to business architecture

The IT related improvements are:

- Business driven information system and data model
- Consolidated IT services aligned with business services and capabilities
- Information system as provider of IT services aligned with business services
- Governance of IT strategy in enterprise wide applications
- Efficient and effective IT enabling business objective
- Higher level of automation with workflow management
- SOA based applications derived from business functionalities
- Controlled and managed change management
- Increased reusability, agility, alignment and integration with SOA

Right business architecture improves the business process, fulfills strategic requirements and leads to world class sophisticated IT solution that enables the business objective.

2.3   Business Architecture Frameworks

The Business Architecture (BA) framework consists of BA Meta-model, BA Methods & Tools and BA Models. BA Meta-model is conceptual model that covers the business domains of an enterprise.

BA methods describe the development process and the techniques that are used in the specific context in which BA is applied. It includes the design principle, reference models, use cases, business scenarios etc. In our approach, we apply SOA to transform business activities into business services realized by business function.   Based on capability based planning approach, our business functionality is represented in terms of business capabilities and business services.

The BA tools support the meta-models, methodologies with engineering tools which provides the functionality to develop, visualize, analyze, and eventually simulate aspects of the BA.

BA models contain a set of elements and their relationship that visualize the business activities to achieve its objectives. BA models are descriptions of the company's current and future states, created using the BA meta-model, methodology and tool.

BA model guides the design of the final solution. Thus, value added business transformation activities in an organization are achieved by using right BA models.

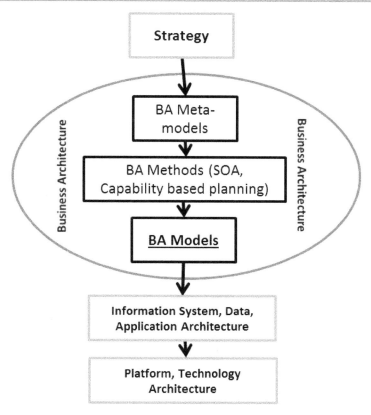

Figure 2.1: © HBS, Business Architecture Framework

BA meta-models receive strategy as its input, on which BA methods and tools are applied to generate final BA models. BA meta-models, BA methods & tools and BA models constitute together business architecture.
Essentially BA models acts as input for designing information system, data and application architecture.

Business Architecture Development

We follow the architecture development method of TOGAF and extend it with our innovative approach of SOA and capabilities based planning to build our business architecture.

We will develop the target architecture of "Haloedscape" assuming that there is currently no existing business architecture. With this assumption, our scope is limited to developing target business architecture without any gap analysis.

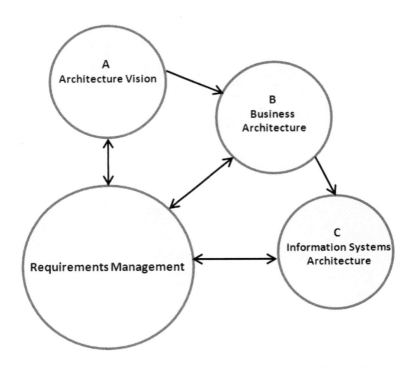

Figure 2.2: Copyright © The Open Group, TOGAF® 9.1, Business Architecture - Architecture Development Cycle

The framework of TOGAF for "Architecture Development Method" guides that Business Architecture gets its input from Architecture Vision- which is essentially part of our Strategy (Refer previous chapter) to generate the BA Model which acts as inputs to Information Systems

Architecture in order to enable the business. All of these phases of Architecture (Architecture Vision/Strategy, Business and Information Systems) interact in bidirectional way with Requirements Management so that each phase of architecture development keeps its essence of fulfilling the requirements as its top objective.

The business architecture in this book is structured with following elements:

- Frameworks for business architecture
- Framework for mapping and aligning IT with business
- Business description
- Organization structure
- Business motivation models
- Business goals and objectives
- Business function and sub-functions
- Business services
- Business capabilities
- Business process model
- KPI allocation
- Process lifecycle
- Value-added chain
- Business data model
- Business tactics, rules
- Business scenario
- Business use-cases

We apply SOA not only to Information System Architecture but to Business Architecture also. This implies that business are modeled as service; and requirements of four core factors - Information, Integration, Governance and QoS are embedded into modeling of each business service.

Business capability is supported, delivered and made aligned to organization by business functions. Capability is matured, value-added business service to efficiently and effectively serve the customers.

> *Business function realizes, possesses and delivers the business services governed by strategy to provide specific services to customer.*
>
> *We present innovative extended frameworks to interrelate and align business functions, services and capabilities.*
>
> *In our approach, business capabilities and business services are all service oriented which are directly transformed into IT-services to achieve services-oriented IT solutions aligned with business.*

2.4   Business Motivation Model

Business Architecture starts with elaboration of the motivating factors for business, the elements of business plan, the inter-relation of these factors & elements. The standardization of these business plans are exactly what the Object Management Group (OMG) has presented in from of Business Motivation Model. The BMM is business driven and methodological neutral realized by different firms in its own method keeping the essence of model intact.

The Business Motivation Model (BMM) contains:

a)   Elements of business plan structured together, which are methodological-neutral – business driven approach for planning a business.

b)   Roles in the business plan structure for business process, business rule and organizational unit.

The core objectives of BMM are to structure, communicate and organize the business plans specified in terms of factors and elements.

Some elements of full business model like following are not specified by business motivation model.

a) Business Process Model (BPM): No business process in BMM description but Reference to BPM in placeholder.
b) Workflow: No design of workflow in BMM but plan to achieve effective workflow
c) Business vocabulary: No description of the concepts and vocabulary used in the elements of business plans in BMM.

For any business's work, there is motivation which addresses enterprise's aspirations and action plans to realize them.

BMM captures business requirements across different dimensions to rigorously capture and justify why the business wants to do something, what it is aiming to achieve, how it plans to get there, and how it assesses the result.

The main elements of BMM are:

- Ends: What (as oppose to how) the business wants to accomplish
- Means: How the business intends to accomplish its ends
- Directives: The rules and policies that constrain or govern the available means
- Influencers: Can cause changes that affect the organization in its employment of its Means or achievement of its Ends. Influencers are neutral by definition.
- Assessment: A judgment of an Influencer that affects the organization's ability to achieve its Ends or use its Means.

For details, refer Business Motivation Model V 1.1- Object Management Group (OMG)

In this book, we use the service driven approach to business functions and business motivations, so that the enterprise-wide top level plans could also be reflected in enterprise architecture. The motivation models are incorporated not only as reference but as real entities in enterprise portfolio. BMM in enterprise portfolio leads the BA model to be more result-oriented, innovative and effective which in turn transformed into enterprise-wide business

> *solution. This approach helps us better align IT with business which starts at motivation level and goes down to capabilities, services and process.*

2.4.1 Vision, Goal and Objectives of Business

Vision

H_EA_VI_01: Be one of the leading firms for specialized business function in the world.

Mission

H_EA_MI_01: Keep acquiring the capabilities, innovation, sophistications and knowledgebase in order to provide best services to stakeholders.

Goals

H_EA_GO_01: Be most promising firm for the clients and stakeholders.

H_EA_GO_02: Possess solutions for innovative, appropriate & suitable functional methods

H_EA_GO_03: Successful business with matured capabilities

H_EA_GO_04: A holistic approach in planning, managing and executing the business deal

Objectives

H_EA_OB_01: To be most supportive and trustworthy business firm for clients.

- Good image, trust in market.
- Technical capabilities for precise analysis to prove the trust worthiness to acquirer and target companies
- Neutral and fair approach to clients.

H_EA_OB_02: Possess broad range of business & IT capabilities

Haloedscape should be successfully active in acquiring and improving the broad range of business and IT capabilities required for business

H_EA_OB_03: Acquire sophisticated capabilities for holistic approach in planning, managing and executing the business

H_EA should acquire and continuously improve the integrated solution for core capabilities of advanced strategy & governance, precise due-diligence, appropriate mode of financing, effective bidding strategy, optimal deal-structuring and well planned integration & synergy to lead successful business for clients.

H_EA_OB_04: High rates of success in business

- High rate of success in business requires best managers, right approach, decision-support, precise analysis, precise valuations, and anticipated market conditions supported by automated real-time solution.
- Haloedscape should acquire specialized managers to deal with business function
- Managers should be accountable for their decisions which are validated by automated solution.

The End, Vision, Mission, Goals and Objectives have been consolidated and interrelated together. Other objectives and performance measures will be presented further.

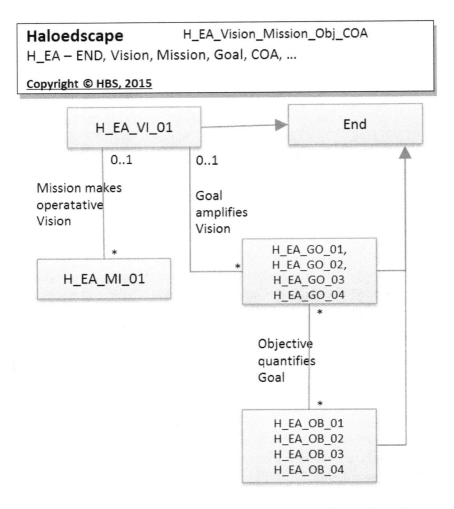

Figure 2.3: © HBS -V1_2014, BMM (OMG)- Interrelating End, Vision, Mission, Goals, Objectives of H_EA

BMM directives and influencers are presented in form of business principles, business strategy and tactics.

2.4.2 Business Principles

Name	Maximize Benefit to the Enterprise
Description / Statement	Focused and agile Enterprise-Architecture is developed which improves the business, applications, technology and platforms for its development, operation and maintenance in a way to maximize benefit to enterprise.
Rationale	Maximum return on investment for whole enterprise is the driving force to formulate strategy which impacts each level of enterprise architecture.
Implications	Achieve maximum enterprise-wide benefits with enterprise architecture. • Business Architecture should be service oriented. Business functionalities and capabilities should be transformed into business services. • Foundation of Information-Architecture should be optimized to be used in optimal way by individual applications. • Develop Enterprise Architecture which leads to effective IT in order to achieve maximum ROI. • Use SOA (loosely coupled, reusable services)

	for optimal use of resources. • Reduce costs & risks and increase agility & effectiveness of IT. • Do everything possible to maximize ROI and long term strategic benefits.

Name	Business Continuity
Description / Statement	Enterprise business operations are continued in spite of system interruptions. The core business processes running on enterprise resources (technology, platforms, hardware) must possess the capability to continue their business functions regardless of internal or external adverse events.
Rationale	Business must be continued in spite of internal and external interruptions. A failure of business continuity results in financial loss leading to business abatement.
Implications	• Acquire mission-critical services to ensure business function continuity. • Acquire sophisticated and improved solution for effective prevention and recovery of business functions. • Maintain the value system integrity with technology supporting fail-over, fault tolerance, cloning, replication etc. • Identify and secure enterprise's exposure to external and internal threats.

Name	Business Ownership

Description / Statement	Each core business function should be under ownership for full accountability.
Rationale	Business function should be maintained and accounted for its proper functioning. The responsibility for proper functioning of business function should be well defined.
Implications	• Identify the functions owners and allocate the responsibility for business functions. • The owners of business functions must possess the resource capabilities to serve the business functions.

Name	Secured Intellectual Property
Description / Statement	The enterprise's intellectual property must be protected. The confidential business tactics and algorithm must be secured.
Rationale	Intellectual property is the basis of existence of a business and must be secured to safeguard the business.
Implications	• State the security policy in business strategy governing human and IT actors to protect the intellectual property and business tactics.

Name	Compliance with Law
Description / Statement	The business functions and processes must comply with all relevant laws, policies and regulations.
Rationale	Failure in legal compliance endangers the business and invites the penalty.
Implications	• Establish a process to validate the business functions fulfilling the legal compliance. • The periodic updates of validation process

	must be automated to include new changes in policies and regulations. • The legal-compliance must be treated as a utility function executed under an ownership necessary to run core business function. • The legal-compliance must be a part of corporate strategy.

Name	Principles Governance
Description / Statement	Govern the principles across all the business units of an enterprise. The governance process must be a part of Business/IT Strategy.
Rationale	Governance of principles assures realization of enterprise wide strategic benefits. Principles provide directions and guidelines in every stage of enterprise architecture. Automated governance of principles ensures a smooth transition to optimal Enterprise-Architecture and consistent growth on maturity curve.
Implications	• Develop governance framework. • Strive for automating the governance process. • The governance process must be treated as a strategic governance function and executed under ownership. • The principles should be enforced in all core applications of an enterprise to realize strategic benefits.

	• The principles governance should be an integral part of corporate strategy.

2.4.3 Business Strategy and Tactics

As mentioned in chapter1 – Refer Business Strategy, Strategic Rules and Tactics.

2.5 Organizational Structure

Organizational structure illustrates the expressed allocation of responsibilities for different functions and processes to different entities such as the branch, department, workgroup and individual. An organization can be structured in many different ways, depending on their objectives. The structure of an organization will determine the modes in which it operates and performs. The functional structure of organization consists of inter-relation between different key sub-functions.

To illustrate the organizational structure with examples, we use investment banking business functions like Private Equity, Mergers and Acquisitions, Venture Capital etc.

Business organization of Private Equity:

The investors are called Limited Partners (LP) and they aim to manage risk and returns with diversified portfolios that aim for a high target return from private equity investment. The private equity firm managing the PE fund is General Partner (GP). The GP acts as PE fund manager responsible for managing the PE fund.

The basic roles of Investment Bank in private equity business are:-

- Introduce the potential acquisition targets to PE firms
- Help negotiate acquisition price
- Provide loans or arrange bond financing
- Arrange exit transaction

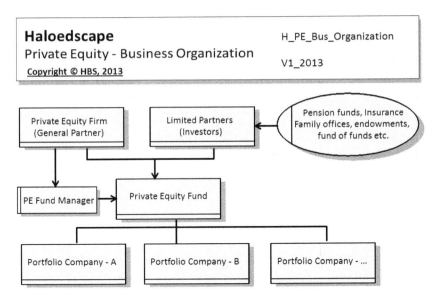

Figure 2.4-A: © HBS, Private Equity Fund Organization

Business organization of Secondary Market of Private Equity:

Secondary Market is purchase of existing commitments in PE funds or portfolio of direct investments. Secondary Market enables the LPs to buy and sell PE investments and commitments to fund.

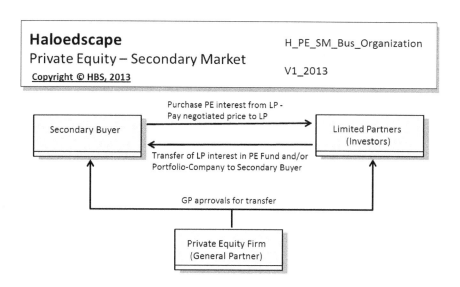

Figure 2.4-B: © HBS, PE-Secondary Market Organizational Roles

Business organization of M&A function:

Buyer/Acquirer categorized under strategic buyers, financial buyers or consolidators. The strategic buyers seek to extend their customer base, boost market shares, expand product lines and business to new locations and expect a big growth on long term. Financial buyers are buyout funds, wealthy individuals and investment funds etc. which are active majorly in M&A activities. Consolidators intend to consolidate their business through M&A. Buyer intends to offer price based on whether transaction will be accretive: increases earnings per share of acquiring company.

Seller seeks premium over its existing stock price (if public) or price in line with public traded comparable or recent public disclosed M&A transaction multiples based on price to earnings, price to EBITDA or price to sales.

Investment bank acts as primary financial advisor for M&A business. Key services of Investment Bank in M&A business are:

- Analyzes the M&A requirements, strategy, target-valuation, synergy and acquisition-benefits in order to offer negotiation-terms and structure the deal
- Prepares financial model to analyze the financial benefits of combined company
- Carries out due diligence to explore M&A opportunity
- Evaluates the target company with pricing techniques
- Offers advice on tax and accounting structure for transaction
- Helps raise capital needed to complete transaction
- Helps in commissioning and post-merger integration

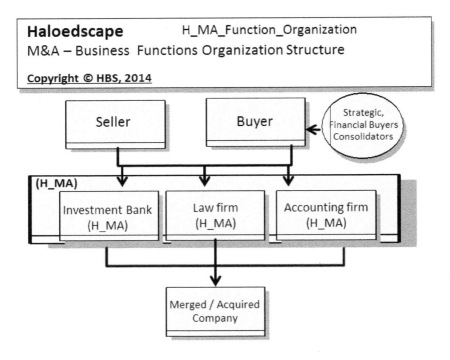

Figure 2.5: © HBS, M&A Organizational Structure

Legal service includes drafting and negotiation of transaction documents, reviews appropriate tax, employment, environmental, corporate governance, securities, real property, and abides by applicable international, federal, state and local laws.

The important accounting services are to advise company on proper tax and accounting treatment of transaction, assist in valuing certain specific assets, preparing comfort-letter on accounting issues, preparing consent-letter if publicly registered securities offering is made related with transaction.

2.6   Business Values

Business values are parameters of financial performance of business. Business values in terms of performance are quantified as KPI Allocation diagram.

To illustrate the Business Values with examples, we use investment banking functions like Private Equity, Mergers and Acquisitions, Venture Capital etc.

2.6.1 Business Strategic Benefits

Ideally companies are motivated to improve long-term competitive advantage in support of strategic goals. The strategic rationale drives the companies to achieve a set of strategic objectives.

In principle, the decisions regarding strategic growth and capital budgeting are taken at corporate level. Corporate decision obviously affects the value of the firm, but they also affect the relative value of the stocks and bonds. The value of an action may depend on things like strategic fits and alignment.

In Investment Banking, following are some of key underlying events or reasons that motivate a course of action in M&A function:

- Stock Market
- Globalization
- Geographical Consolidation
- Asset Diversification
- Sector Pressures

- Capacity Reduction
- Financial Necessity
- Market Control & Competitive Advantage
- Strategic Benefits

An instance of Business Strategic Benefits in terms of KPI allocation for M&A function of Haloedscape is as follows:

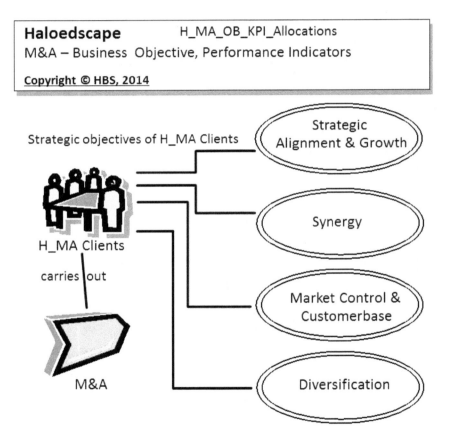

Figure 2.6: © HBS, M&A Strategic Objectives KPI

In M&A function of Investment Banking, synergy value is created from economies of integrating a target with the acquiring company, which is an amount by which the value of combined firm exceeds the sum value of two individual firms.

The value chain diagram of synergy is illustrated below:

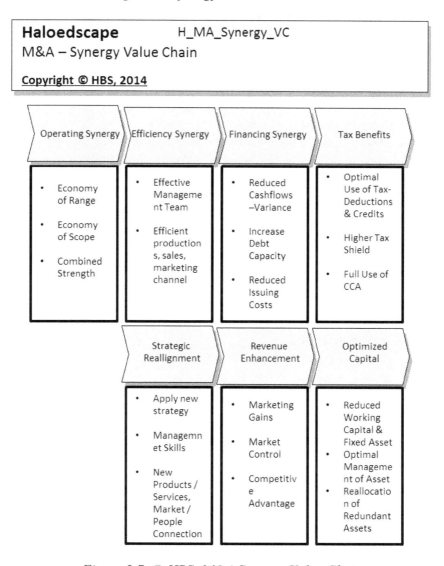

Figure 2.7: © HBS, M&A Synergy Value Chain

Buyer utilizes the acquisition to improve the cash flows of the target, itself, or both to create additional values. In common language, this has come to be known as the concept of "synergy."

Synergy causes the merged company worth more than the sum of the parts. The target and acquiring companies generate more values together then operating separately.

2.6.2 Performance Value as KPIs

Key performance Indicators quantifies the measure of performance. KPIs evaluate the success of an organization for specific set of activities. Key performance indicators define a set of values against which to measure. These raw sets of values, which are fed to systems in charge of summarizing the information, are called indicators. KPI allocation diagrams for private equity and M&A functions of investment banking are illustrated below:

Buyer's Performance & Quantifying Indicators for M&A function

- Ratio of Achieved and Expected Synergy
- Outperformance of combined company
- Revenue Growth
- Diversification
- Free Cashflows
- Strategic Alignment & Values
- Enhanced Market Control & Customer base
- Globalization for new market access, enhanced capabilities and resources
- EPS
- SVAR
- TRR

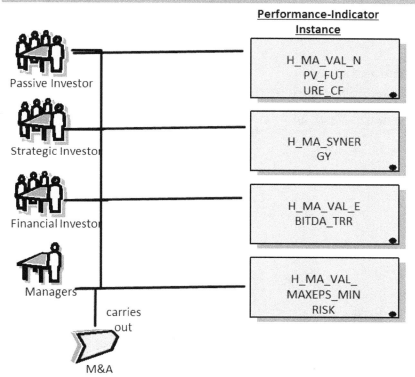

Figure 2.8: © HBS, M&A Buyer KPI Allocation

Seller's Performance & Quantifying Indicators for M&A function

- Stock Premium
- P/E Ratio
- Multiples of EBITDA
- Earn-outs
- Shareholder values - EPS after acquisition
- Liquidity

- Divestiture
- LBOs
- Consolidation
- EPS Growth for shareholders
- Q Ratio

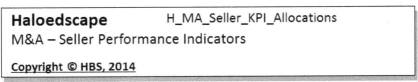

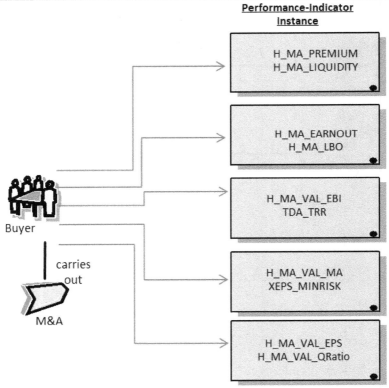

Figure 2.9: © HBS, M&A Seller KPI Allocation

Strategic advantages of Private Equity asset class in terms of KPIs

- Long-term capital growth
- Diversification
- Uncorrelated returns
- Higher returns

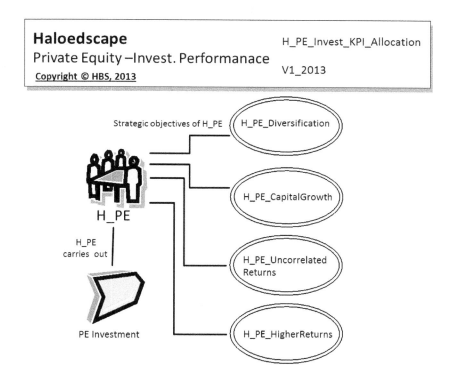

Figure 2.10: © HBS, Private Equity Strategic Objectives KPI

Key Performance Indicators for Leverage Buyouts (LBOs)

LBO is the primary sub-asset of private equity where acquired company's balance sheet is leveraged to reduce the investor's cash commitment.

Key Performance Indicators (KPIs) for LBO are:

- *H_PE_KP_01: Target IRR*

- ***H_PE_KP_02: Debt Reduction***
- ***H_PE_KP_03: Increase in Equity***

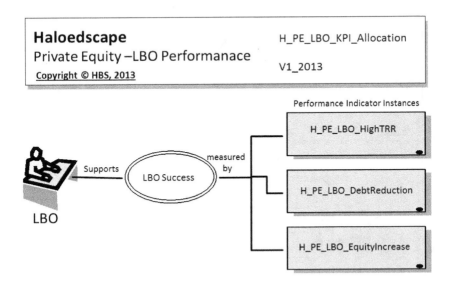

Figure 2.11: © HBS, LBO KPI Allocation

For an LBO transaction to be successful, the target company must generate a significant amount of cash flow to pay high debt interest and principal payments and, sometimes, pay dividends to the private equity shareholders.

Key Performance Indicators for Distressed / Special Situation

Distressed or Special Situation is characterized by investment in debt securities or equity of a company under financial stress. This investment is quite risky and loans are rated BB and below by S&P based on ration debt/EBITDA, EBITDA interest coverage etc.

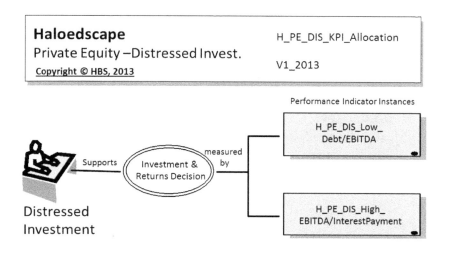

Figure 2.12: © HBS, Distressed Investment KPI Allocation

The performance of company is measured by its ability to pay off its incurred debt. Debt/EBITDA metric approximates the time required by company to pay off all debt, ignoring, interest taxes, depreciation and amortization. EBITDA/Interest-payment ratio approximates the company's ability to pay off its interest expenses.

Key Performance Indicators for Secondary Market
Secondary Market is purchase of existing commitments in PE funds or portfolio of direct investments. Secondary Market enables the LPs to buy and sell PE investments and commitments to fund.

The performance is measured by percentage of liquidity available in secondary market. The valuation of LP interest in PE fund and target-company is also important to measure the performance.

Key Performance Indicators (KPIs) for Secondary Market are:

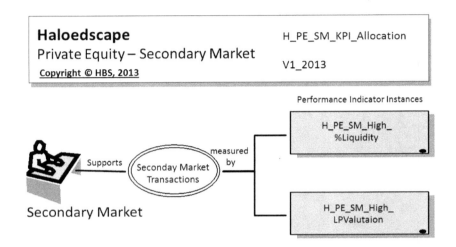

Figure 2.13: © HBS, Secondary Market KPI Allocation

Key Performance Indicators for Mezzanine

Mezzanine is provided by mezzanine fund and sometimes hedge funds. In this investment, debt Instrument is immediately subordinated to equity. Mezzanine deals with debt instrument and receives high yield in return. Mezzanine financing includes equity ownership. Mezzanine is usually reimbursed at exit if not refinanced before.

Returns are generated by:

- Cash interest payment – Fixed rate, float rate attached with index
- PIK interest – Payment is made by increasing the borrowed amount

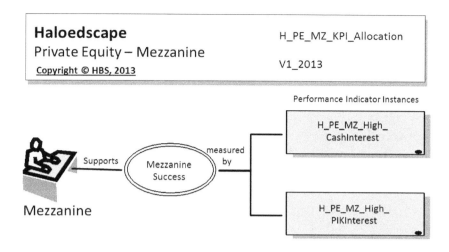

Figure 2.14: © HBS, Mezzanine KPI Allocation

<u>Key Performance Indicators for value creation in Private Equity</u>
The measures of value creation are achieved with following:

- EBITDA generation: Sales expansion, Margin Improvement, GDP growth
- Acquisitions: Add-on acquisitions
- Multiple Expansion (ME): Multiple EV/EBITDA
    - o Multiple expansion is difference between entry and exit multiple.
    - o Measure of expansion = Multiple uplift x Exit EBITDA
    - o Multiple uplift = Exit EV / EBITDA – Entry EV/EBITDA
- Debt reduction (Deleveraging) = Entry net debt – exit net debt

Measures of performance of PE investments are quantified with following:

Multiple of Cost:
- Total value over Paid-in Capital (TVPI)
- (Cash used + Unrealized value) / capital invested
- Total Return: Cash return regardless of timing

Internal Rate of Return (IRR):

- Internal rate of return: Discount rate that makes NPV of all cash-flows equal zero.
- Short term gain: Quick flip leads to high IRR

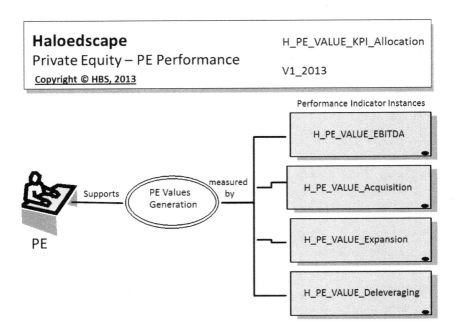

Figure 2.15: © HBS, Private Equity Values KPI Allocation

2.7 Business Process Lifecycle

To illustrate the Business Process Lifecycle with examples, we use investment banking business functions like Private Equity, Mergers and Acquisitions, Venture Capital etc.

The business lifecycle specifies all the stages of business execution, wherein a stage is constituted of a set of events and activities. Each stage of lifecycle comprises a course of events, planning and activities which are required to complete the stage and transit to next stage. The business lifecycle starts with Strategy phase which involves the analysis of business strategy, strategic tactics and business rules to plan, analyze, undertake and validate the business.

Lifecycle of M&A and Private Equity functions of investment banking are illustrated below.

M&A Lifecycle

M&A spans through following stages:
- M&A Strategy
- Selection Criteria, Target Search and Feasibility
- Due Diligence & Valuation
- Financing
- Negotiation & Deal Structure
- Accounting
- Implementation & Closing
- Commissioning - Post-merger Integration

The strategic needs, preferences and selection criteria of buyer-company are the main factors in acquisition criteria and initial selection process.

Due diligence is a process through which a potential acquirer evaluates a target firm in order to make decision for acquisition and thereafter structuring the deal for negotiation. Due diligence involves investigating and analyzing the target company leading to deeper understanding of its financial values, market strength and business potential.

Valuation process involves financial position of acquiring firm and the valuation of the acquisition target. The target company to be acquired is valued to determine what price to offer.

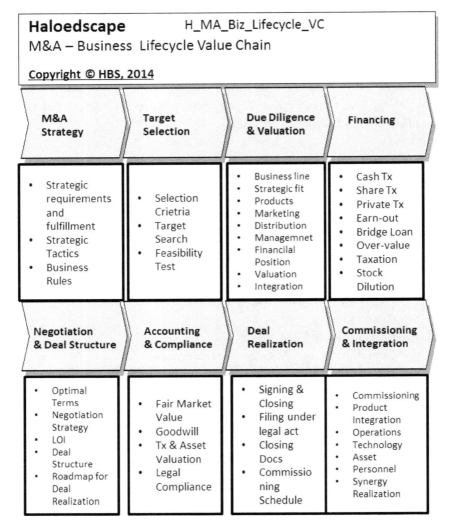

Figure 2.16: © HBS, M&A Lifecycle Value Chain

Structuring an acquisition financing involves financial position and expectations of both companies merging together. Favorable acquisition currency, flexibility and tax-free transactions are normally the wishes of companies joining together.

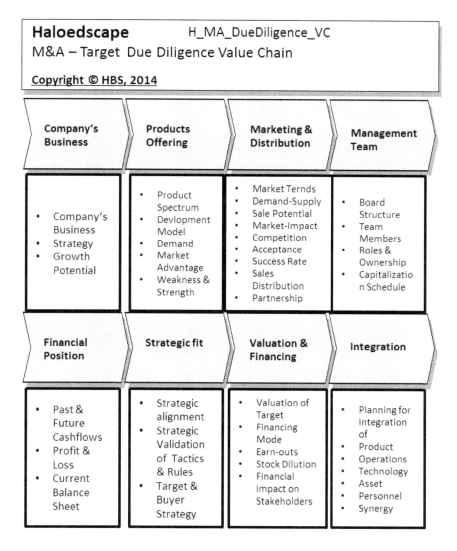

Figure 2.17: © HBS, M&A Due Diligence Process

The pre-merger negotiation phase starts right after the commitment to proceed. In this phase the senior managers of the two organizations enter into negotiations in order to reach agreement on the structure and format of the new combined organization.

Purchase method is used for accounting where all assets and liabilities are expressed as fair market value (FMV) and difference of FMV and target firm's equity is reported as goodwill.

The implementation process starts as soon as the contract is in place. Implementation includes the mechanics of actually making the merger happen.

Stage of Commissioning/Integration is followed by a longer-term phase in which the new organization acclimatizes to the new organizational structure.

Private Equity (PE), Venture Capital (VC) – Process Lifecycle

There are four key process steps for PE transactions categorized under:

- Preparatory Phase: Initial business review and due diligence are carried out. A review of financial, operational and regulatory issues is done. A preferred structure of PE investment is proposed and initial offering is made.
- Marketing Phase: The investors are invited for initial meetings and a potential set of investors are selected for management presentation.
- Buyer/Investor Meetings: Further management and strategic meetings are held. The deal terms and structure are finalized.
- Structuring & Negotiations: Letters of intent are finalized. Negotiations are done for improvement of deal structure. Complete due diligence is done and definitive document is signed.

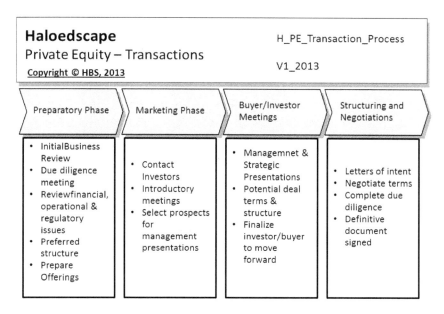

Figure 2.18: © HBS, Private Equity Transaction Process

Private Equity Asset Class – Investment Stages & Financing Lifecycle

The strategies private equity may employ are venture capital, leveraged buyout, mezzanine fund, distressed debt, growth capital etc.

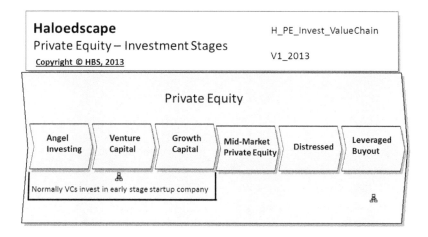

Figure 2.19: © HBS, Stages of Investment in Private Equity

These strategies are structured as sub-asset class of private equity as illustrated in value chain diagram.

Stages of investment in PE business start with Angel Investing where seed capital is invested to give a basic foundation of target-company. Angel investing is done to startup a business from scratch where company structuring and market research for product development takes place.

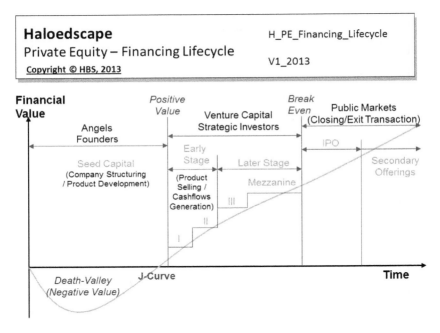

Figure 2.20: © HBS, Financing Lifecycle in Private Equity

The next stage of investment is early stage investment taken by strategic investors where financial value of target-company stands in positive due to small cashflows generation. The PE investment at this stage is considered loss because the little cashflows cannot cross break-even level for investments.

The positive value investment starts with Venture Capital investment where the product selling and cashflows generation start in target-company. This stage of investment happens in target-company funding full-scale operations and selling product and services. The last stage of positive value investment below but close to break-even is Mezzanine. At this stage, target-company expands the funding and adds new products to their product/service inventory.

Last stage of investment crosses the break-even and become profitable. At IPO stage, the target company is transited to public market and PE investment is closed returning a high profit on PE investment. Other form of PE investment is Secondary Offerings where target-company is acquired by third party returning high return on PE investment.

Venture Capital (VC) is treated as a subset class or private equity that falls under alternative assets.

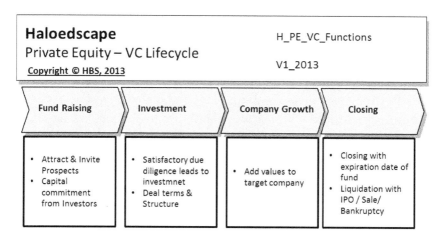

Figure 2.21: © HBS, VC Lifecycle

Venture capital investment lifecycle involves the following stages:
- Raising the fund
- Sourcing and structuring the investment
- Creating and adding values
- Exit strategy – closing the fund

2.8   Pricing and Valuation

Pricing & Valuation methods are illustrated with Business Process Model (BPM) for investment banking functions.

The valuation techniques used in investment banking are comparable methods, breakup valuation, leveraged buyout analysis, gross revenue multiplier, earning per share method, liquidation analysis etc.

To develop a DCF model an acquirer typically forecasts cash flows over some period of time (five to ten years) and a terminal value for a target, and discounts those values at the weighted average cost of capital. The final valuation depends on the weighted average cost of capital chosen, cash flows forecasted (e.g. revenue, cost, net working capital, and investment forecasts), and terminal value.

Fair market value (FMV) is the highest price obtainable in an open and unrestricted market, where all involved parties without any compulsion wish to transact.

Determining fair market value depends on the perspective of the acquirer. Some acquirers are more likely to be able to realize synergies than others and those with the greatest ability to generate synergies are the ones who can justify higher prices.

There are two approaches for pricing, proactive models approach and reactive pricing approach. The proactive models approach involves valuation method to determine what a target firm's value should be based on future values of cash flow and earnings. Reactive pricing approach reacts to general rules of thumb and the relative pricing compared to other securities.

Discounted Cashflows (DCF) Method: To develop a DCF model an acquirer typically forecasts cash flows over some period of time for instance five to ten years, and a terminal value for a target, and discounts those values at the weighted average cost of capital. The final valuation depends on the weighted average cost of capital chosen, cash flows forecasted (e.g. revenue, cost, net working capital, and investment forecasts), and terminal value.

The entity DCF model evaluates of a company as the value of a company's operations less the value of debt and other investor claims, such as preferred stock, that are superior to common equity. The value of operations is the value of operations equals the discounted value of expected future free cash flow.

The key to using the DCF approach to price a target firm is to obtain good forecasts of free cash flow. Free cash flows to equity holders represent cash flows left over after all obligations, including interest payments have been paid.

DCF valuation takes the following steps:

- Forecast free cash flows
- Obtain a relevant discount rate
- Discount the forecast cash flows and sum to estimate the value of the target

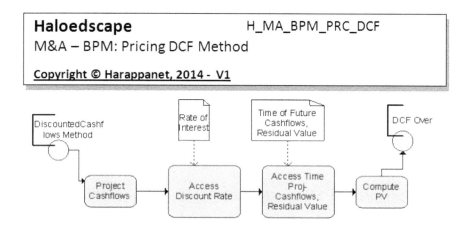

Figure 2.22: © HBS, Biz Process Model - Discounted Cashflow Pricing Method

Following is the generalized version of the DCF model showing how forecast free cash flows are discounted to the present and then summed up.

$$V_0 = \frac{CF_1}{(1+k)^1} + \frac{CF_2}{(1+k)^2} + ... + \frac{CF_\alpha}{(1+k)^\alpha} = \sum_{t=1}^{\alpha} \frac{CF_t}{(1+k)^t}$$

where V_0 = present value of projected cashflows
             CFt = projected cashflows for different time (year)
             k = discounting rate, risk free rate - cost of capital or TRR

For a startup target company, just like venture capital method, negative cashflows and highly uncertain projected cashflows are taken into account. The discounted cashflows method is used for several potential scenarios.

To achieve a target rate of return (TRR), it is used as discounting rate instead of cost of capital.

Synergy Valuation Method: Synergy achieves economic gain which is the PV of increased earnings. Net synergy value is formulated as follows:

$$NSV = V_{ab} - (V_a + V_b) - P - E$$

where V_{ab} = combined value of the both firms
             V_b = market value of the shares of target firm
             V_a = Acquisitor measure of its own value
             P   = premium paid for target
             E   = expenses of the operation

Comparable method: For comparable methods, appropriate comparators are identified. An ideal way is to identify an individual firm that is highly comparable to the target or finding an average of comparable industry. After finding the comparators, data is adjusted and normalized wherein capital structures and accounting differences like LIFO versus FIFO, accelerated versus straight-line deprecation are adjusted.

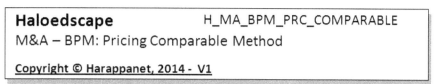

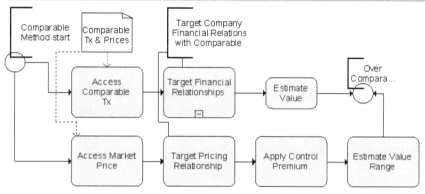

Figure 2.23: © HBS, Biz Process Model - Comparable Pricing Method

A variety of ratios for both the target and the comparator like following are calculated to get a range of justifiable values:

- Price-earnings ratio (trailing)
- Value/EBITDA
- Price/Book Value
- Return on Equity

The comparable transaction method: Under this method, the acquisition candidate is compared with the transactions of publicly traded companies. Acquisition multiples are calculated for comparable transactions and applied to financial results to estimate the value at which the target would likely trade.

The comparable company method: Under this method, the acquisition candidate is compared with the market price of publicly traded companies. A relationship is assessed which compares how the value of target compares with the market price of publicly traded companies. A pricing relationship is also analyzed and applied to acquisition candidate's cashflows, earnings, book value etc. A change of control premium is applied to value, identified by this method to estimate the value-range of the target firm.

The M&A multiples techniques: Benchmark values are based on multiples of earnings, book value etc. It analyze the acquisition multiples and the change of control premium and is used when comparable transactions or companies are not available.

Breakup valuation technique: This method involves analyzing the valuation of each of business units and summing them for up for whole of target's business to estimate the total value.

The book value approach: The net worth of a company is analyzed on the basis of balance sheet. Book Value Multiples are useful for industries where a company's book value plays a role in determining future profitability.

The book value approach is used for companies like following:

> Service industry receiving rate-of-return, such as telephone, electric, and gas utilities, where the company's future earnings are limited to a defined return on the company's equity.

> In financial industry such as banks and insurance companies, where the balance sheet values of most assets and liabilities are reasonably close to market values

Liquidation Analysis: Under this method, analysis is done for amount of cash that could be realized if a company sells all of its assets and pays off its liabilities. Liquidation value is the minimum value of company.

It is amount of proceeds that could be realized by a stockholder, if a company ceases operations, if all assets are sold at prevailing market prices, and if all liabilities and tax obligations are satisfied.

Replacement Value: Replacement value is the maximum value of company which is the cost that would be incurred if one tries to replicate all of the assets and liabilities of a company by building them or purchasing them in the market

Earnings multiples: The technique involves collecting the past or projected earnings per share and multiplying by earnings multiple derived from publicly traded comparable companies.

Earnings Multiples is the gross acquisition price divided by operating earnings.

Gross acquisition price (GAP) is sum of price paid for equity and market value of total debt owed by acquired company. Operating earnings is earnings before interest and taxes (EBIT) and is formulated as sum of pretax earnings and interest expenses.

Price-Earnings Ratio: P/E ratio is measure of investments per dollar of earnings denoting multiple of a stock. It is formulated as follows:

P/E Ratio = Market Value per Share / Earning per Share

Venture Capital Valuation: Terminal value is estimated- The terminal value of target is estimated at a specific time in future planned as closing date. It is calculated using the multiple such as price-earnings ratio applied to projected net income on exit date.

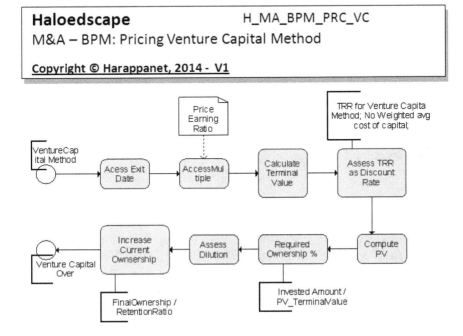

Figure 2.24: © HBS, Biz Process Model – Venture Capital Pricing Method

Terminal value is discounted to present value- Usually the net present value is calculated using weighted average cost of capital is used to discount annual cashflows and terminal value. In venture capital method, the target rate of return (TRR) is used to calculate present value of projected terminal value.

Required ownership percentage is calculated- The required ownership percentage to achieve the target rate of return (TRR) is the amount to be invested by acquirer divided by PV of terminal value of target-company.

Required current ownership percentage is calculated for expected dilution- If additional shares are issued to other investing parties before the closing date, the dilution of equity comes into effect. To counter the dilution effect, the acquirer increase the ownership percentage which is formulated as required current ownership is required final ownership divided by retention ratio.

Required Current Ownership = Req. Final Ownership / Retention Ratio

Economic Profit Model: The value of a firm equals the amount of capital invested and present value of profit generated on capital.

Economic Profit = Invested Capital x ($R_{IC} - C_{WAC}$)
Economic profit = Tax Adjusted Net Profit – (Invested Capital x C_{WAC})
        Where R_{IC} = Return on Invested Capital
            C_{WAC} = Weighted Average Cost of Capital

Return on Invested Capital = Tax Adjusted Net Profit / Invested Capital

Estimating Cost of Capital: The weighted average cost of capital (WACC) is the rate that a company is expected to pay on average to all its security holders to finance its assets. The WACC is the minimum return that a company must earn on an existing asset base.

The WACC is formulated as:

$$WACC = \frac{\sum_{i=1}^{N} r_i \cdot MV_i}{\sum_{i=1}^{N} MV_i}$$

Where N is the number of sources of capital (securities, liabilities etc); r_i is the required rate of return for security; and MV_i is the market value of all outstanding securities.

In the case where the company is financed with only equity and debt, the average cost of capital is computed as follows:

$$WACC = \frac{D}{D+E}K_d + \frac{E}{D+E}K_e$$

Where D is the total debt, E is the total shareholder's equity, K_e is the cost of equity, and K_d is the cost of debt

Cost of Equity: Cost of equity is sum of risk free rate of return and premium expected for risk. It is formulated as:

$$E_s = R_f + \beta_s(R_m - R_f).$$

Where
- E_s is the expected return for a security
- R_f is the expected risk-free return in that market (government bond yield)
- β_s is the sensitivity to market risk for the security
- R_m is the historical return of the stock market/ equity market
- $(R_m - R_f)$ is the risk premium of market assets over risk free assets

Option Valuation Method: The Black-Scholes method involves assigning the uses the quantified value of flexibility that buyer has on making the follow-on decision.

The pricing with Black-Scholes requires a correspondence of variable between option and target-company.

The PV of expenses required to undertake the project corresponds to exercise price of option X. The PV of projected cashflows corresponds to stock price S. The time interval for which the buyer can defer the investment decision corresponds to maturity time T of option. The riskiness of underlying project corresponds to volatility of stock-returns σ. The risk-free rate is r which is time value of money.

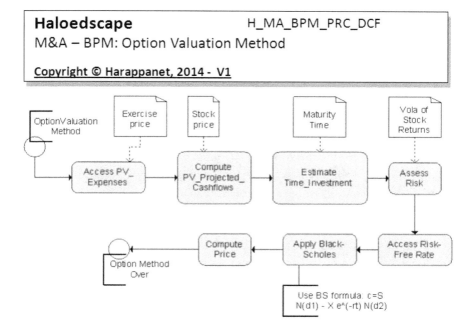

Figure 2.25: © HBS, Biz Process Model –Option Valuation Pricing Method

The price of option to undertake the investment like European call option is c and to sell the option like European put option is p.

The values c & p calculated by Black-Scholes are as follows:

$$c = S_0\, N(d_1) - X\, e^{-rT} N(d_2)$$

$$p = X\, e^{-rT}\, N(-d_2) - S_0\, N(-d_1)$$

$$\text{where}\ \ d_1 = \frac{\ln(S_0 / X) + (r + \sigma^2 / 2)T}{\sigma\sqrt{T}}$$

$$d_2 = \frac{\ln(S_0 / X) + (r - \sigma^2 / 2)T}{\sigma\sqrt{T}} = d_1 - \sigma\sqrt{T}$$

Here $N(x)$ is the probability that a normally distributed variable with a mean of zero and a standard deviation of 1 is less than x.

2.9 Business Deal Realization

Business Deal Realization is most important business event which requires, uses, and invokes most of the business sub-modules. Deal execution dependency requires automated workflow.

Deal realization includes the mechanics of making the business happen. It involves invocation of most of business functionalities. In investment banking, it associates the deal-structure, invokes the pricing functions for valuation and acts as events to trigger the process of isolated modules.

In this book, deal realization is illustrated with examples for investment banking functions like Merger & Acquisitions, and Private Equity.

Deal Execution in M&A

In M&A business function of investment banking, deal structure is prepared with strategic compliance, due diligence and analytical process.

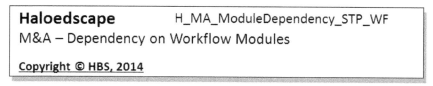

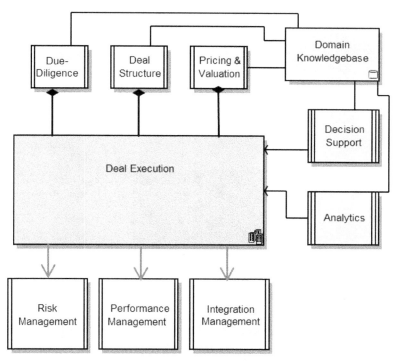

Figure 2.26: © HBS, M&A Module Dependency for STP Workflow

Deal execution is treated as events for invoking the callback functions of remote module like performance management, risk management and post-merger integration so that workflow automation could be achieved.

Deal Execution in Private Equity

In Private Equity function of investment banking, deal execution is treated as events for invoking the callback functions of remote module like portfolio management, risk management and fund administration so that workflow automation could be achieved. Deal execution is function of front office which is integrated with middle/back-office using straight-through-processing (STP) workflow.

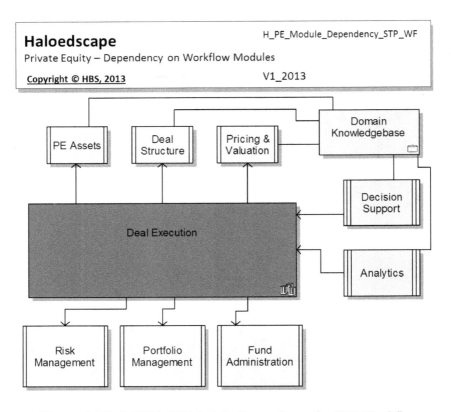

Figure 2.27: © HBS, PE Module Dependency for STP Workflow

Deal execution is most important functionality of business which involves active participation of most of functionalities. Deal realization is dependent on due diligence, deal-structure and pricing functionalities of M&A whereas performance management, risk management and Integration management are dependent on deal-execution.

2.10 Risk and Performance Management

A consistent set of monitoring and benchmarking elements is essential for a coherent assessment of business function, forming the basis for risk management. Early risk identification and active management are crucial in order to secure maximum value for the business.

There should be consolidated automation of risk-management which works in real-time with deal execution so that stakeholders could access their customized dashboards and receive the reports they wish on real time.

Risk management concerns the identification, monitoring and management of the risk profile of the business. Risk management should be in place to track and control the process execution in line with planning and anticipation. Business values planned and realized should be tracked, measured and controlled to promptly take appropriate action as and when any anticipated financial value is lost.

The primary objective of performance management is to formulate the deals and ensure values addition in order to achieve superior returns. The operational and value creation drive are managed effectively and efficiently by real-time performance management system linked to risk management.

Domain of Business Risks

Strategic Risk - Strategic risks are directly linked to business capability statements, business principles, tactics, business rules, strategic guidelines and planning.

Project Risk - Delay in transition to next phase of business function increase the costs and lowers down the value of deal. The prime factors which leads smooth transition of deal are effective completion of business lifecycle; all done in holistic environment with effective project management.

Business Process Risk: Business process is execution of an instance of business lifecycle. Business's risk identification and control mechanism should be handled with comprehensive risk management process. Business process risks adversely affect the financial value realization and expectation of stakeholders, resulting in shortcomings in realizing the business values.

> *It is required to anticipate deviation, promote correcting actions, calculate valuations and ratios and generate summary reports for business process executed so far. The requirements of performance data range from key indictors to more detailed performance drivers. There should be consolidated automation of performance management which works in real-time with deal transition so that stakeholders could subscribe to the reports they wish and receive it on real time.*

Addressing the Business Risks

The immediate and likely long-term performance of the business can be monitored and controlled using risk management tools and techniques.

Business risks of different level and criteria are managed with different methods to assist in decision making and control the risks. Risk management model is categorized into risk identification and risk quantization.

Proper due diligence is carried out including stress tests for target's resilience and growth prospects to ensure, how the business will handle large shifts in demand, its sensitivity to interest rate changes or currency fluctuation, and other macro-economic drivers of the target's business.

Project Management, Analytics and DSS for Risks Management:

Domain-knowledgebase is comprehensive information repository which helps automate different life cycles of business.

Analytics accesses data from knowledgebase and applies the methods to generate required information which is used for decision support.

Decision support module plays important role for optimal strategic recommendations and business planning.

Project management ensures planning of business process and its realization is maintained in form of project where processes are divided into small units of functions and sub-functions.

Analysis of business project planning and process execution are carried out in a consolidated environment so that every process of process is monitored, controlled and managed with automated risk & performance management.

Risk management should be directly linked and well integrated with performance management.

> *Risk & Performance Management is automated with straight through processing workflow. Events like deal execution invoke function of isolated risk-management module which executes the dependent process in real-time to compute the risk associated with new event. Workflow automation with STP enables the real-time risk management integrated with performance management.*

2.11 Business Automation Requirements and Design Perspective

Business automation is required for solution that provides not only a complete system of record to help capture, execute, and monitor business processes and achievements but also helps in decision making and providing optimal business process.

Business Requirements

- Full end to end business process design, playbook development for whole company or individual functions, staff augmentation services & execution readiness assessments.
- Knowledgebase – It provides automated information on request. Analytics for due-diligence, deal structuring, optimizing portfolio, and decision support module use centralized knowledgebase as primary source of information.
  Domain-knowledgebase is comprehensive information repository which helps automate different life cycles of business process. Analytics accesses data from knowledgebase and applies the methods to generate required information which is used for decision support.
- Decision support module – Decision support module aligned with strategy is used for decision making at various points in business process.
- Pricing Module – Precise valuation of financial product/assets using suitable method.
- Analytics Module – Analysis for complete lifecycle of business process. Analytics module is core of automation and most of functions are dependent on analytics.
- Risks and performance management – Integrated risks and performance monitoring and management on real time.
- Tracking and management assistance – Optimal integration is guided by automation wherein combination of resources and operations are optimized.
- Project management tool - Business process is managed in a consolidated environment so that whole process is monitored, controlled and managed. Project tool helps in tracking, managing the business process in terms of strategic planning, process transition, risks, performances and value realization.
  Project management helps track, manage and share all business activities throughout the lifecycle. Effective project management is required for following:
  - Project management for planning and completion of all tasks in holistic manner

- Project management controls the project for smooth transition to next phase.
- Data and processes are managed to improve productivity and simplification.
- Task assignment and monitoring
- Activity dependency identification and impact
- Risk mitigation planning

- Governance - Governance must be ensured across business process with strategic validation.
- Service and capabilities oriented automation - Service oriented design leading to business services delivering sophisticated business process supported by business capabilities.

Requirements for risk and performance management functions

Performance and risk are monitored online to quickly capture the status or correct the efforts to control the risk and improve the performance. Project is managed in a consolidated environment so that every process of business is monitored, controlled and managed with integrated risk and performance modules.

Business automation helps create visible driver measurement to enable early identification of issues and their course corrections. Main requirements of performance and risk automated functions are:

- Key Risk Indicators (KRIs): detailed analysis of risk exposures to determine the key risk indicators. Identified risks are measured and monitored.
- Key Performance Indicators (KPIs): detailed analysis of measure of success in terms of performance indicators to measure and monitor the identified performances.
- Risk Limits: acceptable risk limits are established for each identified segments.
- Dashboards: summarizes the performance and risk monitoring results that includes the KPIs and KRIs control within allowed limits.

- Project Monitoring: a well-structured monitoring framework composed of qualitative and quantitative elements facilitates the management of business process.
- Stress Test & Scenario Analysis: stress and scenarios tests intend to test the state of a business by analyzing what would happen to the portfolio if particularly adverse and unexpected movements hit the portfolio.

  Stress testing is an analysis process by which we explore how the portfolio would react to small (Sensitivity Analysis) or more drastic (Stress Tests) changing conditions in the markets. Sensitivity analysis consists of shocking various risk factors of the portfolio with small upward or downward increments.

  Stress test and scenario analysis indicate an optimal portfolio that delivers highest return at defined risks.

Technical requirements of system

Generic technical requirements of system are summarized as follows:

- Fully configurable system - Intuitive, focused display, changeable to transaction / deal / individual's role. Configurable on-demand or automated batch jobs or delivery of reports. Parameters based configuration adjustment of the system for varying needs.
- Powerful and simplified navigation - View cross transaction data and drill down for deal values with easy navigation.
- Portfolio handling - Supports a single deal team or multiple business lines, a single deal or portfolio of trades.
- Consolidated system – Consolidated business processes are automated in holistic manner
- Security and accessibility - Users organized in different groups are secured with authentication and authorization. Transmitted information uses SSL protocol for encryption. Services are made accessible to valid users based on roles and privileges from anywhere.
- Auditing and tracing - Full audit trail and activity capture for business process and events.

- Transparency - Drill down for every risk or performance
- Integrity - Synchronized process and consistent data
- Scalability - System handles growing amount of work in optimal way without additional effort and time.
- SOA – Business services automated and delivered as IT-services fulfilling SOA design.
- Supporting business capabilities - Automation provides flexibility in creating and adapting new capabilities.

Benefits of Automation

Automation is required for all aspects of the business process including target tracking, due diligence, pre-close planning, integration execution, and post-deal synergy monitoring. Some of benefits of automation are as follows:

- Define, track and manage realization of value drivers in real time
- Methods to create driver and its measure for business performance and success
- Identification and resolution of cross functional issues
- No inconsistencies of data and functions between any phase of business lifecycle
- Integrated risk and performance management
- Real time module update with deal execution
- Increased productivity with automated deal tracking, reporting and management
- Automated data collection, usage and maintenance
- Smooth transition to next phase
- Enforced strategic governance for entire business process

2.12 Business Use-Cases

There are a set of functionalities which are carried out to fulfill the business requirements. These functionalities are business use-cases, where actors and functions or other use-cases interact with each other. Business use-cases used at higher level generally represent a business application.

To elaborate the models of business use-cases precisely, we illustrate the investment banking functions Merger & Acquisitions, and Private Equity.

M&A Business Use Case

In following diagram, an actor H_MA interacts directly with business use-cases. H_MA as an actor requires following business use-cases to fulfill the business requirements.

- Strategy & Governance
- Target Selection & Feasibility
- Due Diligence
- Negotiation & Deal Structure
- Legal Compliance
- Pricing & Valuation
- Deal Realization
- Performance Management
- Risk Management
- Integration Management

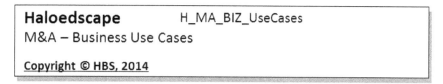

Figure 2.28: © HBS, M&A Business Use Cases

Private Equity Business Use-Case

H_PE as an actor requires following business use-cases to fulfill the business requirements.

- Strategic Governance
- Due Diligence
- Investor Evaluation and Negotiation

- Strategy & Deal Structure
- Legal Compliance
- Pricing & Valuation
- Deal Execution
- Portfolio Management
- Risk management
- Closing Transaction

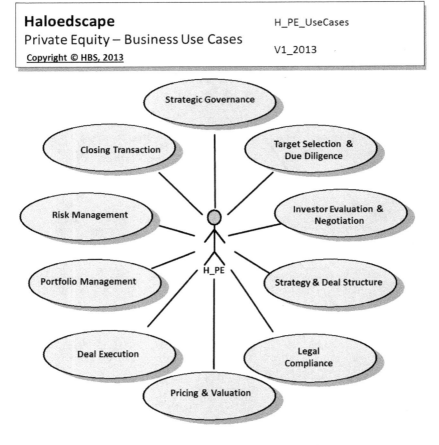

Figure 2.29: © HBS, Private Equity Business Use Cases

Business use-cases mentioned herewith invoke some internal use-cases of pricing, analysis and decision-support to complete their operation.

2.13 Capabilities based Planning

Capability based Planning (CBP) focuses on the planning, designing, and delivery of strategic business capabilities to the enterprise. It is business-driven, business-led methodology to execute a function with superior ability in matured fashion.

Business capability is matured ability possessed by company which helps deliver strategic business-focused outcome efficiently and effectively and is measured in terms of value addition to the enterprise.

Each capability is ensured through the right combination of processes, tools, knowledge, skills and organization; all focused on meeting the desired result.

CBP is handled by attaching the capabilities to business service to improve the ability and increase the business values. The core capabilities as identified in business-strategy and capabilities-model are some specific business-services whose abilities and values are improved by CBP.

Generic Capabilities attached to business services are:
- Automated governance of strategy, tactics and business rules to concerned business service so that functions and services are compliant and fulfill the requirements of strategic alignment.
- Sophisticated analysis and decision-support capabilities help in decision-making and formulating action plans.
- Full-fledged domain knowledgebase is used for analysis and decision-making.
- Agile SOA-based process automation increases the quality of decisions and the effectiveness of business.

- Real-time integrated performance and risk management
- Automated workflow with STP to integrate the isolated modules
- Business process performance is improved with streamlined processes, structured collaboration, real-time updates and non-redundant processing.
- Advanced pricing functionalities
- Full end-to-end business-aligned SOA based automation and real-time integration

In our scope, Capabilities based Planning (CBP) is referred as a methodology of enterprise architecture to accomplish structured operating model for mission critical business services. Under CBP, capability is a set of associated services whose main objective is to improve the ability and values of a business service. A business service categorized as business capability uses some capability-based services to be executed efficiently and effectively under any adverse circumstances addressed under CBP.

2.13.1 Capabilities Driven Strategy

A clear strategic direction of matured capabilities, a system of differentiating capabilities consistent with strategic direction, continuous improvement of capabilities and application of capabilities help achieve the leadership position in market.

A company's chance to win in any market depends on external market positioning, internal resource allocation and most importantly on a coherent capability strategy that aligns these factors at every level.

Firms achieve superior business performance by developing certain distinctive and robust capabilities. Companies with core capabilities that deliver mature and sophisticated services achieve better results in all dimensions. Capabilities possessing firms are more likely to deliver projects on time within budget with better values, and are more successful in achieving the financial and strategic targets.

Companies with better capabilities are better able to balance external and internal growth, and adapt their resources and core competencies to the threats and opportunities of dynamic market.

> *The core capabilities of business function are identified in business strategy and are elaborated in business architecture. The capabilities as a set of services are part of information system of enterprise so that it is available to enterprise-wide applications.*

2.13.2 Business Capabilities Model

> *Business capabilities are matured ability possessed by company which helps deliver business-focused outcome efficiently and effectively. Capability is always measured in terms of value addition to the enterprise.*
>
> *In our approach, Business Capabilities are built with explicitly defined internal business services and delivers strategically governed, matured business services to customers. Capability is built by choreographing the internal discrete services to fulfill the specific goals to improve the ability, efficiency and effectiveness of business services.*
>
> *Capability model is an organized representation of comprehensive capabilities possessed by organization unit, which serves the business services to enable the business objectives.*

Capability generally originates from strategic planning and encapsulates different activities to acquire an effective, sophisticated ability to handle market situation, customer requirements or special business tasks.

Examples of business capabilities are: capability to increase customer base, capability for e-commerce, capability for rapid merger and acquisition, capability to survive the financial crunch and capability to achieve strategic enterprise architecture.

To illustrate the business capability model with examples, we use investment banking functions like M&A, Private Equity etc.

Capability Model of M&A

Consolidated capability model of M&A is depicted below:-

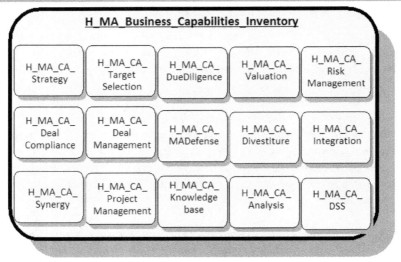

Figure 2.30: © HBS, M&A Capabilities Model

The capabilities owned are:

- H_MA_CA_Strategy - Strategy, tactics and rules are developed and governed.
- H_MA_CA_TargetSelection – Target criteria, target search and feasibility
- H_MA_CA_DueDiligence – Comprehensive due-diligence
- H_MA_CA_Valuation – Valuation and pricing of target
- H_MA_CA_RiskManagement – Risk management
- H_MA_CA_DealCompliance – Accounting, taxation and legal compliance
- H_MA_CA_DealManagement – Deal management
- H_MA_CA_MADefense – Defense from hostile takeover
- H_MA_CA_Divestiture – Divestiture and spin-off
- H_MA_CA_Integration – Post merger integration
- H_MA_CA_Synergy – Synergy planning, realization & measurement
- H_MA_CA_ProjectManagement – Integrated project management for M&A business
- H_MA_CA_Knowledgebase – Knowledgebase for strategy, analysis, valuation, DSS
- H_MA_CA_Analysis – Analysis of due-diligence, bidding strategy, pricing, financing
- H_MA_CA_DSS – Decision support for optimal deal structure, negotiation terms etc.

Capability Model for Private Equity

The capabilities owned for Private Equity function are:

- Strategic Governance
- Analysis
- Decision-Support
- Valuations
- Legal obligations
- Customer relations
- Domain knowledge

- Strategy Assets
- Deal Management
- Value Addition
- Exit/Closing Management
- Trading
- Portfolio Management and
- Risk Management

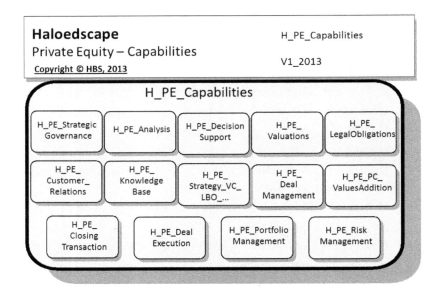

Figure 2.31: © HBS, Private Equity Capabilities Model

Capability model evolves from capability-based planning approach where change activities can be sequenced and grouped in order to harness continuous and incremental business value even in adverse circumstances addressed under CBP.

2.13.3 Capabilities Maturities Model (CMM)

Maturity Model is a comprehensive framework that covers several business processes, sub-processes, resources etc, that helps companies evaluate and improve their capabilities. It contains a set of criteria, key performance indicators, and detailed process descriptions referring to four maturity stages (basic, established, advanced and high performance) that represent the real-life capability spectrum.

Using the Maturity Model, a company can assess the maturity of each sub-process, rapidly find performance gaps in terms of benchmarking with sophisticated capabilities, and define appropriate improvement initiatives to close those gaps. Mature and sophisticated business processes constitute capabilities that significantly increase a company's fitness on all dimensions of achieving better performance

Companies with business capabilities of above-average maturity outperform their industry peers in terms of overall growth and value generation.

2.14 Alignment of Business Functions, Business Services and Capabilities

2.14.1 Business Function & Services

Business function represents the business behavior associated with an organization unit, specifying the top level objectives and delivered capabilities of that organizational unit.

In our approach, the top level of business function is an organizational unit (department) involved in particular activities to deliver department specific business capabilities. Common examples of Business Functions are: Sales, Marketing, Supply Chain Management, Financial Management, Operations, Customer Relationship Management etc.

Business Functions can be decomposed into components as business sub-functions resulting in a business function hierarchy.

These decompositions are based on behavior specific several activities of the top level business function. For example the business function - Sales are decomposed into sub-functions like Product Management, Customer Management, Marketing, Order Management and Support.

Each behavioral entity in form of business function realizes and possesses Business Services as depicted in following diagram.

As an example, alignment of Business Function and Services are illustrated for M&A function of investment banking.

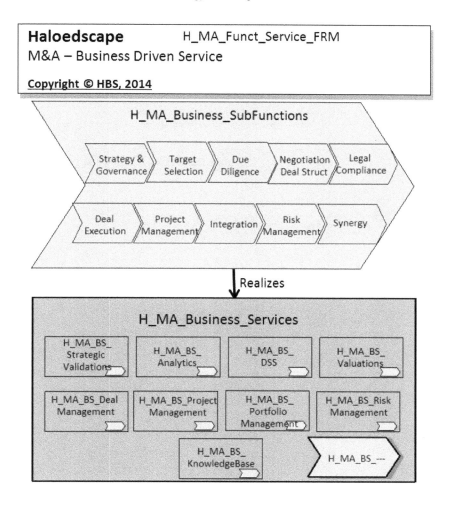

Figure 2.32: © HBS, M&A Biz Functions and Services

To enable a business function, several inter-dependent business services are required. The M&A business functions and the corresponding business services are as follows:

Haloedscape	H_MA_Business_Funct_Services_MTX
M&A – Business Function-Services Matrix	
Copyright © HBS, 2014	

	M&A Business Service
M&A Business Sub-Function	
M&A Combination Forms	H_EA_BS_MergerAnalysis H_EA_BS_Combination H_EA_BS_Category H_EA_BS_ReverseMA H_EA_BS_Takeover
Strategy and Governance	H_EA_BS_StrategicValidations H_EA_BS_Strategy H_EA_BS_SynergyAnalysis H_EA_BS_SellerStrategy H_EA_BS_BuyerStrategy H_EA_BS_ProjectPlanning H_EA_BS_Closing_Commissioning
MA Target Selection, Selection Criteria	H_EA_BS_StrategicValidations H_EA_BS_SynergyAnalysis H_EA_BS_DueDiligence H_EA_BS_Analysis H_EA_BS_DSS H_EA_BS_TermsNegotiation H_EA_BS_DealStructuring
M&A Synergy	H_EA_BS_SynergyAnalysis H_EA_BS_BuyerValues H_EA_BS_SellerValues H_EA_BS_SynergyRealization H_EA_BS_KPI_Analysis
M&A Due Diligence	H_EA_BS_DueDiligence H_EA_BS_StartegicValidation H_EA_BA_SynergyAnalysis H_EA_BS_Financing H_EA_BS_GrowthPotential H_EA_BS_ShareHolderImpact H_EA_BS_CommercialValues H_EA_BS_OperationalValues H_EA_BS_IntegrationAnalysis H_EA_BS_Pricing H_EA_BS_Taxation

Negotiation & Deal Structuring	H_EA_BS_DealStructuring H_EA_BS_TermsNegotiation H_EA_BS_Strategy H_EA_BS_DueDiligence H_EA_BS_Analysis H_EA_BS_Financing H_EA_BS_Taxation H_EA_BS_Accounting H_EA_BS_Pricing H_EA_BS_Closing_Commissioning H_EA_BS_IntegrationAnalysis
M&A Deal Execution	H_EA_BS_DealExecution H_EA_BS_DealStructuring H_EA_BS_ProjectManagement H_EA_BS_RiskManagement H_EA_BS_SynergyRelaization
M&A Legal Compliance	H_EA_BS_Registration H_EA_BS_Taxation H_EA_BS_Accounting H_EA_BS_MergerLegalValidations
M&A Closing, Commissioning, Integration	H_EA_BS_Integration H_EA_BS_SynergyRealization H_EA_BS_Closing_Commissioning
M&A Project	H_EA_BS_ProjectManagement H_EA_BS_ProjectPlanning H_EA_BS_RiskManagement H_EA_BS_DealStructuring H_EA_BS_Closing_Commissioning H_EA_BS_Integration
M&A Pricing, Valuation	H_EA_BS_Pricing
Risk Management	H_EA_BS_RiskManagement
Takeover Defense	H_EA_BS_Takeover_Defense
Divestiture	H_EA_BS_ReverseMA H_EA_BS_Takeover H_EA_CombinationForms
M&A Analysis	H_EA_BS_Analysis
M&A Decision Support	H_EA_BS_DSS

Figure 2.33: © HBS, M&A Function-Services Matrix

Business Function is a higher level behavioral view of an organization which realizes and possesses several Business Services to support and enable its business objectives.

2.14.2 Functions, Business Services and Capabilities

In our scope, we use an innovative framework to interrelate the business function, business services, business capabilities, IT services etc.

We apply SOA to transform business activities into business services realized by business function. Based on capability based planning approach, our business functionality is represented in terms of business capabilities and business services.

Business function represents the business behavior associated with an organization unit. It specifies the top level objectives and delivered capabilities of organizational unit.

Business capability is an effective ability possessed by business-units to execute a specified course of action to achieve specific strategic goals and objectives. It defines purpose of business unit and its core competencies. A business capability generally measures the objectives and maturity level of business and is therefore bound directly to business enablement and strategy.

Business function delivers business capabilities closely aligned to an organization, but not necessarily explicitly governed by the organization.

Business service represents an external view of the services, an organization provides or sells to its customers to achieve business objective. Technically, business service encompasses and uses business capabilities, enables business function to achieve business objectives; is transformed into and realized by IT service. Business service is explicitly governed by an organization.

Business process is an instance of execution that describes how the organization performs its business tasks.

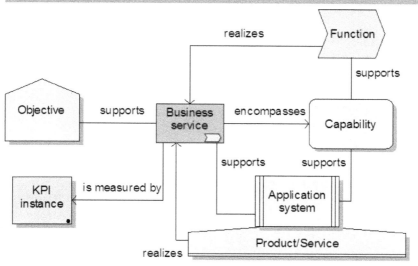

Figure 2.34: © HBS, Framework for Biz Function, Services & Capabilities

In our approach, Business Capabilities are built with explicitly defined internal Business Services to deliver improved Business Services to customers. Business Capability is supported, delivered and made aligned to organization by Business Functions. Capability is built with private business services and is invoked by public business services to efficiently and effectively serve the customers.

Explicit internal interfaces of Business-Services are made available to support and acquire the Business Capabilities.

Business-Function realizes, possesses and delivers the Business-Service governed by strategy to provide specific services to customer.

Business-Service encompasses and uses Business-Capability to deliver an improved service to customer to achieve and support Business-Objectives.

The Business-Service is measured by performance indicators which quantifies the level of achieving the business objectives.

Application running on IT-system supports the automation of business service. A logical unit of software transformed from and tightly aligned with Business Service is IT Service which represents, realizes and enables the Business Service.

It is to be noted that Business-Capabilities and Business-Services are modeled with SOA (service-oriented) which are transformed into IT-services to acquire services-oriented IT solutions.

As an example, the alignment of M&A Business-Functions and the corresponding Business-Services & Capabilities are shown below:

Haloedscape	**H_MA_Biz_Funct_Services_Cap_MTX**
M&A – Business Functions-Services-Capabilities Matrix	
Copyright © HBS, 2014	

Business Function	Business Service	Capability
M&A Combination Forms	H_EA_BS_MergerAnalysis H_EA_BS_Combination H_EA_BS_Category H_EA_BS_ReverseMA H_EA_BS_Takeover	H_EA_CA_Analysis
Strategy and Governance	H_EA_BS_StrategicValidations H_EA_BS_Strategy H_EA_BS_SynergyAnalysis	H_EA_CA_Strategy

	H_EA_BS_SellerStrategy H_EA_BS_BuyerStrategy H_EA_BS_ProjectPlanning H_EA_BS_Closing_Commissioning	
MA Target Selection, Selection Criteria	H_EA_BS_StrategicValidations H_EA_BS_SynergyAnalysis H_EA_BS_DueDiligence H_EA_BS_Analysis H_EA_BS_DSS H_EA_BS_TermsNegotiation H_EA_BS_DealStructuring	H_EA_CA_TargetSelection
M&A Synergy	H_EA_BS_SynergyAnalysis H_EA_BS_BuyerValues H_EA_BS_SellerValues H_EA_BS_SynergyRealization H_EA_BS_KPI_Analysis	H_EA_CA_Synergy
M&A Due Diligence	H_EA_BS_DueDiligence H_EA_BS_StartegicValidation H_EA_BA_SynergyAnalysis H_EA_BS_Financing H_EA_BS_GrowthPotential H_EA_BS_ShareHolderImpact H_EA_BS_CommercialValues H_EA_BS_OperationalValues H_EA_BS_IntegrationAnalysis H_EA_BS_Pricing H_EA_BS_Taxation	H_EA_CA_DueDiligence
Negotiation & Deal Structuring	H_EA_BS_DealStructuring H_EA_BS_TermsNegotiation H_EA_BS_Strategy H_EA_BS_DueDiligence H_EA_BS_Analysis H_EA_BS_Financing H_EA_BS_Taxation H_EA_BS_Accounting H_EA_BS_Pricing H_EA_BS_Closing_Commissioning H_EA_BS_Integration	H_EA_CA_DealManagement
M&A Deal Execution	H_EA_BS_DealExecution H_EA_BS_DealStructuring H_EA_BS_ProjectManagement H_EA_BS_RiskManagement H_EA_BS_SynergyRelaization	H_EA_CA_DealManagement
M&A Legal Compliance	H_EA_BS_Registration H_EA_BS_Taxation H_EA_BS_Accounting H_EA_BS_MergerLegalValidations	H_EA_CA_DealCompliance
M&A Closing, Commissioning, Integration	H_EA_BS_Integration H_EA_BS_SynergyRealization H_EA_BS_Closing_Commissioning	H_EA_CA_Integration
M&A Project	H_EA_BS_ProjectManagement H_EA_BS_ProjectPlanning H_EA_BS_RiskManagement H_EA_BS_DealStructuring	H_EA_CA_ProjectManagement

	H_EA_BS_Closing_Commissioning H_EA_BS_Integration	
M&A Pricing, Valuation	H_EA_BS_Pricing	H_EA_CA_Valuation
Risk Management	H_EA_BS_RiskManagement	H_EA_CA_RiskManagement
Takeover Defense	H_EA_BS_Takeover_Defense	H_EA_CA_MADefense
Divestiture	H_EA_BS_ReverseMA H_EA_BS_Takeover H_EA_CombinationForms	H_EA_CA_Divestiture
M&A Analysis	H_EA_BS_Analysis	H_EA_CA_Analysis H_EA_CA_Knowledgebase
M&A Decision Support	H_EA_BS_DSS	H_EA_CA_DSS H_EA_CA_Analysis H_EA_CA_Knowledgebase

Figure 2.35: © HBS, M&A Biz Function-Services-Capability Matrix

2.14.3 Business Service Alignment

The interrelation of Business Objectives, Business Functions, Business Services and Business Capabilities are formulated so that they remain absolutely aligned with each other and fulfill their target to achieve strategic enterprise architecture.

Alignment of IT with business requires precise alignment of business objectives, business functions, business services and capabilities. This alignment is illustrated below with an example for M&A business function.

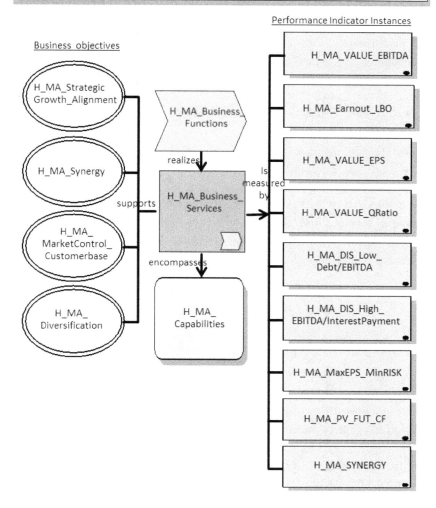

Figure 2.36: © HBS, M&A Biz Service Allocation; Objective/Capability KPI

Business-Objectives supported by Business-Services are set to achieve the fulfillment of business. As stated earlier, the behavioral entity of organization grouped under different business functions possesses the business service, which encompasses and invokes business capabilities to provide improved services to customers.

The performance and ability of Business Service are measured by key performance indicators. Core business objectives of M&A as mentioned in business details earlier are:

- H_MA_StrategicGrowth_Alignment
- H_MA_Synergy
- H_MA_MarketControl_Customerbase
- H_MA_Diversification

These objectives are supported and enabled by business services. Business services use the business capabilities to provide improved services which are measured and benchmarked with key performance indicators like H_MA_VALUE_EBITDA, H_MA_VALUE_EPS etc.

2.15 Conclusion - Business Architecture

In essence, sophisticated business architecture allows companies to show the present situation of business and strive for service based delivery, business capabilities, business aligned IT, agile automation, loosely-coupled integration besides other SOA advantages.

A holistic approach in planning, managing and executing the business is of utmost importance. To achieve automation of end-to-end business for all departments, one needs a consolidated service inventory containing all services for enterprise. This leads business architecture in the form of enterprise architecture, where business architecture acts as input for development of enterprise information system architecture.

Our approach in this book is to develop business architecture which is aligned and compatible with strategic enterprise architecture.

Business Architecture (BA) fulfills the strategic requirements, improves business process, optimizes the business models with capabilities and services, and specifies the requirements to develop information system architecture.

We start this chapter with Business Architecture Framework where BA meta-model receives strategy as its input, on which BA methods and tools are applied to generate BA models. BA meta-model is conceptual model that covers the business domains of an enterprise. BA meta-models, BA methods & tools and BA models constitute together business architecture.

As next, we present our approach and scope towards Business Architecture Development. Overview of framework TOGAF for Business Architecture Development and our approach and innovative extension of framework are presented.

In next section, Business Motivation Model (BMM) for M&A business of Haloedscape is described. The core objectives of BMM are to structure, communicate and organize the business plans. The elements of BMM like End, Vision, Mission, Goals and Objectives have been consolidated and interrelated together.

Business principles mentioned in the chapter includes: maximize benefits to enterprise, business continuity, business ownership, secured intellectual property, compliance with law, and principles governance.

Business strategy and corresponding tactics are elaborated which specifies the directions, rules and guidlines for operation, planning, control and development of business service.

For precise illustration, we have used the investment banking business domain with examples of M&A, Private Equity, Venture Capital etc.

Organization structures of business are illustrated. Business transaction process is shown with value-added chain diagram. Strategic Objectives is shown with KPI allocation diagram which includes the performance of business.

Business lifecycle are modeled together in value-added chain. Due diligence process includes the investigation and analysis of target company to justify the negotiation terms and structure the deal. Pricing & valuation is elaborated with Business Process Modeling (BPM). Core event like deal execution is elaborated together with STP workflow integrating the isolated modules of performance management, risk management and integration. Deal execution is dependent on due diligence, deal structure and pricing functionalities. Requirements of risk & performance management are elaborated where it is essential to anticipate deviation, promote correcting actions, calculate valuations and ratios and generate reports. Risk Management requires early risk identification and active risk management in order to control and manage the risks.

We used capability based planning (CBP) for planning, designing, and delivery of strategic business capabilities to the enterprise. It is business-driven, business-led methodology to execute a function with superior ability in matured fashion, which enhances the ability and values of business services.

To possess better capabilities for successful business, we infer that business requires consolidated automation of remote modules which work in real-time with core event like deal execution using STP workflow.

Business use cases are depicted with examples where core functionalities and actors are interlinked for high level business process.

Throughout this chapter, we have intensively elaborated the frameworks for interrelating and aligning the business function, business capabilities & business services.

This chapter presents the framework to align the business functions, business services, business capabilities and business objectives. Business function realizes, possesses and delivers the business services governed by strategy to provide specific services to customer.

Business service encompasses and invokes/calls business capability to deliver an improved service to customer to achieve and support business objectives.

Capability model is shown, which is capability-based planning approach where change activities can be sequenced and grouped in order to provide continuous and incremental business value.

The interrelations of business objectives, business functions, business services and business capabilities are formulated so that they remain absolutely aligned with each other and fulfill their target to achieve strategic enterprise architecture.

It is noteworthy that business capabilities and business services are modeled as SOA which are directly transformed into IT-services to achieve services-oriented IT solutions described in later chapters. In this chapter, we developed service-oriented business architecture which acts as input for developing SOA based Information System, Data and Application Architecture in the next chapter.

Chapter 3: Information System, Data & Application Architecture

Acronyms & Definitions used in this chapter:

API: Application Programming Interface – A library which provides the function interface to develop the required application.

CORBA: Common Object Request Broker – A standard specification defined by OMG for object oriented middleware which supports platform independent distributed objects to be accessed by any client application supported on agent called Object Request Broker (ORB).

J2EE: Java Platform Enterprise Edition – Full-fledged Java platform which natively integrates enterprise framework and platform together for enterprise IT solution.

JMS: Java Message Service – Java API for accessing a MOM messaging system including the event capabilities.

MOM: Message Oriented Middleware – Most elegant technology for supporting the distributed application to exchange message with sophisticated techniques.

OOM: Object Oriented Middleware – OOM facilitates distributed objects accessed by distributed applications to achieve process and functional level interoperability and enterprise integration.

P&L: Profit and Loss – A financial summary of financial performance of business over time.

STP: Straight through Processing – A methodology to automate the Workflow.

UC: Use Case – Modeling of actors, functionalities and interactions between them.

UI: User Interface– An input/output interface aligned with process-flow displayed to user in text or graphical form. The graphical form of user interface is GUI.

UML: Unified Modeling Language – General purpose modeling language to create visual models of software systems using software engineering.

H_EA: Enterprise Architecture (IT) wing of Haloedscape.

In this chapter, we will elaborate the development of Information System Architecture, Data Architecture and Application Architecture, based on our IT Strategy and Business Architecture, as discussed in previous chapters. The concept of Information System, Application and Data Architecture are illustrated with examples of investment banking business function.

3.1   Executive Summary

Our SOA based Information System Architecture, Data Architecture and Application Architecture leads us to strategic Enterprise Architecture for whole business.

Data Architecture includes the architecture of core enterprise data which are used by services of information system & applications

Information System services includes the core enterprise IT Services which are collaborated together by enterprise wide applications of different business units.

Application Architecture includes different business-unit applications which access the enterprise data and functionalities IT services from Information Systems to develop and deploy their own application.

The strategic governance is automated with applications accessing enterprise resources only through Information System which fulfills all strategic requirements for enterprise architecture.

The alignment of IT with business, loosely-coupled component based agile design, simplified and optimal services are achieved with SOA.

In the context of IT, Service oriented Architecture (SOA) is defined as architecture of software component based on service oriented design principles, which transforms business functionalities into IT services to enable business services.

Information system services make interfaces available to enterprise wide application to access the enterprise services and capabilities.   Our Information System is completely SOA based supported by innovative platform with required technology.

Consolidated data services and functional services of information system fulfill the most of data and computational principles. SOA based information system achieves strategic objective of business-aligned, agile IT which maximize the ROI while reducing overall risks and costs.

The business services and capabilities explained in previous chapter are transformed into IT services, so that there is effective alignment of IT with business.

Our application architecture is primarily motivated from J2EE based solution which natively integrates with event based object/message oriented middleware. Many components of our generic business application like pricing engine and simulation for valuation, analysis etc. are made available in form of distributed objects supported with OOM programmed in C++ for efficient computation.

IT services, concern of this chapter, are language and platform independent being accessed by any standard client or applications thus achieving a high level of functional integration.

Application is designed to be secured with encryption, authentication and authorization. Authorization includes resource based access-control, which is configured and enabled. Some of the sequential tasks which need manual intervention are automated with workflow using parallel split and synchronize patterns. Application is also facilitated with session and transaction management supported by platform so that application could maintain its state and also the critical operations are guaranteed maintaining the consistent data and synchronized process.

Application is computed in real time besides efficiently computing for the changes by subscribing to receive notification for required events in specific topic/content mode.

The services are implemented on distributed computing platform supported with object oriented and message oriented middleware. Application is equipped with advanced capabilities to provide innovative and sophisticated solution.

Data management is crucial for enterprise where data unification, centralization, access, non-redundancy, sharing, security and consistency are managed to maintain high quality data.

In Business Architecture, we have used framework for capability based planning approach to model the inventory of capabilities, which delivers improved business services to customers. Business capability is an effective ability possessed by business-units to execute a specified course of action to achieve specific strategic goals and objectives. We will use framework to model the IT capability in form of IT services and align it to business capability. Capability generally measures the objectives and maturity level of business and is therefore bound directly to business enablement and strategy.

Business function delivers business capabilities closely aligned to an organization. Business service encompasses business capabilities to enable business function and achieve business objectives. Business services and capabilities are transformed directly into and realized by IT services.

High level design and architecture of information system as well as applications are presented with use-cases, logical diagrams, activity diagram, workflow, components diagram, frameworks etc. Low level design for implementation is not considered in the context of architecture, hence is beyond the scope of this book.

For illustration and design of application components, we will present the examples of investment banking business functions like M&A, Private Equity etc.

3.2 Overview of Information System, Data & Application Architecture

Focused enterprise architecture derived from IT strategy is a key to achieve highest ROI where only core business functions are considered and transformed into enterprise architecture. Enterprise Architecture concerns enterprise wide complete functionalities to be considered in holistic way to achieve effective IT solution. In this book, we develop the meta-models and business function models (instances/examples) illustrating "Focused Enterprise Architecture" aligned with strategy.

The framework of TOGAF for "Architecture Development Method" guides that Information Systems Architecture gets its input from Business Architecture to automate the data, services and applications and sends the outputs to Technology Architecture to identify and acquire right platform empowered with required technology in order to achieve strategic IT solution to enable the business. All of these phases of Architecture (Business, Information Systems and Technology) interact in bidirectional way with Requirements Management, so that each phase of architecture development keeps its essence of fulfilling the requirements as its top objective.

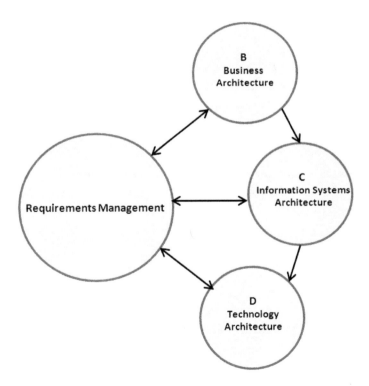

Figure 3.1: Copyright © The Open Group, TOGAF® 9.1, Architecture Development Cycle

Our approach to Information System Architecture is more innovative and slightly different from some of the most successful open frameworks like TOGAF; As per TOGAF, Information System is constituted of Data Architecture and Application Architecture.

In our scope, the Information System is constituted of enterprise functional services and enterprise data services. Information System contains all enterprise core services to fulfill all strategic requirements to achieve the enterprise capabilities.

Application uses the information system to access the enterprise resources (data and services) to build their own applications, hence inheriting all strategic capabilities from information system.

All enterprises services (data & functionalities) are consolidated together in information system. The enterprise resources like core data, enterprise functionalities are available to applications only through information system. All strategic requirements are fulfilled with services of information systems, wherein accessibility of enterprise resources (data & functions) through Information System governs the fulfillment of strategic requirements in the applications to achieve enterprise capabilities in automated way. Simply stated, this is our approach to automated governance.

As part of Information System Architecture, we will present the architecture of the frameworks, data models, logical diagrams in UML and consolidated service inventory. We will describe the static and dynamic data models and its interaction with services. The architecture of business services, IT Services and service-collaboration are also presented.

Application Architecture shows the service inventory, application's components, interaction with information system, components activity diagram etc. The business logic of functionalities like pricing functions is elaborated in Business Architecture using business process modeling.

The Information System, Data and Application Architecture are

> *modeled and described in general-purpose, language independent and platform independent manner so that most appropriate and sophisticated platform can be identified and acquired for implementation of solution.*

3.3 Framework for aligning Business Services, Capabilities and IT Services

Business services realizing/enabling the concerned business functions are identified in Business Architecture.

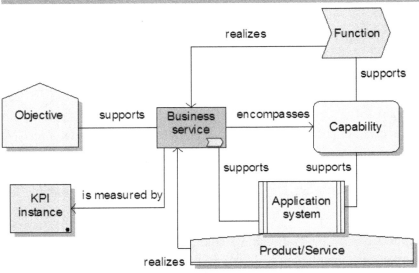

Figure 3.2: © HBS, Framework aligning Business Services, Capabilities, Function and IT

The business objectives and Key-Performance Indicators (KPI) assessing and measuring the business services are also identified and defined in Business Architecture. The business service supports the business objective and success rate of business service is measured with KPI. Business services consolidate the business-functionalities, categorize them to be granularly defined and realize them. Business service encompasses and invokes the primary capabilities and both the business services and capabilities are realized by IT services of information system collaborated together in different applications. The realization of business services are achieved by IT product (platform) supporting and delivering IT services.

Business function represents the business behavior associated with an organization unit. It specifies the top level objectives and delivered capabilities of organizational unit.

Business capability is an effective & matured ability possessed by business-units to execute a specified course of action to achieve specific value-added, strategic goals and objectives. It defines purpose of business unit and its core competencies. A business capability generally measures the objectives and maturity level of business and is therefore bound directly to business enablement and strategy.

Business function delivers business capabilities closely aligned to an organization, but not necessarily explicitly governed by the organization.

Business service represents an external view of the services, an organization provides or sells to its customers to achieve business objective. Technically, business service encompasses business capabilities to realize business function and support business objectives. Business service is transformed into and realized by IT service. Public business service accessed by external client is explicitly governed by an organization.

3.4   SOA Layers Architecture & System-Components

SOA solution as proposed by OMG, for an enterprise business is depicted as a meta-model in form of a set of logical layers. OMG based SOA layer architecture has five separated horizontal layers for business computation; and four vertical layers for transforming the system into strategic enterprise system. The vertical layers are embedded into each of horizontal layers to transform our computational system into enterprise based strategic system.

End-user accesses Consumer-Interface possessing a graphical or text based display accessing the layer Business-Process using well defined interfaces.

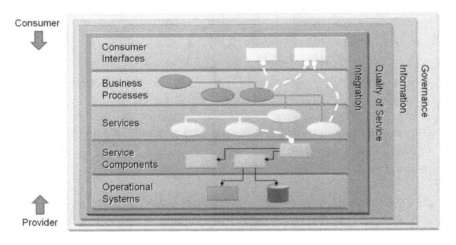

Figure 3.3: © OMG, SOA Layers Architecture

Three of the layers address the implementation and interface with a service (the Operational Systems Layer, the Service Component Layer, and the Services Layer), whereas three of them support the consumption of services (the Business Process Layer, the Consumer Layer, and the Integration Layer). Four of them support cross-cutting concerns of a more supporting (sometimes called non-functional or supplemental) nature (the Information Layer, the Quality of Service Layer, the Integration Layer, and the Governance Layer).

SOA System Components

Overall structure for system is organized as logical grouping of components into separate layers that communicate with each other and also with external clients and applications. Our solution is SOA based wherein a group of services interacting together via message to provide access to business data & functionalities.

- Presentation Layer: The user interface & presentation logic make clients communicate with application and services. The presentation layer is dedicated to format and display the information with input-output (I/O) data of system to clients, aligned with navigation of business process.
- Application Layer: Application layer typically access the multiple services collaborated together required for a specific business function and makes it available to presentation layer.
- Service Layer: Service layer entirely belongs to information system which provides enterprise level data and functionalities in form of services to different application and to clients. Collaboration and orchestration of services also deliver value-added, matured capabilities. The services are implemented using lower layer of business components containing business logic. Service exposes its interface as an access point that allows client to access the service.
- Business Layer: The business layer encompasses the IT components that contain the business logic required to implement the services of upper layer. Business logic is embedded into service implementation that computes the process specific to business logic and rules.

Business layer is categorized into business entity and workflow components. Business entity components encapsulate the business logic and data necessary to represent the real world entity. The Business workflow components involve the processes that have multiple activities and interaction which must be performed in correct order through service orchestration.

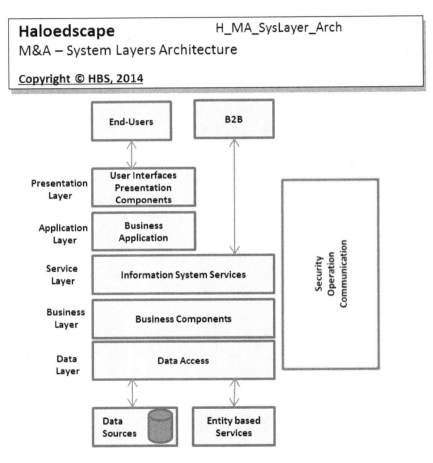

Figure 3.4: © HBS, System Component Layers

- Data Layer: Enterprise data and its access components reside at this layer. Data is modeled in a way to increase the level of information, governance, integration and data quality.

As illustrated in figure, the service, business sand data layers are part of our enterprise Information System. Application layer access the Information System to build their solution for specific need.

3.5 Information System /Application and Data Principles

Information System / Application Principles

Name	Shared Application Components
Description / Statement	The applications and/or its components should be used across whole enterprise on shared basis to optimize the resource utility and reduce the costs.
Rationale	Components of application should be shared to lower down the cost on redundant components and increase the shared usage across business functions.
Implications	• The components of application should be loosely-coupled and component based in form of services, so that it could be used across different applications without investing resources.

	• The design and implementation of applications should follow SOA approach to realize shared & unique services that are accessible across enterprise. • The application components in form of granular services and choreographed services should be consolidated to avoid resource and computational redundancy. • The capabilities developed for a business unit should be unified and shared across enterprise to realize the capability based planning.

Name	Service Orientation
Description / Statement	The enterprise architecture must be based on design of business driven services leading to business-aligned IT which provides full business agility. The design and implementation of business and IT solutions must fulfill service oriented principles.
Rationale	• Service Oriented Architecture (SOA) ensures business-aligned effective IT. SOA also leads to business agility due to optimized, simplified, loosely-coupled and reusable services. SOA is the core foundation of Enterprise Architecture. SOA is a leading market standard capability which world-wide corporates strive to achieve.

Implications	• SOA transforms the business functions into optimized, standardized and integrated services.
	• Service orientation optimizes the uses of infrastructure with scalability.
	• Service orientation delivers maximum returns to enterprise and delivers strategic capabilities.
	• SOA achieves the alignment of IT solution with business.
	• SOA achieves effective and efficient IT returning maximum ROI on long term.
	• Service oriented applications should be supported by service platform empowered with open-standard technology to realize SOA benefits.
	• Essence of SOA approach is that governance / Integration / Information / QoS are supported at each horizontal layers of system architecture.

Name	Computational Efficiency & Non-Redundancy
Description / Statement	The computation of business process must be made efficient and effective. Redundant computation must be avoided to optimize the resource usage and execution.
Rationale	Redundant computation must be avoided to lead to efficient and effective computation. Computation

	should be done only for new or changed events.
Implications	• Acquire the capability to compute only for the dependent process of module which changes on occurrence of events. This is delta computation which computes only for changing process, but no computation is done for other processes of module which are free from change of events. The delta computation capability is essential to optimize the resource usage and produce the results efficiently.
	• Real time platform for delta computation changes the computational paradigm and leads to high performance IT.
	• Messaging platform is essential to receive the sync/asynchronous mode of guaranteed delivery for distributed computing.
	• Redundant computation should be avoided using delta computation technology on distributed computing platform. Handling it on silo based monolithic applications leads to non-standard, unmanaged, uncontrolled and error-prone computing environment.

Data Principles

Name	Secured Data
Description / Statement	The Enterprise data must be secured from internal and external threat. The information flow must be made secured. The computation must be done in secured environment to protect sensitive data.
Rationale	Data are critical to business and must be protected from unauthorized use and disclosure to avoid unwarranted speculation, misinterpretation and inappropriate use. Processes must be kept synchronized.
Implications	• Acquire the capability to compute in secured environment to protect data. • Access to system must be well defined and allowed only for valid users & processes. • Set up an authentication & authorization features to verify the user of business process and allow them access to data for which they are qualified. • Set up an encryption platform to secure the data flow. • Enforce a data protection process to secure data from internal threats. • Data must be persistent in secured manner so that it is not lost due to any failure. The data storage device must be protected from failure and should possess data recovery

	capability.

Name	Shared Data
Description / Statement	Enterprise data should be shared to reduce the resource cost and achieve the data integration. Enterprise data integration is required for optimized and effective computation.
Rationale	Data sharing provides the basis of data integration and reduces the risks of data redundancy. Data sharing across business functions achieves the enterprise benefits.
Implications	<ul><li>Acquire the capability to share the data in a standard way.</li><li>Sharing of data should be handled in controlled way, such as user-groups based roles and privileges.</li><li>Sharing of data must not result in inconsistency of integrity-violation of data. The platform should provide the basis of data synchronization.</li><li>Data management concept should provide the policies and procedures for data sharing.</li><li>Data sharing should improve the efficiency of enterprise computation.</li><li>Enterprise Service Bus (ESB) should be provided by platform to simplify and</li></ul>

	optimize the sharing of data services.

Name	Accessible Data
Description / Statement	Enterprise data must be accessible to business users to perform their functions.
Rationale	Simplified and efficient data accessibility is essential to complete the primary tasks of business functions.
Implications	• Acquire capability to keep the data accessible for business. • Data recovery process must be available and efficient to restore the data and make them accessible in short time in case of failure. • The infrastructure (hardware, software and networks) must be scalable and optimal to keep the data accessibility efficient. • Process must be available to monitor the data availability and report the consequences of resource hogging, deadlocks etc. which affects the data availability adversely. • Data management concept should be in place which plans, guides and regulates the data accessibility concept for business users. • Enterprise Service Bus (ESB) should be acquired which provides the data services from

	central access point, simplifies the format and communication across different platforms.

Name	Non Redundant Data
Description / Statement	The enterprise data must not be redundant to avoid inconsistency and increase data quality.
Rationale	Redundant data takes unnecessarily resources and increases the costs for maintenance. Data redundancy adversely affects the data quality which causes the results of computation to be error-prone.
Implications	• Acquire the capability to access, share, unify and integrate data to avoid redundancy and achieve the enterprise benefits. • Data redundancy causes the quality degradation of data and impacts the whole enterprise with error-prone computed results due to inconsistent, redundant data. • Data redundancy unnecessarily takes more hardware, software and human-ware resources to handle and manage the data which increases costs and risks. • Manually copying the enterprise data for business tasks from one place to another which does not guarantee real-time data consistency and integrity must be prohibited. If system copies the data at

	different places to deliver some capability and ensures the data consistency & integrity with technology, then it causes no harm to enterprise, rather provides additional capabilities and benefits to enterprise.

There are several platforms and technologies which duplicates some amount of data (redundancy) internally to provide some benefits like efficiency, security, availability, recoverability, fail-over, load balancing. These technologies which deliver some capabilities are extensively tested and certified to ensure high quality data. Even if system fails, process gets killed, power fails, the technology guarantees consistency and integrity of data. Such data-redundancy which are supported and guaranteed by technologies to maintain data integrity and consistency are allowed in company.

Name	High Quality Data
Description / Statement	Data must possess high quality standards fulfilling the data principles.
Rationale	The business functions depend upon data where high quality data ensures authentic and reliable results.
Implications	• Acquire capability to guarantee high data quality. • Develop a process to safeguard the data in terms of consistency and integrity. • Data sharing and its usage in computations should not reduce the data quality.

	<ul><li>Data must be secured and accessible only by valid users and processes.</li><li>Data management process should plan, guide and regulate high quality of data.</li><li>Data principles must be governed.</li></ul>

3.6   Requirements of Automation

For optimizing the business process, the system should provide a standard review, analysis and optimal decision-support for possible scenarios. This approach should include a strategic review (rationale and achievements), a financial review (performance, valuation, and assumptions), an operational review (operating performance and issues) and a project management review of functional modules, business services, capabilities, time, risks, effort, and budget.

Business Requirements
- Full end to end business process design, playbook development for whole company or individual functions, staff augmentation services & execution readiness assessments.
- Knowledgebase – It provides automated information on request. Analytics for due-diligence, deal structuring, optimizing portfolio, and decision support module use centralized knowledgebase as primary source of information.
Domain-knowledgebase is comprehensive information repository which helps automate different life cycles of business process. Analytics accesses data from knowledgebase and applies the methods to generate required information which is used for decision support.

- Decision support module – Decision support module aligned with strategy is used for decision making at various points in business process.
- Pricing Module – Precise valuation of financial product/assets using suitable method.
- Analytics Module – Analysis for complete lifecycle of business process. Analytics module is core of automation and most of functions are dependent on analytics.
- Risks and performance management – Integrated risks and performance monitoring and management on real time.
- Tracking and management assistance – Optimal integration is guided by automation wherein combination of resources and operations are optimized.
- Project management tool - Business process is managed in a consolidated environment so that whole process is monitored, controlled and managed. Project tool helps in tracking, managing the business process in terms of strategic planning, process transition, risks, performances and value realization.

  Project management helps track, manage and share all business activities throughout the lifecycle. Effective project management is required for following:

  - Project management for planning and completion of all tasks in holistic manner
  - Project management controls the project for smooth transition to next phase.
  - Data and processes are managed to improve productivity and simplification.
  - Task assignment and monitoring
  - Activity dependency identification and impact
  - Risk mitigation planning

- Governance - Governance must be ensured across business process with strategic validation.
- Service and capabilities oriented automation - Service oriented design leading to business services delivering sophisticated business process supported by business capabilities.

Requirements for risk and performance management functions

Performance and risk are monitored online to quickly capture the status or correct the efforts to control the risk and improve the performance. Project is managed in a consolidated environment so that every process of business is monitored, controlled and managed with integrated risk and performance modules.

Business automation helps create visible driver measurement to enable early identification of issues and their course corrections. Main requirements of performance and risk automated functions are:

- Key Risk Indicators (KRIs): detailed analysis of risk exposures to determine the key risk indicators. Identified risks are measured and monitored.
- Key Performance Indicators (KPIs): detailed analysis of measure of success in terms of performance indicators to measure and monitor the identified performances.
- Risk Limits: acceptable risk limits are established for each identified segments.
- Dashboards: summarizes the performance and risk monitoring results that includes the KPIs and KRIs control within allowed limits.
- Project Monitoring: a well-structured monitoring framework composed of qualitative and quantitative elements facilitates the management of business process.
- Stress Test & Scenario Analysis: stress and scenarios tests intend to test the state of a business by analyzing what would happen to the portfolio if particularly adverse and unexpected movements hit the portfolio.
  Stress testing is an analysis process by which we explore how the portfolio would react to small (Sensitivity Analysis) or more drastic (Stress Tests) changing conditions in the markets. Sensitivity analysis consists of shocking various risk factors of the portfolio with small upward or downward increments.

Stress test and scenario analysis indicate an optimal portfolio that delivers highest return at defined risks.

Technical requirements of system

Generic technical requirements of system are summarized as follows:

- Fully configurable system - Intuitive, focused display, changeable to transaction / deal / individual's role. Configurable on-demand or automated batch jobs or delivery of reports. Parameters based configuration adjustment of the system for varying needs.
- Powerful and simplified navigation - View cross transaction data and drill down for deal values with easy navigation.
- Portfolio handling - Supports a single deal team or multiple business lines, a single deal or portfolio of trades.
- Consolidated system – Consolidated business processes are automated in holistic manner
- Security and accessibility - Users organized in different groups are secured with authentication and authorization. Transmitted information uses SSL protocol for encryption. Services are made accessible to valid users based on roles and privileges from anywhere.
- Auditing and tracing - Full audit trail and activity capture for business process and events.
- Transparency - Drill down for every risk or performance
- Integrity - Synchronized process and consistent data
- Scalability - System handles growing amount of work in optimal way without additional effort and time.
- SOA – Business services automated and delivered as IT-services fulfilling SOA design.
- Supporting business capabilities - Automation provides flexibility in creating and adapting new capabilities.

Business Capabilities Requirements

Matured and value-added services form capabilities to increases the business values and abilities of business. There are following capabilities are requirements in general:

- Business services attached with capabilities enabling improved business delivery

- Value-drivers identified and linked to activities to measure business performance, objectives, direction and maturity
- Process tracking and reporting with management of whole business process
- Strategic governance
- Decision support
- Functional analysis
- Sophisticated Knowledgebase
- IT services enabling business capabilities
- Automated workflow for remote modules integration
- Real time process updates
- Secured, scalable, high-performance service
- Process tracing & auditing

Benefits of Automation

Automation is required for all aspects of the business process including target tracking, due diligence, pre-close planning, integration execution, and post-deal synergy monitoring. Some of benefits of automation are as follows:

- Define, track and manage realization of value drivers in real time
- Methods to create driver and its measure for business performance and success
- Identification and resolution of cross functional issues
- No inconsistencies of data and functions between any phase of business lifecycle
- Integrated risk and performance management
- Real time module update with deal execution
- Increased productivity with automated deal tracking, reporting and management
- Automated data collection, usage and maintenance
- Smooth transition to next phase
- Enforced strategic governance for entire business process

3.7 Information Systems Services with applied SOA

The service orientation is a revolutionary architecture style to align the IT with business. It lowers down the risks & maintenance costs. The agile design of SOA guarantees efficient time to market. The services designed with right SOA principles are assets to whole enterprise. SOA fulfills the computational and business principles and offers a highest level of effectiveness.

In our scope, we use SOA based solution to achieve strategic enterprise architecture.

Service Oriented Architecture (SOA) in IT context is defined as architecture of IT software based on service oriented design principles that transforms business functionalities into IT services.

IT service designed with SOA principles is self-contained autonomous software that alone or in combined form gives logical representation of enterprise business functionalities.

Important SOA design principles are: Standardized service contract, loose coupling, abstraction, reusability, autonomy, statelessness, discoverability and composability.

Besides being compliant to major parts of the application and data principles, SOA significantly fulfills strategic requirements. The alignment of IT with business, loosely- coupled component based agile design, simplified and optimal processes are achieved with SOA.

SOA delivers better ROI on long run while reducing the overall risks.

Enterprise data services are illustrated with example of M&A business function.

The enterprise data services of M&A business as a part of information system are:

- H_MA_DS_StrategicReq
- H_MA_DS_Synergy_KPI
- H_MA_DS_Market

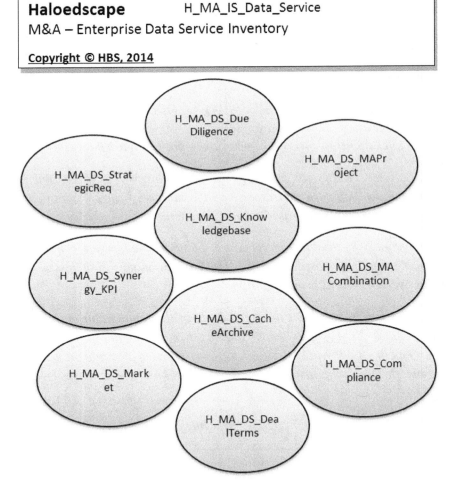

Figure 3.5: © HBS, Data Service Inventory

- H_MA_DS_DueDiligence
- H_MA_DS_DealTerms
- H_MA_DS_MAProject
- H_MA_DS_MACombination
- H_MA_DS_Compliance
- H_MA_DS_Cache
- H_MA_DS_Knowledgebase

The data-service module containing granular or choreographed data-services of M&A business function are depicted below:

Data-Service Module	Data Services Basic / Choreographed
H_MA_DS_StrategicReq	<ul><li>H_MA_DS_TargetCrieteria</li><li>H_MA_DS_BuyerNeed</li><li>H_MA_DS_SellerNeed</li><li>H_MA_DS_TargetFeasibility</li><li>H_MA_DS_ClientValues</li><li>H_MA_DS_TargetCompanies</li><li>H_MA_DS_Tactics</li><li>H_MA_DS_Rules</li><li>H_MA_DS_ClientStrategy</li></ul>
H_MA_DS_Synergy_KPI	<ul><li>H_MA_DS_BenefitsKPI</li><li>H_MA_DS_AcquirerValues</li></ul>

	• *H_MA_DS_SynergyValues*
	• *H_MA_DS_Risks*
	• *H_MA_DS_Performance*
H_MA_DS_Market	• *H_MA_DS_MarketPricing*
	• *H_MA_DS_MarketTransaction*
	• *H_MA_DS_MarketSnapshots*
H_MA_DS_DueDiligence	• *H_MA_DS_TC_Business*
	• *H_MA_DS_TC_Product*
	• *H_MA_DS_TC_Marketing*
	• *H_MA_DS_TC_Distribution*
	• *H_MA_DS_TC_StrategicFit*
	• *H_MA_DS_TC_Synergy*
	• *H_MA_DS_TC_Integration*
H_MA_DS_DealTerms	• *H_MA_DS_DealFinancing*
	• *H_MA_DS_DealContracts*
	• *H_MA_DS_DealRegulations*
	• *H_MA_DS_DealSchedule*
	• *H_MA_DS_DealValue*
	• *H_MA_DS_DealValidation*
	• *H_MA_DS_DealIntegration*
	• *H_MA_DS_DealSynergy*
	• *H_MA_DS_FinancialValues*
	• *H_MA_DS_OptimalFinancing*

H_MA_DS_MAProject	• *H_MA_DS_DealPlanning* • *H_MA_DS_DealStructure* • *H_MA_DS_ProjectTasks* • *H_MA_DS_ProjectSchedule* • *H_MA_DS_Validation* • *H_MA_DS_RisksPerf* • *H_MA_DS_BenefitsBenchmark* • *H_MA_DS_IntegrationPlanning* • *H_MA_DS_SynergyPlanning*
H_MA_DS_MACombination	• *H_MA_DS_MergeAnalysis* • *H_MA_DS_AcqisitionData* • *H_MA_DS_CombinationForms* • *H_MA_DS_Takover* • *H_MA_DS_ReverseMA*
H_MA_DS_Compliance	• *H_MA_DS_Accounting* • *H_MA_DS_Tax* • *H_MA_DS_Regulation* • *H_MA_DS_Laws*
H_MA_DS_CacheArchive	*Optimized data-service for performance & accessibility*
H_MA_DS_KnowledgeBase	*Knowledgebase for all Data-Services*

Each data-service module is used by a set of granular/choreographed services to fulfill the task of business functionality. The enterprise data are accessed via data-services exposed through standard interfaces.

Data services are identified and selected through SOA modeling of business functionalities and capabilities. The primary focus of data-services is to fulfill the requirements of functionalities and capabilities.

Mapping of business functionalities, capabilities and corresponding data-services of M&A business function:

Functionalities	Capabilities	Data-Service Modules
Client Management (Buyer, Seller, Target Company) Target Selection Target Criteria	H_MA_CA_TargetSelectio n	H_MA_DS_MAStrategicReq H_MA_DS_Knowledgebase
Business Strategy, Rules & Tactics, Strategic Alignment & Governance	H_MA_CA_Strategy	H_MA_DS_StrategicReq H_MA_DS_Knowledgebase
M&A Due-Diligence	H_MA_CA_DueDiligence	H_MA_DS_DueDiligence H_MA_DS_Knowledgebase
Financing	H_MA_CA_DealManagem ent	H_MA_DS_StrategicReq H_MA_DS_DueDiligence H_MA_DS_DealTerms H_MA_DS_Knowledgebase
Negotiation & Deal Structuring	H_MA_CA_DealManagem ent	H_MA_DS_StrategicReq H_MA_DS_DueDiligence H_MA_DS_DealTerms H_MA_DS_MACombination H_MA_DS_Knowledgebase H_MA_DS_Compliance H_MA_DS_Synergy_KPI
Deal Execution	H_MA_CA_DealManagem ent	H_MA_DS_DealTerms H_MA_DS_MAProject H_MA_DS_Synergy_KPI

M&A Legal Compliance	H_MA_CA_DealComplian ce	H_MA_DS_Compliance
Project Management	H_MA_CA_ProjectManag ement	H_MA_DS_MAProject H_MA_DS_DealTerms H_MA_DS_Synergy_KPI
Pricing, Valuation	H_MA_CA_Valuation	H_MA_DS_DealTerms H_MA_DS_Market H_MA_DS_Knowledgebase
Risk & Performance Management	H_MA_CA_RiskManagem ent	H_MA_DS_Synergy_KPI H_MA_DS_DealTerms H_MA_DS_MAProject H_MA_DS_Market H_MA_DS_Knowledgebase
Takeover Defense	H_MA_CA_MADefense	H_MA_DS_MACombination H_MA_DS_Synergy_KPI
Divestiture	H_MA_CA_Divestiture	H_MA_DS_MACombination H_MA_DS_Synergy_KPI
Acquisition Strategy- Merger Analysis, Bid Strategy, Combination Forms	H_MA_CA_DealManagem ent	H_MA_DS_StrategicReq H_MA_DS_MACombination H_MA_DS_Synergy_KPI H_MA_DS_DealTerms H_MA_DS_MAProject
M&A Closing, Integration Management	H_MA_CA_Integration	H_MA_DS_Synergy_KPI H_MA_DS_DealTerms H_MA_DS_MAProject
M&A Synergy	H_MA_CA_Synergy	H_MA_DS_MAProject H_MA_DS_DealTerms H_MA_DS_Synergy_KPI
M&A Info Base	H_MA_CA_Knowledgeba se	H_MA_Data_KnowledgeBase
M&A Analysis	H_MA_CA_Analysis	H_MA_Data_KnowledgeBase H_MA_Data_CacheArchive
M&A DSS	H_MA_CA_DSS	H_MA_Data_KnowledgeBase H_MA_Data_CacheArchive

> *Business and IT strategy require that information system consolidates the enterprise-wide services together which are used by different applications. All the strategic requirements will be part of information systems so that strategy will be automatically governed in different applications using the information systems.*
>
> *Information system possesses functional services and data services for maximal integration, computation efficiency and overall effectiveness.*
>
> *The enterprise resources like core process and data are made available to applications only through the information systems. In no way, applications are allowed to access the enterprise data and process directly surpassing the information systems.*
>
> *Business functionalities are transformed into enterprise IT-services (Information System) which are configured, parameterized, extended and deployed in form of applications to enable the business services.*

In the Business Architecture, we have discussed the business functionalities represented and modeled in form of corresponding business services. The strategic framework that transforms the business services into IT services effectively aligns the IT with business.

We consolidate the IT services together and build the service inventory. These IT services form a key part of Information System. Service inventory for Private Equity and M&A are illustrated below.

Private Equity Service Inventory

In Information System Services Architecture of Private Equity, there are nine key IT Service groups which expose different services under its scope.

The service group H_PE_IS_ClientManagement exposes the services H_PE_IS_TargetSelection and H_PE_IS_InvestorSelection.

H_PE_IS_Strategy exposes H_PS_IS_Strategy, H_PE_IS_Tactics and H_PE_IS_Rules.

H_PE_IS_DecisionSupport exposes H_PE_IS_DueDiligence, H_PE_IS_ClientDecision, H_PE_IS_DealStructure, H_PE_IS_Financing, H_PE_IS_Contracts.

H_PE_IS_Regulations exposes H_PE_IS_GovRules, H_PE_IS_StrategicCompliance, H_PE_IS_ExternalRules and H_PE_IS_BusinessRules.

H_PE_IS_Financing exposes H_PE_IS_CashAffect, H_PE_IS_StockAffect and H_PE_IS_FinAnalysis.

H_PE_IS_Analysis exposes H_PE_IS_DueDiligence, H_PE_IS_ClientDecision, H_PE_IS_DealStructure, H_PE_IS_Financing, H_PE_IS_Contracts.

H_PE_IS_PortfolioManagement exposes the H_PE_IS_PortfolioPosition, H_PE_IS_StrategicPortfolio, H_PE_IS_HedgedPortfolio and H_PE_IS_PortfolioRisks.

H_PE_IS_RiskAnalysis exposes H_PE_IS_Sensi, H_PE_IS_P&L, H_PE_IS_VAR, H_PE_IS_Statistics, H_PE_IS_MarketRisks and H_PE_IS_RiskIndicators.

H_PE_IS_DealStructure exposes H_PE_IS_DealFinancing, H_PE_IS_DealContracts, H_PE_IS_DealRegulations, H_PE_IS_DealForecast, H_PE_IS_DealAssets and H_PE_IS_DealStrategy.

H_PE_IS_Pricing exposes H_PE_IS_Market_DealData, H_PE_IS_PricingMethod, H_PE_IS_ControlPremium, H_PE_IS_IRR, H_PE_IS_TRR and H_PE_IS_IR.

H_PE_IS_DealTrading exposes H_PE_IS_Deal_MarketData, H_PE_IS_DealExecution, H_PE_IS_AutomatedSTP, H_PE_IS_DealPosition and H_PE_IS_DealRisks.

H_PE_IS_DealAdministration exposes H_PE_IS_DealValidation, H_PE_IS_DealClearing, H_PE_IS_DealRecordManagement, H_PE_IS_DealReporting and H_PE_IS_DealPosition.

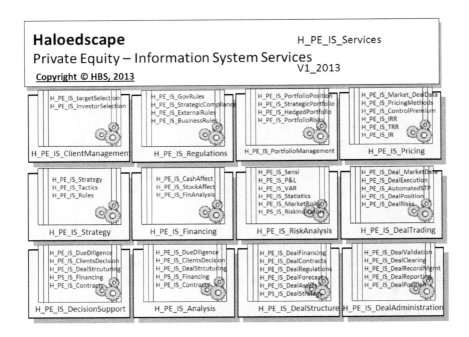

Figure 3.6: © HBS, Private Equity Information System - Service Inventory

M&A Service Inventory

In Information System Architecture of M&A, there are twelve key IT-service groups which expose different services under its scope.

The service group H_MA_IS_ClientValues exposes the services for target-selection, target-feasibility, client's need, and client's value.

Service group H_MA_IS_Strategy is used to exposes the services for business & IT strategy, business rules, tactics, client's strategy and strategic alignment.

Service group H_MA_IS_DecisionSupport exposes the decision related services for mode of merger, due diligence, optimal financing mode, bidding strategy, negotiation terms and deal-structuring.

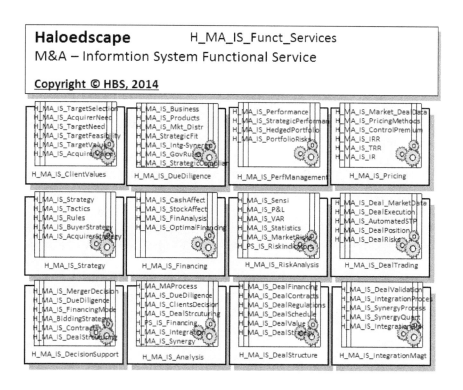

Figure 3.7: © HBS, M&A Information System - Functional Service Inventory

Service group H_MA_IS_DueDiligence exposes the service for due-diligence analysis of target-company in terms of product sales, marketing, distribution, market control, customer-base, synergy potential and compliance with business & legal rules.

Service group H_MA_IS_Financing exposes service for evaluating impact of different mode of financing and optimal proportion of financing.

Service group H_MA_IS_Analysis are used for most of M&A functionalities. The core services exposed by this group are due-diligence, seller's & buyer's business strategy, deal-structuring, financing, integration & synergy.

Service group H_MA_IS_PerformanceManagement exposes the services for performance management, strategic performance, hedged-risk and portfolio risk.

Service group H_MA_IS_RiskAnalysis exposes the services for sensitivities, P&L, VAR, statistics, market-risks and risk-indicators.

Service group H_MA_IS_DealStructure exposes the services for deal financing, deal contracts, deal regulations, deal schedule, deal value and deal strategy.

Service group H_MA_IS_Pricing exposes the services for market data of deal, pricing method, control-premium, IRR, TRR, IR etc.

Service group H_MA_IS_DealTrading exposes the services for deal market data, deal execution, automated-STP, deal position and deal risks.

Service group H_MA_IS_IntegrationManagement exposes the services for deal validation, integration planning, synergy realization, synergy measurement and integration-risks.

The services exposed here are in the namespace of service group so name clash is prevented with the specification of global service group. Application is a complex business service that is built through choreography of basic granular services.

Interlinking Functionalities, Capabilities and Services

Inter-related business functionalities, capabilities and corresponding functional services of M&A are mapped as below:

Functionalities	Capabilities	Functional-Service
Business Strategy, **Business Rules-Tactics,** **Strategic Alignment-Governance**	H_MA_CA_Strategy	H_MA_IS_Strategy *H_MA_IS_Tactics* *H_MA_IS_Rules* *H_MA_IS_ClientStrategy*
Client Management **(Buyer, Seller, Target Company)** **Target Selection** **Target Criteria**	H_MA_CA_TargetSelection	H_MA_IS_ClientValues *H_MA_IS_TargetSelection* *H_MA_IS_BuyerNeed* *H_MA_IS_SellerNeed* *H_MA_IS_TargetFeasibility* *H_MA_IS_ClientValues*
M&A Due- Diligence	H_MA_CA_DueDiligence	H_MA_IS_DueDiligence *H_MA_IS_TC_Business* *H_MA_IS_TC_Product* *H_MA_IS_TC_Marketing* *H_MA_IS_TC_Distribution* *H_MA_IS_TC_StrategicFit* *H_MA_IS_TC_Synergy* *H_MA_IS_TC_Integration*
Financing	H_MA_CA_DealManagement	H_MA_IS_Financing *H_MA_IS_CashAffect*

		H_MA_IS_StockAffect
		H_MA_IS_FinAnalysis
		H_MA_IS_OptimalFinancing
Negotiation & Deal Structuring	H_MA_CA_DealManagement	H_MA_IS_DealStructure
		H_MA_IS_DealFinancing
		H_MA_IS_DealContracts
		H_MA_IS_DealRegulations
		H_MA_IS_DealSchedule
		H_MA_IS_DealValue
		H_MA_IS_DealStrategy
Deal Execution	H_MA_CA_DealManagement	H_MA_IS_DealTrading
		H_MA_IS_DealExecution
		H_MA_IS_AutomatedSTP
		H_MA_IS_DealPosition
		H_MA_IS_DealRisks
M&A Legal Compliance	H_MA_CA_DealCompliance	H_MA_IS_DealStructure
		H_MA_IS_DealRegulations
Project Management	H_MA_CA_ProjectManagement	H_MA_IS_DealStructure
		H_MA_IS_DealSchedule
		H_MA_IS_DealStrategy
		H_MA_IS_DealValue
Pricing, Valuation	H_MA_CA_Valuation	H_MA_IS_Pricing
		H_MA_IS_Market
		H_MA_IS_PricingMethod

		H_MA_IS_ControlPremium
		H_MA_IS_IRR/TRR/IR
Risk & Performance Management	H_MA_CA_RiskManagement	H_MA_IS_PerfManagement
		H_MA_IS_StrategicPerformance
		H_MA_IS_HedgedPortfolio
		H_MA_IS_PortfolioRisk
Risk Management	H_MA_CA_RiskManagement	H_MA_IS_RiskAnalysis
		H_MA_IS_Sensi
		H_MA_IS_P&L
		H_MA_IS_VAR
		H_MA_IS_Statistics
		H_MA_IS_MarketRisk
		H_MA_IS_RiskIndicator
Takeover Defense	H_MA_CA_MADefense	H_MA_IS_Analysis
		H_MA_IS_DecisionSupport
Divestiture	H_MA_CA_Divestiture	H_MA_IS_Analysis
		H_MA_IS_DecisionSupport
Acquisition Strategy-Merger Analysis, Bid Strategy, Combination Forms	H_MA_CA_DealManagement	H_MA_IS_Analysis
		H_MA_IS_DealStructure
		H_MA_IS_DecisionSupport
M&A Closing, Integration Management	H_MA_CA_Integration	H_MA_IS_IntegrationMagt
		H_MA_IS_DealValidation

		H_MA_IS_IntegrationProcess
		H_MA_IS_SynergyProcess
		H_MA_IS_SynergyQuant
		H_MA_IS_IntegrationRisk
M&A Synergy	H_MA_CA_Synergy	H_MA_IS_IntegrationMagt
		H_MA_IS_SynergyProcess
		H_MA_IS_SynergyQuant
M&A Info Base	H_MA_CA_Knowledge base	H_MA_IS_Analysis
		H_MA_IS_DecisionSupport
M&A Analysis	H_MA_CA_Analysis	H_MA_IS_Analysis
		H_MA_IS_MAProcess
		H_MA_IS_DueDiligence
		H_MA_IS_ClientDecision
		H_MA_IS_DealStructure
		H_MA_IS_Financing
		H_MA_IS_OptimalBidding
		H_MA_IS_Integration
		H_MA_IS_Synergy
M&A DSS	H_MA_CA_DSS	H_MA_IS_DecisionSupport
		H_MA_IS_DS_MergerDecision
		H_MA_IS_DS_DueDiligence
		H_MA_IS_DS_Financing
		H_MA_IS_DS_BiddingStrategy
		H_MA_IS_DS_Contract

Information system services make interfaces available to enterprise wide application to access the enterprise resources. Our Information System is SOA based supported with sophisticated platform with required technology.

Consolidated Data and functional services of information system fulfill the service orientation and shared application components principles.

As mentioned earlier, the SOA based information system achieves strategic objective of business aligned agile IT which maximizes the ROI while reducing risks for enterprise-wide IT.

In our approach, the strategic principles and policies are governed across enterprise applications with our Information System.

3.8 Information System/Application – Use Cases & Class Diagram

Use-cases and logical diagrams are presented for different functionalities of business. Interrelation of use-Case, service, application, data and process are also mentioned. Use-cases and class diagram are modeled in UML.

We illustrate below the use-cases, class diagrams, associations etc using UML with example of M&A business function.

Use-Case Inventory

M&A Use-Case Inventory

Use Cases	H_MA_F_TC_Do mainBusiness	H_MA_F_TC_M arketing	H_MA_F_TC_ Distribution
H_MA_F_TC_M anagementTea m	H_MA_F_TC_Fin ancial CashBook	H_MA_F_TC_In vestment	H_MA_DueDili gence
H_MA_F_TC_P roductOfferings	H_MA_Strategic Governance	H_MA_InvestorS elction	H_MA_Busine ssTactics
H_MA_Analysis _Decision	H_MA_Strategy_ Deal_Structure	H_MA_LegalCo mpliance	H_MA_F_EX_ Rules_Regulat ion
H_MA_Pricing_ Valuation	H_MA_RiskMana gement	H_MA_Performa nceManagement	H_MA_Integra tionManagem ent
H_MA_DealExe cution	H_MA_TargetSel ection		

Packages	H_MA_DueDili gence	H_MA_Target Selection	H_MA_Deal
H_MA_StrategicGo vernance	H_MA_Investo rSelection	H_MA_Pricing	H_MA_Risk_Perf _Management
H_MA_Integration_ Management	H_MA_Analysi s	H_MA_Decisi onSupport	

Classes	H_MA

H_MA, an actor for business function is Mergers and Acquisitions wing of our virtual investment bank "Haloedscape".

Business Strategy Governance – Business Strategy, Tactics, Rules

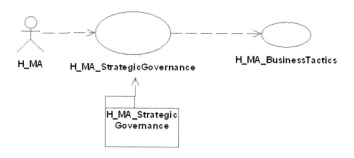

Figure 3.8: © HBS, UC-Strategic Governance

H_MA as an actor calls use-case H_MA_Strategic_Governance which invokes another function H_MA_BusinessTactics. The package H_MA_StrategicGovernance includes this use-case.

The function H_MA_BusinessTactics instantiates class H_MA_IB_BusinessTactics_Rules.

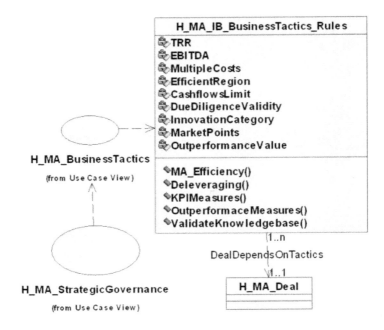

Figure 3.9: © HBS, UC/Class-Business Tactics

The dependency relationship named as DealDependsOnTactics shows that one or many entity of H_MA_IB_BusinessTactics_Rules is associated with one entity of H_MA_Deal.

Class H_MA_IB_BusinessTactics_Rules

Operations

Name	Signature	Class
◆MA_Efficiency	◆MA_Efficiency ()	H_MA_IB_BusinessTactics_Rules
◆Deleveraging	◆Deleveraging ()	H_MA_IB_BusinessTactics_Rules
◆KPIMeasures	◆KPIMeasures ()	H_MA_IB_BusinessTacti

		cs_Rules
◈ OutperformaceMeasures	◈ OutperformaceMeasures ()	H_MA_IB_BusinessTactics_Rules
◈ ValidateKnowledgebase	◈ ValidateKnowledgebase ()	H_MA_IB_BusinessTactics_Rules

Attributes

Name	Class
TRR	H_MA_IB_BusinessTactics_Rules
EBITDA	H_MA_IB_BusinessTactics_Rules
MultipleCosts	H_MA_IB_BusinessTactics_Rules
EfficientRegion	H_MA_IB_BusinessTactics_Rules
CashflowsLimit	H_MA_IB_BusinessTactics_Rules
DueDiligenceValidity	H_MA_IB_BusinessTactics_Rules
InnovationCategory	H_MA_IB_BusinessTactics_Rules
MarketPoints	H_MA_IB_BusinessTactics_Rules
OutperformanceValue	H_MA_IB_BusinessTactics_Rules

Associations

Name	My Role	My Class	Other Role	Other Element
TacticsAppliedOnDeal	TacticsIncludedInDeal	H_MA_IB_BusinessTactics_Rules	DealIncludesTactics	H_MA_Deal

Dependencies

Name	Class	Supplier
DealDependsOnTactic s	H_MA_IB_BusinessTactics_Rule s	H_MA_D eal

Realize Relationships

Class	Supplier
H_MA_IB_BusinessTactics_Rules	H_MA_Deal

Business and Strategic Requirements

H_MA as an actor invokes use-case H_MA_TargetSelection, which invokes another function H_MA_Analysis_Decision to compute the process. The package H_MA_TargetSelection contains the functionality H_MA_TargetSelection.

H_MA_Analysis_Design function is handled by class H_MA_Analysis and H_MA_DSS which are modeled later. H_MA_Analysis for target selection depends upon functionality H_MA_StrategicRequirements.

The model H_MA_StrategicRequirements acts as aggregate containing the subordinate classes H_MA_BusinessRequirements, H_MA_InvestmentType, H_MA_SellerStrategy and H_MA_BuyerStrategy.

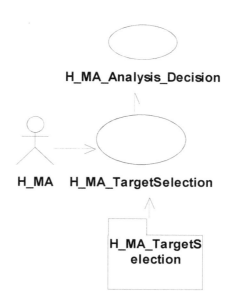

Figure 3.10: © HBS, UC-Target Selection

Models   H_Ma_BenefitAnalysis,   H_MA_SynergicValues,
H_MA_TermsNegotiations   and   H_MA_Project   associate
H_MA_StrategicRequirements.   This implies that associating model
H_Ma_BenefitAnalysis or H_MA_SynergicValues needs input from
model H_MA_StrategicRequirements.

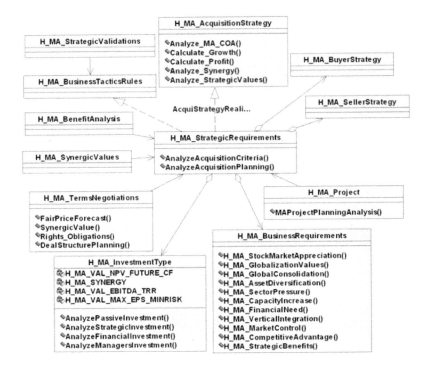

Figure 3.11: © HBS, Class-Strategic Requirements

H_MA_StrategicRequirements   realizes   H_MA_BusinessTacticsRules
and H_MA_AcquisitionStrategy.

Class H_MA_StrategicRequirements

Operations

Name	Signature	Class
◈ AnalyzeAcquisitionCriteria	◈ AnalyzeAcquisitionCriteria ()	H_MA_StrategicRequirements
◈	◈	H_MA_StrategicRequ

AnalyzeAcquisitionPlanning	AnalyzeAcquisitionPlanning ()	irements
◆Analyze_MA_COA	◆ Analyze_MA_COA ()	H_MA_AcquisitionStrategy
◆Calculate_Growth	◆Calculate_Growth ()	H_MA_AcquisitionStrategy
◆Calculate_Profit	◆Calculate_Profit ()	H_MA_AcquisitionStrategy
◆Analyze_Synergy	◆Analyze_Synergy ()	H_MA_AcquisitionStrategy
◆ Analyze_StrategicValues	◆ Analyze_StrategicValues ()	H_MA_AcquisitionStrategy

Associations

My Class	Other Element
H_MA_StrategicRequirements	H_MA_TermsNegotiations
H_MA_StrategicRequirements	H_MA_PricingMethods
H_MA_StrategicRequirements	H_MA_Synergy
H_MA_StrategicRequirements	H_MA_TakeoverDefence
H_MA_StrategicRequirements	H_MA_IntegrationCapabilities
H_MA_StrategicRequirements	H_MA_AcquisitionStrategy
H_MA_StrategicRequirements	H_MA_TermsNegotiations
H_MA_StrategicRequirements	H_MA_DealStructure
H_MA_StrategicRequirements	H_MA_Pricing_Valuation
H_MA_StrategicRequirements	H_MA_Takeover
H_MA_StrategicRequirements	H_MA_Project
H_MA_StrategicRequirements	H_MA_SynergicValues
H_MA_StrategicRequirements	H_MA_BuyerStrategy
H_MA_StrategicRequirements	H_MA_SellerStrategy
H_MA_StrategicRequirements	H_MA_ClassificationAnalysis
H_MA_StrategicRequirements	H_MA_BenefitAnalysis

H_MA_StrategicRequirements	H_MA_IntegrationCapabilities
H_MA_StrategicRequirements	H_MA_Project
H_MA_StrategicRequirements	H_MA_BusinessRequirements
H_MA_StrategicRequirements	H_MA_InvestmentTypes
H_MA_StrategicRequirements	H_MA_InvestmentType
H_MA_StrategicRequirements	H_MA_DueDiligence
H_MA_StrategicRequirements	H_MA_BusinessRequirements
H_MA_StrategicRequirements	H_MA_InvestmentType
H_MA_StrategicRequirements	H_MA_BuyerStrategy
H_MA_StrategicRequirements	H_MA_SellerStrategy
H_MA_StrategicRequirements	H_MA_Analysis
H_MA_StrategicRequirements	H_MA_AcquisitionStrategy

Dependencies

Name	Class	Supplier
StrategyInvokesRequirements	H_MA_AcquisitionStrategy	H_MA_StrategicRequirements

Generalization Relationships

Name	Class	Supplier
--Not Named--	H_MA_StrategicRequirements	H_MA_AcquisitionStrategy

Realize Relationships

Class	Supplier
H_MA_StrategicRequirements	H_MA_StrategicValidations
H_MA_StrategicRequirements	H_MA_BusinessTacticsRules
H_MA_StrategicRequirements	H_MA_AcquisitionStrategy

Class H_MA_AcquisitionStrategy

Operations

Name	Signature	Class
◈Analyze_MA_COA	◈ Analyze_MA_COA ()	H_MA_AcquisitionStrategy
◈Calculate_Growth	◈Calculate_Growth ()	H_MA_AcquisitionStrategy
◈Calculate_Profit	◈Calculate_Profit ()	H_MA_AcquisitionStrategy
◈Analyze_Synergy	◈Analyze_Synergy ()	H_MA_AcquisitionStrategy
◈ Analyze_StrategicValues	◈ Analyze_StrategicValues ()	H_MA_AcquisitionStrategy

Class H_MA_BusinessRequirements

Operations

Name	Signature	Class
◈ H_MA_StockMarketAppreciation	◈ H_MA_StockMarketAppreciation ()	H_MA_BusinessRequirements
◈ H_MA_GlobalizationValues	◈ H_MA_GlobalizationValues ()	H_MA_BusinessRequirements
◈ H_MA_GlobalConsolidation	◈ H_MA_GlobalConsolidation ()	H_MA_BusinessRequirements
◈ H_MA_AssetDiversification	◈ H_MA_AssetDiversification ()	H_MA_BusinessRequirements
◈ H_MA_SectorPressure	◈ H_MA_SectorPressure (	H_MA_BusinessRequirements

	)	
◈ H_MA_CapacityIncrease	◈ H_MA_CapacityIncrease ()	H_MA_BusinessRequirements
◈ H_MA_FinancialNeed	◈ H_MA_FinancialNeed ()	H_MA_BusinessRequirements
◈ H_MA_VerticalIntegration	◈ H_MA_VerticalIntegration ()	H_MA_BusinessRequirements
◈ H_MA_MarketControl	◈ H_MA_MarketControl ()	H_MA_BusinessRequirements
◈ H_MA_CompetitiveAdvantage	◈ H_MA_CompetitiveAdvantage ()	H_MA_BusinessRequirements
◈ H_MA_StrategicBenefits	◈ H_MA_StrategicBenefits ()	H_MA_BusinessRequirements

Class H_MA_InvestmentType

Operations

Name	Signature	Class
◈ AnalyzePassiveInvestment	◈ AnalyzePassiveInvestment ()	H_MA_InvestmentType
◈ AnalyzeStrategicInvestment	◈ AnalyzeStrategicInvestment ()	H_MA_InvestmentType
◈ AnalyzeFinancialInvestment	◈ AnalyzeFinancialInvestment ()	H_MA_InvestmentType
◈ AnalyzeManagersInvestment	◈ AnalyzeManagersInvest	H_MA_InvestmentType

	ment ()	

Attributes

Name	Class
🔖H_MA_VAL_NPV_FUTURE_CF	H_MA_InvestmentType
🔖H_MA_SYNERGY	H_MA_InvestmentType
🔖H_MA_VAL_EBITDA_TRR	H_MA_InvestmentType
🔖 H_MA_VAL_MAX_EPS_MINRISK	H_MA_InvestmentType

Interrelation of Use-Case, Service, Application and Data

Use-Case / Business Functionality	Service	App / System Components	Data Model
H_MA_Strategic_Governance H_MA_Strategic_Requirementse	H_MA_IS_Strategy	H_MA_SYS_Strategy	H_MA_Data_Strategy

Class H_MA_Pricing_Valuation

Operations

Name	Signature	Class
🔷DCFMethod	🔷DCFMethod ()	H_MA_PricingMethods
🔷SynergyValuation	🔷SynergyValuation ()	H_MA_PricingMethods
🔷 ComparableMethod	🔷 ComparableMethod ()	H_MA_PricingMethods
🔷MultipilesMethod	🔷MultipilesMethod ()	H_MA_PricingMethods
🔷BreakupMethod	🔷BreakupMethod ()	H_MA_PricingMethod

235

		ds
◆BookValue	◆BookValue ()	H_MA_PricingMetho ds
◆ LiquidationAnalysis	◆LiquidationAnalysis ()	H_MA_PricingMetho ds
◆ReplacementValue	◆ReplacementValue ()	H_MA_PricingMetho ds
◆EarningMultiples	◆EarningMultiples ()	H_MA_PricingMetho ds
◆PERatioMethod	◆PERatioMethod ()	H_MA_PricingMetho ds
◆ EconomicProfitModel	◆ EconomicProfitModel ()	H_MA_PricingMetho ds
◆ CostOfCapitalMethod	◆ CostOfCapitalMethod ()	H_MA_PricingMetho ds
◆ CostofEquityMethod	◆ CostofEquityMethod ()	H_MA_PricingMetho ds

Attributes

Name	Class
◈ ComarableFactor	H_MA_PricingMethods
◈BreakupVal	H_MA_PricingMethods
◈LBO	H_MA_PricingMethods
◈GRM	H_MA_PricingMethods
◈EPS	H_MA_PricingMethods
◈LiquidationVal	H_MA_PricingMethods
◈DiscountFactor	H_MA_PricingMethods

Associations

My Class	Other Element

H_MA_Pricing_Valuation	H_MA_PricingMethods
H_MA_Pricing_Valuation	H_MA_Accounting
H_MA_Pricing_Valuation	H_MA_DealStructure
H_MA_Pricing_Valuation	H_MA_StrategicRequirements
H_MA_Pricing_Valuation	H_MA_Project
H_MA_Pricing_Valuation	H_MA_Analysis
H_MA_Pricing_Valuation	H_MA_Project
H_MA_Pricing_Valuation	H_MA_TC_Value
H_MA_PricingMethods	H_MA_StrategicRequirements
H_MA_PricingMethods	H_MA_Accounting
H_MA_PricingMethods	H_MA_DealStructure
H_MA_Pricing_Valuation	H_MA_PricingMethods

Dependencies

Class	Supplier
H_MA_Pricing_Valuation	H_MA_TC_Value

Generalization Relationships

Name	Class	Supplier
PricingGeneralizesMethods	H_MA_Pricing_Valuation	H_MA_PricingMethods

Realize Relationships

Name	Class	Supplier
ValuationRealized	H_MA_Pricing_Valuation	H_MA_TC_Value

Class H_MA_TC_Value

Attributes

Name	Class
Pricing	H_MA_TC_Value
FMV	H_MA_TC_Value
NegotiatedValue	H_MA_TC_Value
ComparedPriceValue	H_MA_TC_Value
ComparedTxValue	H_MA_TC_Value
DCFValue	H_MA_TC_Value
MultiplesValue	H_MA_TC_Value
OptionValue	H_MA_TC_Value
VCValue	H_MA_TC_Value

Associations

My Class	Other Element
H_MA_TC_Value	H_MA_Pricing_Valuation

Interrelation of Use-Case, Service, Application and Data

Use-Case / Business Functionality	Service	App / System Components	Data Model
H_MA_Pricing	H_MA_IS_Pricing	H_MA_SYS_Pricing	H_MA_Data_DealTerms H_MA_Data_Knowledgebase

Deal Execution & Workflow

H_MA as an actor invokes the function H_MA_DealExecution. The deal structure is inherited from function H_MA_Stratey_Deal_Structure. H_MA_Deal_Execution is associated with functionality H_MA_Pricing_Valuation. The dependent functionalities on H_MA_DealExecution are H_MA_RiskManagement and H_MA_Integration_Management. This dependency constitutes a workflow wherein deal-execution causes processing of two functionalities, integration-management and risk-management.

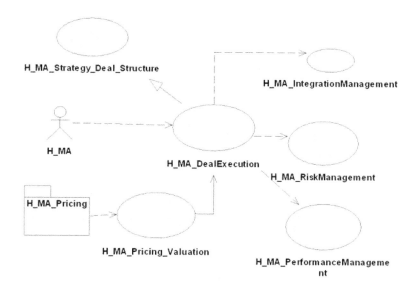

Figure 3.12: © HBS, UC-Deal Execution

Interrelation of Use-Case, Service, Application and Data

Use-Case / Business Functionality	Service	App / System Components	Data Model
H_MA_DealExecution	H_MA_IN_Deal_Trading	H_MA_SYS_DealTrading	H_MA_Data_MA_Project H_MA_Data_Syn

			ergy KPI H MA Data Deal Terms

Integration, Performance & Risk management

Functionality risk-management is integrated with functionality performance-management. Not only deal-execution functionality but H_MA actor also may invoke the functionalities risk-management and integration-management.

H_MA as an actor interacts with functionalities H_MA_RiskManagement and H_MA_RiskManagement associated together bidirectionally, both included in package H_MA_Risk_Perf_Management.

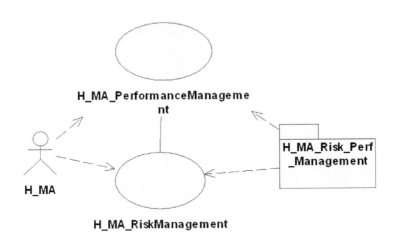

Figure 3.13: © HBS, UC-Risk Performance Management

Integration & Synergy

Besides functionality deal-execution invoking integration-management with automated workflow, actor H_MA may directly interact with functionality H_MA_IntegrationManagement which is associated with H_MA_Analysis_Design and H_MA_Strategy_Deal_Structure.

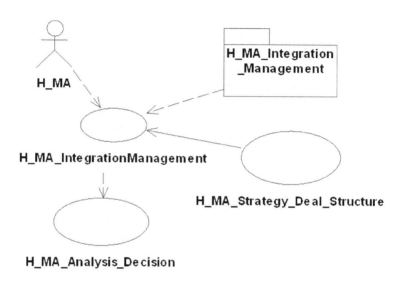

Figure 3.14: © HBS, UC-Integration Management

Model H_MA_Synergy aggregates H_MA_Acquirer_Values and realizes the model H_MA_SynergyValues.

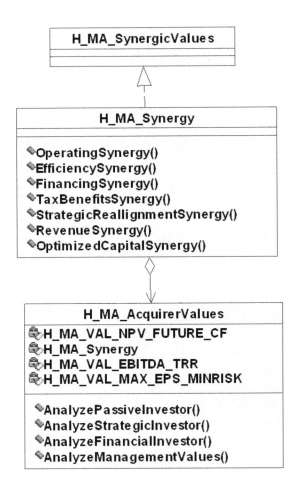

Figure 3.15: © HBS, Class-Synergy

Class H_MA_Synergy

Operations

Name	Signature	Class
OperatingSynergy	OperatingSynergy ()	H_MA_Synergy

EfficiencySynergy	EfficiencySynergy ()	H_MA_Synergy
FinancingSynergy	FinancingSynergy ()	H_MA_Synergy
TaxBenefitsSynergy	TaxBenefitsSynergy ()	H_MA_Synergy
StrategicRealignmentSynergy	StrategicRealignmentSynergy ()	H_MA_Synergy
RevenueSynergy	RevenueSynergy ()	H_MA_Synergy
OptimizedCapitalSynergy	OptimizedCapitalSynergy ()	H_MA_Synergy
AnalyzePassiveInvestor	AnalyzePassiveInvestor ()	H_MA_Acquirer Values
AnalyzeStrategicInvestor	AnalyzeStrategicInvestor ( )	H_MA_Acquirer Values
AnalyzeFinancialInvestor	AnalyzeFinancialInvestor ()	H_MA_Acquirer Values
AnalyzeManagementValues	AnalyzeManagementValues ()	H_MA_Acquirer Values

Attributes

Name	Class
H_MA_VAL_NPV_FUTURE_CF	H_MA_AcquirerValues
H_MA_Synergy	H_MA_AcquirerValues
H_MA_VAL_EBITDA_TRR	H_MA_AcquirerValues
H_MA_VAL_MAX_EPS_MINRISK	H_MA_AcquirerValues

Associations

My Class	Other Element
H_MA_Synergy	H_MA_StrategicRequirements
H_MA_Synergy	H_MA_BenefitAnalysis
H_MA_AcquirerValues	H_MA_BenefitAnalysis

Generalization Relationships

Class	Supplier
H_MA_Synergy	H_MA_AcquirerValues

Realize Relationships

Class	Supplier
H_MA_Synergy	H_MA_SynergicValues

Class H_MA_AcquirerValues

Operations

Name	Signature	Class
AnalyzePassiveInvestor	AnalyzePassiveInvestor ( )	H_MA_AcquirerValues
AnalyzeStrategicInvestor	AnalyzeStrategicInvestor ()	H_MA_AcquirerValues
AnalyzeFinancialInvestor	AnalyzeFinancialInvestor ()	H_MA_AcquirerValues
AnalyzeManagementValues	AnalyzeManagementValues ()	H_MA_AcquirerValues

Attributes

Name	Class
📚H_MA_VAL_NPV_FUTURE_CF	H_MA_AcquirerValues
📚H_MA_Synergy	H_MA_AcquirerValues
📚H_MA_VAL_EBITDA_TRR	H_MA_AcquirerValues
📚 H_MA_VAL_MAX_EPS_MINRISK	H_MA_AcquirerValues

Associations

My Class	Other Element
H_MA_AcquirerValues	H_MA_BenefitAnalysis

Interrelation of Use-Case, Service, Application and Data

Use-Case / Business Functionality	Service	App / System Components	Data Model
H_MA_Performanc eManagement H_MA_RiskManag ement H_MA_Integration	H_MA_IS_Perf Management H_MA_IS_RiskA nalysis H_MA_IS_Syner gyProcess H_MA_IS_Integ rationMagt	H_MA_SYS_Perfor manceMangament H_MA_SYS_RiskAn alysis H_MA_SYS_Integra tionManagement	H_MA_DS_Syn ergy_KPI H_MA_DS_Deal Terms H_MA_DS_MA Project H_MA_DS_Mar ket H_MA_DS_Kno wledgebase

Domain Knowledgebase

The model H_MA_DomainKnowledgeBase is a core business model which is used by all of the core functionalities for processing.

Functionalities like due-diligence, analysis, acquisition strategy, financing and decision-support use domain-knowledgebase for achieving their processing.

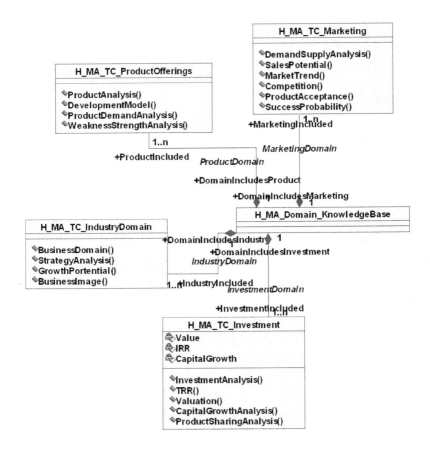

Figure 3.16: © HBS, Class-DomainKnowledgebase-1

The model H_MA_DomainKnowledgeBase as parent class aggregates child classes:

- H_MA_TC_ProductOfferings

- H_MA_TC_Marketing
- H_MA_TC_IndustryDomain
- H_MA_TC_Investment

The model H_MA_DomainKnowledgeBase as parent class aggregates some more child classes as follows:

- H_MA_TC_Finance
- H_MA_TC_ManagementTeam
- H_MA_TC_Distribution

Figure 3.17: © HBS, Class-DomainKnowledgebase-2

Class H_MA_AcquirerValues

Associations

Name	My Role	My Class	Other Role	Other Element
IndustryDomain	DomainIncludesIndustry	H_MA_Domain KnowledgeBase	IndustryIncluded	H_MA_TC_IndustryDomain
ProductDomain	DomainIncludesProduct	H_MA_Domain KnowledgeBase	ProductIncluded	H_MA_TC_ProductOfferings
MarketingDomain	DomainIncludesMarketing	H_MA_Domain KnowledgeBase	MarketingIncluded	H_MA_TC_Marketing
ManagementDomain	DomainIncludesManagement	H_MA_Domain KnowledgeBase	ManagementIncluded	H_MA_TC_Management Team
FinanceDomain	DomainIncludesFinance	H_MA_Domain KnowledgeBase	FinanceIncluded	H_MA_TC_Finance
InvestmentDomain	DomainIncludesInvestment	H_MA_Domain KnowledgeBase	InvestmentIncluded	H_MA_TC_INTEGRATION
IndustryDomain	DomainIncludesIndustry	H_MA_Domain KnowledgeBase	IndustryIncluded	H_MA_TC_IndustryDomain
ProductDomain	DomainIncludesProduct	H_MA_Domain KnowledgeBase	ProductIncluded	H_MA_TC_ProductOfferings
MarketingDomain	DomainIncludesMarketing	H_MA_Domain KnowledgeBase	MarketingIncluded	H_MA_TC_Marketing
ManagementDomain	DomainIncludesManagement	H_MA_Domain KnowledgeBase	ManagementIncluded	H_MA_TC_Management Team
FinanceDomain	DomainIncludesFinance	H_MA_Domain KnowledgeBase	FinanceIncluded	H_MA_TC_Finance

Investme ntDomain	DomainInclud esInvestment	H_MA_Domain _KnowledgeBa se	Investmen tIncluded	H_MA_TC_I nvestment
Distributio nDomain	DomainInclud esDistribution	H_MA_Domain _KnowledgeBa se	Distributio nIncluded	H_MA_TC_ Distribution

Analysis

The model H_MA_Analysis provides core functionalities for analysis of M&A business and decision making.

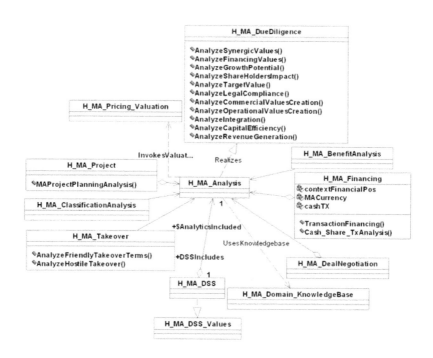

Figure 3.18: © HBS, Class-Analysis

249

H_MAAnalysis is used by H_MA_ClassificationAnalysis, H_MA_Takeover and H_MA_BenefitAnalysis. It calls the model H_MA_Pricing_Valuation for pricing and H_MA_Domain_Knowledgebase for information on which the analysis is based upon. H_MA_Project, H_MA_Financing, H_MA_DealNegotiation act as aggregate and contain the model H_MA_Analysis. H_MA_Analysis realizes the model H_MA_DusDiligence on which whole M&A business is based. H_MA_DSS uses the H_MA_Analysis to realize the model H_MA_DSS_Values which supports the decision- making.

Class H_MA_Analysis

Associations

My Class	Other Element
H_MA_Analysis	H_MA_DSS
H_MA_Analysis	H_MA_Pricing_Valuation
H_MA_Analysis	H_MA_Project
H_MA_Analysis	H_MA_BenefitAnalysis
H_MA_Analysis	H_MA_ClassificationAnalysis
H_MA_Analysis	H_MA_DealNegotiation
H_MA_Analysis	H_MA_SynergicValues
H_MA_Analysis	H_MA_Takeover
H_MA_Analysis	H_MA_Financing
H_MA_Analysis	H_MA_StrategicRequirements

Dependencies

Name	Class	Supplier
InvokesValuation	H_MA_Analysis	H_MA_Pricing_Valuation
	H_MA_Analysis	H_MA_Domain_KnowledgeBa

UsesKnowledgebase	s	se ·

Realize Relationships

Name	Class	Supplier
Realizes	H_MA_Analysis	H_MA_DueDiligence

Decision Support

H_MA_DSS is the core model for decision support functionality. It provides the decision-inputs and realizes optimal-values for the models H_MA_Bidding_Strategy, H_MA_NegotiationTerms, H_MA_DealStructure, H_MA_Synergy, H_MA_AcquisitionStrategy and H_MA_Financing. H_MA_DSS uses some of analytical functionalities for decision making and acts as aggregate containing the models H_MA_Strategy, H_MA_Analysis, H_MA_BenefitAnalysis and H_MA_DueDiligence. H_MA_DSS uses the model H_MA_Domain_Knowledgbase for information on which decision-making is based.

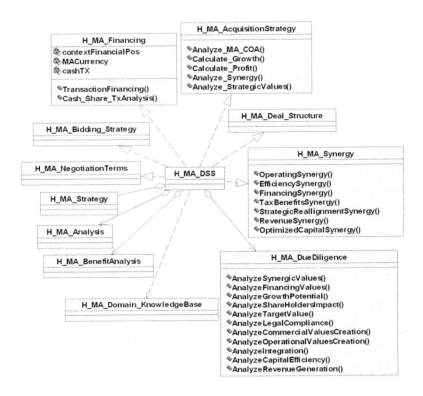

Figure 3.19: © HBS, Class-Decision Support

Class H_MA_DSS

Associations

My Class	Other Element
H_MA_DSS	H_MA_Analysis
H_MA_DSS	H_MA_Analysis
H_MA_DSS	H_MA_Analysis
H_MA_DSS	H_MA_BenefitAnalysis
H_MA_DSS	H_MA_Analysis
H_MA_DSS	H_MA_Strategy

252

H_MA_DSS	H_MA_DueDiligence

Dependencies

Class	Supplier
H_MA_DSS	H_MA_Analysis
H_MA_DSS	H_MA_Bidding_Strategy
H_MA_DSS	H_MA_Domain_KnowledgeBase

Realize Relationships

Class	Supplier
H_MA_DSS	H_MA_DSS_Values
H_MA_DSS	H_MA_Bidding_Strategy
H_MA_DSS	H_MA_Financing
H_MA_DSS	H_MA_AcquisitionStrategy
H_MA_DSS	H_MA_Deal_Structure
H_MA_DSS	H_MA_NegotiationTerms
H_MA_DSS	H_MA_Synergy

Logical Class Inventory

M&A Class Inventory

Classes	H_MA_Contracts	H_MA_EX_Regulations	H_MA_CT_LetterOfIntents
H_MA_Assets_Strategy	H_MA_ST_Angel_Investing	H_MA_ST_VentureCapital	H_MA_ST_GrowthCapital
H_MA_ST_MidMarket	H_MA_ST_Distressed	H_MA_ST_SecondaryMarket_Val	H_MA_ST_LBO
H_MA_CT_NegotiatedTerms	H_MA_CT_DefinitiveDoc	H_MA_Deal	H_MA_Deal_Closing
H_MA_Deal_Fina	H_MA_TC_Due	H_MA_TC_Prici	H_MA_LP_R

ncing	Diligence	ng	eturns
H_MA_Bus_Anal ysisValue	H_MA_Bus_Portf olioManagement	H_MA_LP_Opti malPortfolio	H_MA_LP_C apitalGrowth
H_MA_Bus_Deci sionSupportValue	H_MA_ST_IPO	H_MA_Deal_Fin ancing_Equity	H_MA_Deal_ Financing_D ebt
H_MA_Deal_Fina ncing_Cash	H_MA_ST_LBO Val	H_MA_ST_Distr essed_Val	H_MA_ST_S ecodaryMark et
H_MA_ST_Mezz anine	H_MA_ST_Mezz anine_Val	H_MA_TC_Targ etSelection	H_MA_LP_In vestors
H_MA_Domain_ KnowledgeBase	H_MA_Domain_ Expertise	H_MA_EX_RG_ SEC	H_MA_EX_R G_FASB157
H_MA_Asset_Str ategy_Val	H_MA_IB_Busin essTactics_Rule s	H_MA_TC_Val	H_MA_Bus_ RiskManage ment
H_MA_Bus_Acco unting	F_PE_Bus_Bala nceSheet	F_PE_Bus_FinSt atement	H_MA_Bus_ Risk_KRI
H_MA_Bus_PM_ CF_Bal	H_MA_LP_Inves torSelection	H_MA_TC_Portf olioCompany	H_MA_TC_In dustryDomai n
H_MA_TC_Mana gementTeam	H_MA_TC_Prod uctOfferings	H_MA_TC_Mark eting	H_MA_TC_D istribution
H_MA_TC_Finan ce	H_MA_TC_Inves tment		

3.9 Security and Availability of System

Security service provided by platform provides security and availability services to applications. Some of key features of security are the capability to authenticate the users; encrypt the data; and secure resources by providing the access-control to authorized clients.

The availability services are capabilities to overcome denial of services to valid users and to keep the applications up & running for computing the business process efficiently.

Requirements of Security and Availability

Information Integrity: The reliability of content and origin of information must be maintained. Integrity deals with prevention of unauthorized modification of intentional or accidental modification. Goal is to provide trustworthiness of data and its origin.

Non-Repudiation: Data consumers need to trust that the data has not been altered, and that its source is authentic. Through the use of security related mechanisms, producers and consumers of data can be assured that the data remains trustworthy across untrusted networks such as the internet, and even internal intranets.

Digital Signature: Assures the identity of data source if data is signed by its publishers. Data is signed and encrypted using a public-private key pair. The user application presents a hash code (message digest) to be encrypted by the digital signing algorithm using the private key. The target user decrypts the message using the public key and verifies the authenticity of hashed digest which ensures the integrity and non-repudiation of data.

Confidentiality: The information in transit must be encrypted to prevent the confidentiality of information. Confidentiality also includes limited access to authorized users based on roles and privileges and prevention of unauthorized access or disclosure. The goal is the concealment of information and resources, which is attained by keeping data confidential which is critical to staying competitive in current business environments. Loss of confidentiality jeopardizes system and corporate integrity.

Authentication: User presents his identity used to authenticate him to the system using user's credentials. The common methods of authentication are: -

- User ID and Password: The system compares the supplied ID/password with stored login data. If the supplied data matches with stored data then the user is authentic.

- Biometrics: Retinal scanners and fingerprint readers are used where parts of the body are considered unique enough to allow authentication to computer systems.
- Digital Certificate: An encrypted piece of data which contains information about its owner, creator, generation and expiration dates, and other data to uniquely identify a user.
- Swipe Card: It has a magnetic strip containing user's info so that no physical data entry takes place, or just PIN is entered.

Authorization: Access to information resources are allowed only to the extent user is allowed for. Authorization controls the resources by allowing the full access, limited access or no access based on the roles and privileges of user as configured in the system. Authorization uses Access Control List (ACL) which contains the user's identity and the highest allowed level of usage. Levels of usage or access levels can be one of following:

- None- No access is granted to the specified resource
- Execute- Execute access allows users and groups to execute programs from the library, but they cannot read or write to the library.
- Read- Read access is the lowest level of permission to a resource. This allows users and groups to view the resource but not to alter its contents
- Update- Update access allows users and groups to change the contents of resource. The user is not authorized to delete the resource.
- Alter- Alter access allows users and groups full control over the resource

Availability: Manages to keep the applications up & running for computing the business process efficiently besides assuring the continuous authorized access of information services to valid users. Availability is supported with:

- Design of information system with aspect of reliability and robustness

- Protection of resources from external and internal attempts of hacking and cracking
- Resource protection from virus, spyware, malware etc. by using security software
- The system platform protection with firewall building demilitarize zone
- Workload management to route the request for computation only on healthy and reliable server to protect the system resources from hogging and upkeep the high performance.
- The servers supported on clusters and clones to support fail-over, fault-tolerance mechanism to keep the system up & running.

Accountability: Access to any resources is traced in detail to identify faults, failure, intrusion etc. Complete system tracing for process based on severity levels are provided.

Illustration of security and availability with UML based use-cases and class diagram are given below with example of M&A system, designed by H_EA.

Use-Cases & Logical Diagram

Actor H_MA_SystemSecurity requires different use-cases to secure and keep the IT services available for users to enable business execution in secured environment.

Security and Availiabilities funtions are:

- H_MA_IS_Confidentiality
- H_MA_IS_Integrity
- H_MA_IS_NonRepudiation
- H_MA_IS_Authentication
- H_MA_IS_Authorization
- H_MA_IS_Availability

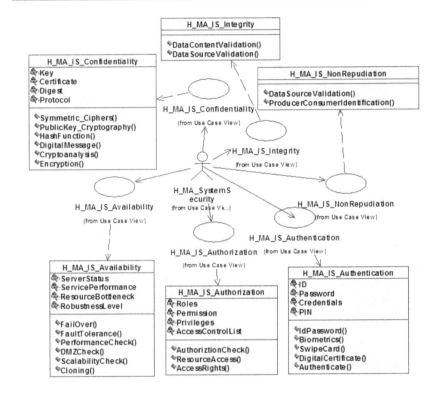

Figure 3.20: © HBS, UC/ Class-System Security

Use Cases	H_MA_IS_Authentication	H_MA_IS_Authorization	H_MA_IS_Confidentiality
H_MA_IS_Integrity	H_MA_IS_NonRepudiation	H_MA_IS_Availability	

Classes	H_MA_IS_Confidentiality	H_MA_IS_Integrity	H_MA_IS_NonRepudiation
H_MA_IS_Authentication	H_MA_IS_Authorization	H_MA_IS_Availability	

Class H_MA_IS_Integrity

Operations

Name	Signature	Class
◈ DataContentValidation	◈ DataContentValidation ()	H_MA_IS_Integrity
◈ DataSourceValidation	◈ DataSourceValidation ()	H_MA_IS_Integrity

Class H_MA_IS_NonRepudiation

Operations

Name	Signature	Class
◈ DataSourceValidation	◈ DataSourceValidation ()	H_MA_IS_NonRepudiation
◈ ProducerConsumerIdentification	◈ ProducerConsumerIdentification ()	H_MA_IS_NonRepudiation

Class H_MA_IS_Authentication

Operations

Name	Signature	Class
IdPassword	IdPassword ()	H_MA_IS_Authentication
Biometrics	Biometrics ()	H_MA_IS_Authentication
SwipeCard	SwipeCard ()	H_MA_IS_Authentication
DigitalCertificate	DigitalCertificate ()	H_MA_IS_Authentication
Authenticate	Authenticate ()	H_MA_IS_Authentication

Attributes

Name	Class
ID	H_MA_IS_Authentication
Password	H_MA_IS_Authentication
Credentials	H_MA_IS_Authentication
PIN	H_MA_IS_Authentication

Class H_MA_IS_Authorization

Operations

Name	Signature	Class
AuthoriztionCheck	AuthoriztionCheck ()	H_MA_IS_Authorization
ResourceAccess	ResourceAccess ()	H_MA_IS_Authorization
AccessRights	AccessRights ()	H_MA_IS_Authorization

Attributes

Name	Class
Roles	H_MA_IS_Authorization

Permission	H_MA_IS_Authorization
Privileges	H_MA_IS_Authorization
AccessControlList	H_MA_IS_Authorization

Class H_MA_IS_Confidentiality

Operations

Name	Signature	Class
Symmetric_Ciphers	Symmetric_Ciphers ()	H_MA_IS_Confidentiality
PublicKey_Cryptography	PublicKey_Cryptography ()	H_MA_IS_Confidentiality
HashFunction	HashFunction ()	H_MA_IS_Confidentiality
DigitalMessage	DigitalMessage ()	H_MA_IS_Confidentiality
Cryptoanalysis	Cryptoanalysis ()	H_MA_IS_Confidentiality
Encryption	Encryption ()	H_MA_IS_Confidentiality

Attributes

Name	Class
Key	H_MA_IS_Confidentiality
Certificate	H_MA_IS_Confidentiality
Digest	H_MA_IS_Confidentiality
Protocol	H_MA_IS_Confidentiality

Class H_MA_IS_Availability

Operations

Name	Signature	Class
FailOver	FailOver ()	H_MA_IS_Availability
FaultTolerance	FaultTolerance ()	H_MA_IS_Availability
PerformanceCheck	PerformanceCheck ()	H_MA_IS_Availability
DMZCheck	DMZCheck ()	H_MA_IS_Availability
ScalabilityCheck	ScalabilityCheck ()	H_MA_IS_Availability
Cloning	Cloning ()	H_MA_IS_Availability

Attributes

Name	Class
ServerStatus	H_MA_IS_Availability
ServicePerformance	H_MA_IS_Availability
ResourceBottleneck	H_MA_IS_Availability
RobustnessLevel	H_MA_IS_Availability

3.10 Information System – Enterprise Data Model

Functional and data services as discussed in consolidated service inventory require managed data models. The core data models required for information system services are enterprise data which forms the content of enterprise repository.

As an example, we illustrate below the enterprise data model for M&A system.

The consolidated enterprise data contained in enterprise repository of M&A system are:

- Model H_MA_Data_StrategicReq containing data for target-criteria, buyer-needs, seller-needs, target-feasibility, client-values, target-companies, business tactics & rules and complete business & IT strategy.
- Model H_MA_Data_DueDiligence containg data for analyzing the target company regarding its business, product, marketing, distribution and analyzing the M&A strategic alignment, deal process, synergy and integration.
- Model H_MA_Data_Project containing data for deal plan, deal structure, M&A process, project schedule, resources, risks & performance, benchmarking, synergy & integration planning.
- Model H_MA_Data_DealTerms containing data for deal structure and negotiations regarding deal financing, contracts, schedule, value and planned synergy & integration.
- Model H_MA_Data_MACombination containing data for M&A types and its forms regarding merger analysis, acquisition, combination-forms, take over, reverse M&A etc.
- Model H_MA_Data_LegalCompliance containing data for accounting, taxation, regulation and laws.
- Model H_MA_Data_Market containing data for current and historical price and transaction.

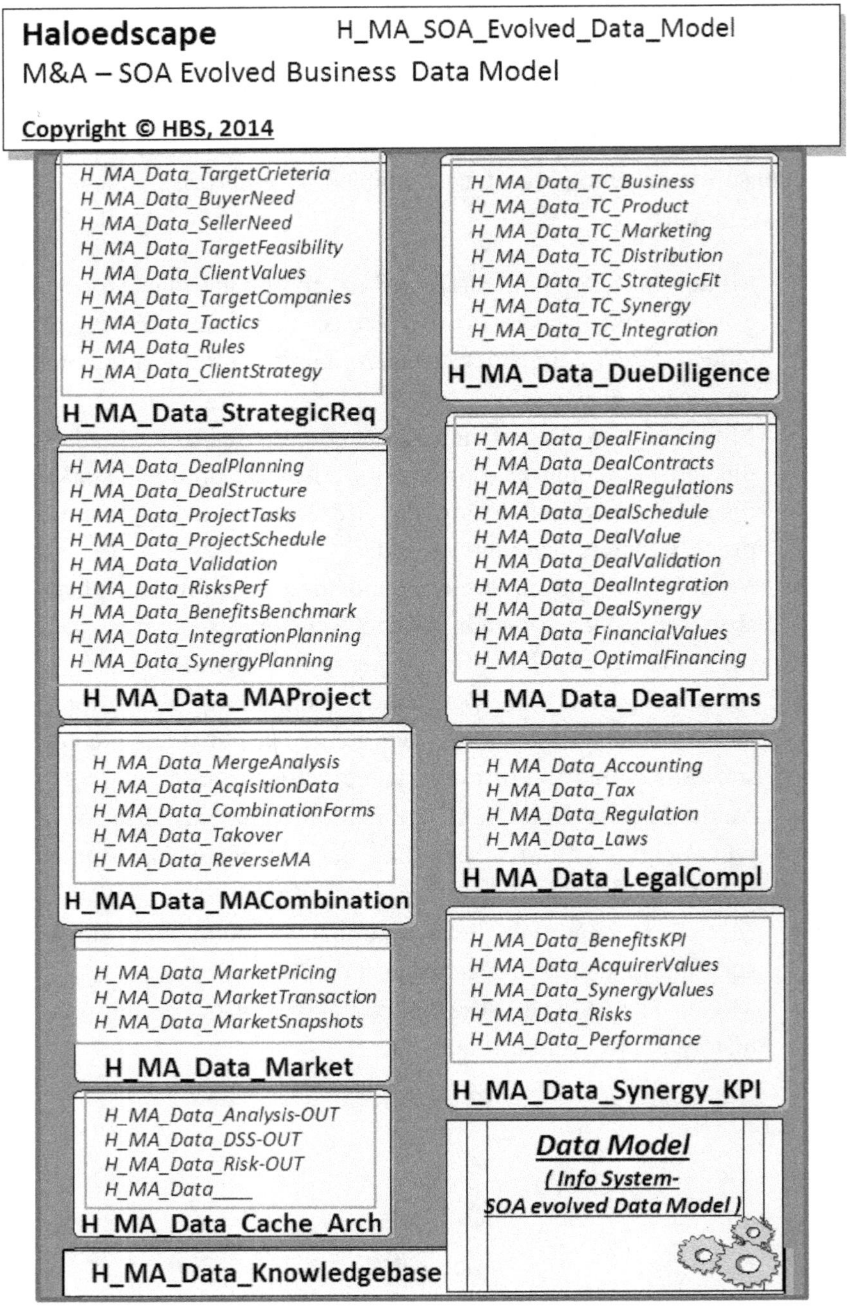

Haloedscape   H_MA_SOA_Evolved_Data_Model

M&A – SOA Evolved Business Data Model

H_MA_Data_TargetCrieteria
H_MA_Data_BuyerNeed
H_MA_Data_SellerNeed
H_MA_Data_TargetFeasibility
H_MA_Data_ClientValues
H_MA_Data_TargetCompanies
H_MA_Data_Tactics
H_MA_Data_Rules
H_MA_Data_ClientStrategy

H_MA_Data_StrategicReq

H_MA_Data_DealPlanning
H_MA_Data_DealStructure
H_MA_Data_ProjectTasks
H_MA_Data_ProjectSchedule
H_MA_Data_Validation
H_MA_Data_RisksPerf
H_MA_Data_BenefitsBenchmark
H_MA_Data_IntegrationPlanning
H_MA_Data_SynergyPlanning

H_MA_Data_MAProject

H_MA_Data_MergeAnalysis
H_MA_Data_AcqisitionData
H_MA_Data_CombinationForms
H_MA_Data_Takover
H_MA_Data_ReverseMA

H_MA_Data_MACombination

H_MA_Data_MarketPricing
H_MA_Data_MarketTransaction
H_MA_Data_MarketSnapshots

H_MA_Data_Market

H_MA_Data_Analysis-OUT
H_MA_Data_DSS-OUT
H_MA_Data_Risk-OUT
H_MA_Data____

H_MA_Data_Cache_Arch

H_MA_Data_Knowledgebase

H_MA_Data_TC_Business
H_MA_Data_TC_Product
H_MA_Data_TC_Marketing
H_MA_Data_TC_Distribution
H_MA_Data_TC_StrategicFit
H_MA_Data_TC_Synergy
H_MA_Data_TC_Integration

H_MA_Data_DueDiligence

H_MA_Data_DealFinancing
H_MA_Data_DealContracts
H_MA_Data_DealRegulations
H_MA_Data_DealSchedule
H_MA_Data_DealValue
H_MA_Data_DealValidation
H_MA_Data_DealIntegration
H_MA_Data_DealSynergy
H_MA_Data_FinancialValues
H_MA_Data_OptimalFinancing

H_MA_Data_DealTerms

H_MA_Data_Accounting
H_MA_Data_Tax
H_MA_Data_Regulation
H_MA_Data_Laws

H_MA_Data_LegalCompl

H_MA_Data_BenefitsKPI
H_MA_Data_AcquirerValues
H_MA_Data_SynergyValues
H_MA_Data_Risks
H_MA_Data_Performance

H_MA_Data_Synergy_KPI

Data Model
(Info System-
SOA evolved Data Model)

Figure 3.21: © HBS, SOA evolved Business Data Models

- Model H_MA_Data_Synergy_KPI containing data for benefits in terms of KPI, acquirer values, synergy, risks and performance.
- Model H_MA_DS_CacheArchive contains the computed data of analysis, decision support, accounting, risks etc. These are normally temporary data organized in cache to optimize performance.
- Model H_MA_DS_Knowledgebase containing data for due diligence, investment, financing, analysis, risks etc.

Data Management with Enterprise Repository

Data management makes the data secured, accessible, shared, consistent, fault tolerant, persisted and essentially delivers interface of service to clients. Besides achieving logical unification, singularity, centralization, Enterprise Repository (ER) is capable of delivering the core data in a uniform secured way across the organization.

Data models are logically organized together as an enterprise repository. ER is an enterprise data container which logically centralizes the core data of enterprise fulfilling the data principles and provides the accessibility of data in form of data service to valid users and applications.

ER secures the enterprise data under its scope. It also maintains the accessibility and audit-control of data.

Data management includes an intelligent background agent which administrates ER with predefined logic. The ER is equipped with sophisticated service and message broker supported with event based processing which makes it intelligent and efficient. The services of ER interact through efficient service-broker to constitute a complex service to be consumed by client. The availability of broker with service architecture makes it possible for ER to provide accessibility to the entity contained in ER physically or logically. The metadata of entity provides the information of entity.

Different processes access the data services from enterprise repository through service bus which provides a central point of access and manages the format compatibility and communication.

The data access layer implemented with enterprise service bus (ESB) is used for designing and implementing the interaction and communication between mutually interacting application in SOA environment. ESB assures the enterprise service integration though a common interface to all available services where service choreography is designed with ESB.

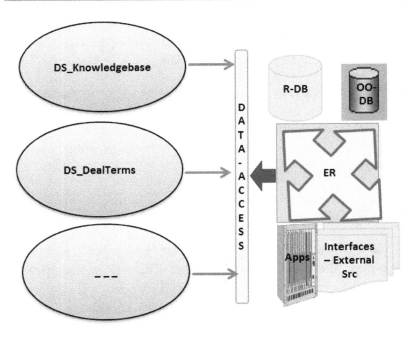

Figure 3.22: © HBS, Enterprise Repository

The enterprise data of information system is managed with enterprise repository. Enterprise Repository is supported with Enterprise Service Bus (ESB) which makes data available for services from a single point of access.

Data management with enterprise repository fulfills the strategic data principles of data being secured, logically consolidated, non-redundant, persisted, shared and accessible. Enterprise repository acts as an effective platform for data management.

3.11 Framework for Aligning Services and Applications

Applications are software components built for smaller business units for their specific needs with the help of enterprise resources accessed from enterprise information system. Our framework for linking the application with information system (enterprise services), and subsystems is depicted in figure.

The application system implements the program module, is interfaced with GUI, configures and parameterizes the apps, accesses the information system services and is supported by subsystem, platform and technology.

The user interface & presentation logic make clients communicate with application, services and business components. The presentation layer is dedicated to format & display the I/O data, navigate the business process, and interface the clients (users) with system.

Application accesses the multiple business components, selected services required for a specific business function, and makes it available to presentation layer.

The basis of IT system & subsystems is essentially provided by the platform supported with required technology providing technical infrastructure to information system and applications.

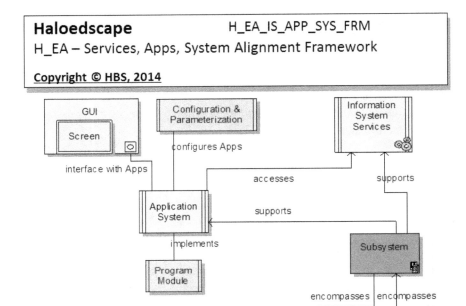

Figure 3.23: © HBS, Framework aligning Services, Apps, System

Aligning Application, Services Data and Capabilities

The application accesses the services of data and business components required to compute business functionality and interfaces with presentation layer to make it available to UI. Functional service supports and enables the capability used by business-service, which is transformed into information-system based IT service.

An illustration of aligning the application, services and capabilities is explained with example of M&A system below.

The application H_MA_SYS_DueDiligence invokes the information-system based functional service H_MA_IS_DueDiligence which uses the data-service H_MA_DS_DueDiligence accessing the data model H_MA_Data_DueDiligence to automate the business functionality required by a business-unit. Functional service H_MA_IS_DueDiligence supports and enables the capability H_MA_CA_DueDiligence, which is used by business-service H_MA_DueDiligence being transformed into information-system functional service H_MA_IS_DueDiligence and data service H_MA_DS_DueDiligence.

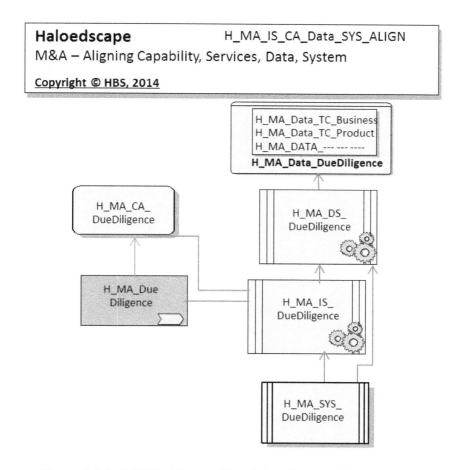

Figure 3.24: © HBS, Aligning Capability, Service, Data & System

In this way the relationship of all applications, business services, capabilities, information-system based functional & data services and data-models are established to align IT with business effectively.

> *The application architecture must have a clear vision to interrelate the application, business services, information-system services and capabilities which ensure our goal of attaining capability-based, business-aligned IT services.*

3.12 Activity Diagram

The IT services of information system are made up of system components, process and data. The activity diagram of component, process and data are illustrated in activity diagram to explain their interactions. Activity diagrams describe parallel, sequential, conditional activities and interrelates it with component and model at a detailed level.

An example of Activity Diagram for M&A system is illustrated below.

The business service (business functionality) H_MA_Strategy starts activity with building the business strategy, tactics and rules in data entity set H_MA_Data_Strategy.

H_MA_Data_Strategy is used by:

- Component H_MA_DealTrading for evaluating and analyzing the deal,
- Component H_MA_ClientValues for target-selection, synergy, values KPI and M&A feasibility of target-companies.
- Component H_MA_DueDiligence for consolidated due-diligence process.

The component H_MA_Client_Values does its tasks of identifying and analyzing the synergy and value-KPIS for the acquirers and sellers leading to data model H_MA_Data_Synergy_KPI. The information of acquirers and buyers are built into data model H_MA_Data_Acquirer_Target.

The data sets generated are used for activity of analyzing the selection of target, feasibility of target, strategy alignment, expected synergy etc.

The component H_MA_DueDiligence starts its activity with building the domain knowledgebase for due diligence in data entity set H_MA_Data_Knowledgebase, a part of enterprise data.

H_MA_Data_Knowledgebase is used by due-diligence activity to generate the output in cache data set H_MA_Data_DealValue which is a part of H_MA_Data_CacheArchive.

Due-Diligence activity is validated with data set H_MA_Data_Strategy. Due-Diligence activity is utilized by component H_MA_Analysis for different kinds of business analysis.

The component H_MA_DealStructure starts its activity with structuring the deal using the data model H_MA_Data_Knowledgebase and due-diligence results. The optimized deal as guided by H_MA_DueDiligence and H_MA_Strategy shapes the deal structure & terms which is organized in data model H_MA_Data_DealTerms, a part of enterprise data.

Data model H_MA_Data_DealTerms is used by activity AnalyzeDealFinancing, which is further used by activity H_MA_Analysis and activity Negotiate_StructureDeals, which are supported with decision support H_MA_DSS. Activity Negotiate_StructureDeals leads to data set H_MA_Data_Deal. The component H_MA_DealTrading starts activity with pricing and analyzing the deal using activity Price-Analyze using the data set H_MA_Data_Deal leading to activity Execute-Deal, which is maintained and tracked using data model H_MA_Data_MAProject.

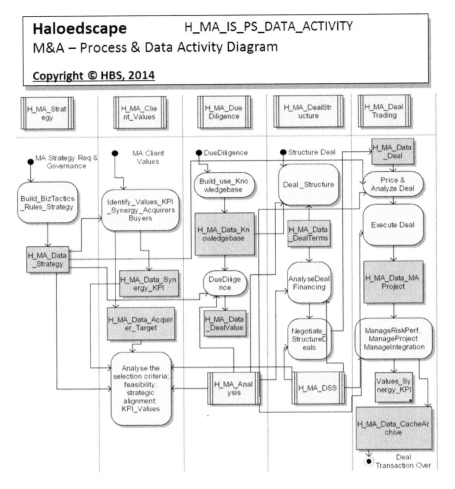

Figure 3.25: © HBS, Process Data Activity Diagram

The activity Execute-Deal triggers the activities Risk_Performance Management, Project Management and Integration Management. Deal execution leading to project-management generates an instance of synergy-KPI as planned and expected benchmark for actual synergy.

Components H_MA_Analysis and H_MA_DSS use the activities Risk_Performance Management, Project Management and Integration Management, which generate the cache data set H_MA_Data_CacheArchive and at last deal trading gets over.

Due-diligence, pricing, deal-structuring, analysis and decision-support are primary functions of M&A which are associated with many other functions. We need object oriented middleware for pricing and valuations because OOM is highly efficient as compared to MOM. Resource intensive simulation and complex algorithm of pricing, analysis and decision-support require efficient, high performance platform.

3.13 STP Workflow for Remote Modules

Deal execution is treated as an event for invoking the callback functions of remote module like performance & risk management and project management so that workflow automation could be achieved with STP (straight-through-processing). Deal execution is function of front office which is integrated with middle/back-office using workflow.

Deal execution is front-office activity treated as event. Remote modules of middle/back office like risk management, performance management and project management subscribe to distribution server to get real-time notification as the events of new/changed deal-execution occur. Upon notification, the callback function of remote module gets activated which synchronizes the activities of middle/back office with front-office.

The computation is carried out with delta calculation process which computes only the changes required and adds it up to already computed results to fulfill computational principle of efficiency and non-redundancy.

An example of STP Workflow for M&A System is illustrated below.

Deal execution is core functionality of M&A business which involves active participation of most of M&A functionalities. Deal execution is dependent on due diligence, deal terms, deal -structure and pricing functionalities of M&A; whereas performance management, risk management and project management are dependent on deal-execution.

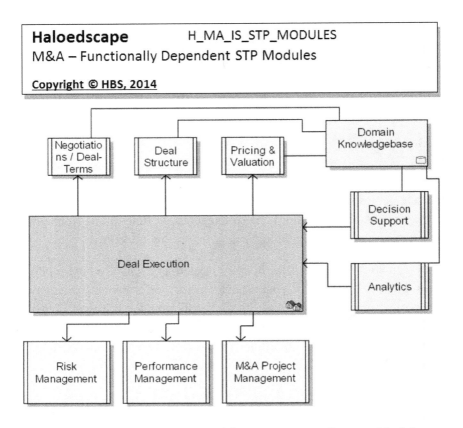

Figure 3.26: © HBS, STP Workflow to integrate Remote Modules

3.14 Anatomy of Real-Time Delta Process

The run-time process of core functionalities are facilitated with (straight through processing) STP workflow, information system services, delta computation, configurable process instances, view attachment and distributed parallel computation of process.

The configurable workflow defines the instances to automate the isolated business function processing, which achieves the integration of front office with middle and back offices.

Configured process leads to a process instance originating from process-repository which defines the calculation graph.

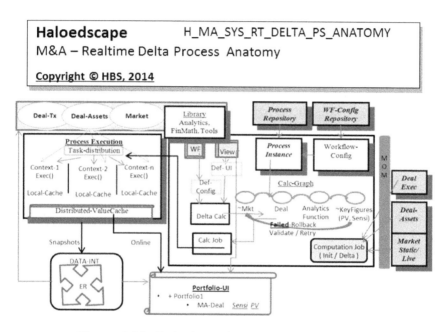

Figure 3.27: © HBS, Real-Time Process Anatomy

The delta computation is a mechanism to compute only a part of function which is dependent on the new events. The delta computational process subscribes to receive notification for new events. New or changed deal-execution, deal-assets and market data are considered important events. The subscribed process receives the notification, when the event occurs and then triggers a computational job which is defined in calculation-graph. For example, delta computation is applied to compute the

275

portfolio P&L in real time where change in market price and transaction (events) triggers pricing module to compute only the new pricing value which is affected to the portfolio P&L with new results. In this way, computation is done only for pricing due to change in market but computation of whole P&L generated earlier is not processed again, as it is resource intensive and time consuming.

Delta computation is transaction based, either whole process succeeds to be committed or whole process is rolled back if failure occurs, which ensures the consistency of data and process. The delta computation is supported with event based message and object oriented middleware.

Pricing and analysis are primary functionalities of investment banking, associated with many other functions. We need delta computation for pricing and analytics besides object oriented middleware platform because OOM is highly efficient as compared to J2EE based MOM. Resource intensive simulation, complex algorithm of pricing and analysis require efficient and high performance platform.

The computational job is distributed on different nodes for execution with parallel processing design and workload management, which are synchronized after completion and pushed into distributed value-cache.

The distributed value-cache contains the computed results which are monitored online or the snapshots are persisted into enterprise-repository to be accessed from application.

Business functions are automated with (straight through processing) STP workflow, information system services, delta computation, configurable process instances, view attachment and distributed parallel computation of process.

The delta computation is a mechanism to trigger a process when an event occurs. Delta process is an efficient way to compute on real time only for the required changes of functionality but not the whole functionality which is already processed earlier. Delta computation is essentially event based trigger which fulfills the strategic principle

> *— "Computational Efficiency and Non-Redundancy"*
>
> *Automated workflow with STP also achieves effectiveness in computation where new events notify the subscribed isolated-module for integrated real-time functional processing.*
>
> *Additionally, distributed parallel computation achieves computational efficiency and optimal resource usage, which also enhances availability of system.*

3.15 Application Components Diagram

Requirements of User Interface

The appropriate software and technology are selected for user-interface. In advanced system, the presentation layers are normally thin client realized with relevant patterns like Model-View-Presenter (MVP) and separation of components using architectural pattern Model-View-Controller (MVC). The observer pattern efficiently improves the dynamics of GUI leading to better efficiency.

The application performance and user-interface responsiveness are improved with caching. Data caching in presentation layer is used to optimize data lookups, avoid initialization of data access object (DAO), and prevent unnecessary network round trips.

The asynchronous communications and worker threads avoid blocking the UI, thus improving the overall performance for client. The design of UI composition pattern achieves the composition of modules and views at run-time, which are easier to develop and maintain. The UI should be able to handle the system and application exceptions to be presented to user with error message for troubleshooting.

Applications and Its Components

System components are business driven. Business logic is implemented as functional service and choreographed as application-component that computes the process specific to business logic and rules. Component diagrams show the dependencies and interactions between software components

An example of Components Diagram of M&A system is illustrated below.

H_MA_SYS_Strategy system component uses the component H_MA_SYS_ Knowledgebase and is used by component H_MA_SYS_ClientValues.

H_MA_SYS_ClientValues uses the components H_MA_SYS_ Knowledgebase, H_MA_SYS_Analysis and H_MA_SYS_DSS.

H_MA_SYS_DealStructure uses the components H_MA_SYS_DealTerms, H_MA_SYS_DSS, H_MA_SYS_Pricing and is used by H_MA_SYS_DealTrading.

H_MA_SYS_DueDiligence uses the H_MA_SYS_ Knowledgebase and H_MA_SYS_DSS and is used by H_MA_SYS_Analysis.

H_MA_SYS_Risk_Perf_Management uses the H_MA_SYS_Analysis and H_MA_SYS_Knowledgebase.

H_MA_SYS_ProjectManagement uses the H_MA_SYS_DealTrading and H_MA_SYS_Analysis.

H_MA_SYS_Pricing uses the H_MA_SYS_ Knowledgebase and is used by H_MA_SYS_Analysis, H_MA_SYS_DSS and H_MA_SYS_DealStructure. It calls the H_MA_SYS_MarketData interface to access market data.

H_MA_SYS_DealTrading is used by H_MA_SYS_ProjectManagement and H_MA_SYS_Risk_Perf_Management. It uses the H_MA_SYS_DealStructure and calls the H_MA_SYS_MarketData interface to access market data.

H_MA_SYS_ProjectManagement uses the H_MA_SYS_DealTrading that effectively persists and tracks the deal with corresponding risks, positions etc.

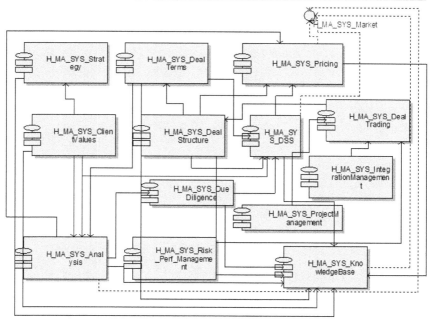

Figure 3.28: © HBS, M&A Components Diagram

H_MA_SYS_DSS is used by all functional components and uses the H_MA_SYS_Analysis.

H_MA_SYS_Analysis is used by all functional components and it uses the H_MA_SYS_Pricing and calls the H_MA_SYS_MarketData interface to access market data.

H_MA_SYS_Knowledgebase is used by all functional components for information and it calls the H_MA_SYS_MarketData interface to access market data.

The applications of business function are interdependent and they are allowed to access the enterprise resources like enterprise data and services only through information systems.

The core applications shown here are essentially parameterized and configured services available in information system but the services accessed at business-unit could also be extended by them at their local site to fulfill their business objective. If the business-unit's extension to fulfill certain objective is considered important and useful for whole enterprise, then it becomes part of information systems and is made available to whole company as an enterprise service.

3.16 Conclusion – Information System, Data and Application Architecture

To develop the Information System and Application Architecture, TOGAF's framework is extended to enhance capabilities of IT solution.

In our approach, all strategic requirements are fulfilled by information system. Enterprise resources like core data and functional services are accessed by applications only through information system which governs the fulfillment of strategic requirements in the applications to achieve enterprise capabilities in automated way.

As next, the layered system design is shown where overall structure of system in terms of logical grouping of components is depicted into separate layers interacting with each other.

Information system, data and application principles provide the directions and guidelines for realizing right information system and application.

SOA for information system is described in this chapter where data services and functional services are consolidated together in inventory of information system. Information system possesses functional services and data services for maximal integration, computation efficiency and overall effectiveness. SOA based information system achieves strategic objective of business aligned agile IT which maximizes the ROI while reducing risks for overall IT.

In the next section, use-cases (UC) and class diagrams of business functionalities are modeled. We have illustrated the use-cases, class diagrams and interactions with examples of investment banking business function of M&A. This includes: Strategy, Due Diligence, Deal Structure, Deal Execution, Pricing, Project Management, Performance & Risk Management, Integration Management, Synergy, Domain Knowledgebase, Analysis & Decision Support.

Security and availability act as support functions for business operation and continuity, which are elaborated with use-cases and logical diagrams.

Data management is shown in next section where enterprise repository acts as logical data container supported with service bus for single point of access managing the access, format compatibility and communication. Different services access the data services from enterprise repository through service bus. Data management with enterprise repository keeps the data consistent, consolidated, secured, non-redundant, shared and accessible which are our strategic principles for enterprise data.

As next, the activity diagram of component, process and data of business functionalities are described to explain their interactions and flow of activities.

Applications are choreographed services built for business units for their specific needs with the help of functional & data services accessed from information system. Framework for linking the application with information system and subsystems has been shown.

Relation between business service, business capability, information system services and application are shown. Application architecture inter-relates the business services, capabilities, IT-services, and applications, which ensures IT alignment with business.

Workflow automation with STP is shown where remote modules of middle/back office are integrated together with front office function – deal execution.

Delta process anatomy is elaborated where a callback process is triggered when an event occurs. Delta process is an efficient way to compute on real time only for the required changes, but not the whole application which is already computed earlier. Delta computation is essentially event based trigger which fulfills the strategic principle – "Computational Efficiency and Non-Redundancy"

At last the applications components and interactions between them are depicted with examples of investment banking system.

To summarize our efforts in this chapter, we have elaborated following in this chapter:-

- Frameworks for aligning IT with business
- Transformation of Business Services into IT Services
- Mapping Business Services, Business Capabilities with IT Services and Applications
- Core functionalities and data delivered as services
- Service based Information System and Application
- Applications accessing enterprise resources only through Information System
- Information System as service provider and governing agent
- Data Management with Enterprise Repository
- Automated Workflow with STP
- Delta Process Anatomy
- Activity diagram for interaction between components, process and data

- Application components and their interaction

We have illustrated the Information System, Data and Application Architecture based on input from Strategy and Business Architecture. To acquire IT solution with enterprise characteristics and strategic capabilities, information system and applications described in this chapter should be supported with right platform possessing required technology, which we will present in next chapter.

Chapter 4: Technology & Platform Architecture

Acronyms & Definitions used in this chapter:

API: Application Programming Interface – A library which provides the function interface to develop the required application.

B2B: Business-to-Business – If services are accessed by valid external application, referred as B2B.

B2C: Business-to-Consumer - If services are accessed by end-user client, referred as B2C.

CORBA: Common Object Request Broker – A standard specification defined by OMG for Object oriented Middleware which supports platform independent distributed objects to be accessed by any client application supported on agent called Object Request Broker (ORB).

EAI: Enterprise Application Integration – ESB is primarily used for EAI to integrate the service inventory of whole enterprise at functionalities and process level.

EAS: Enterprise Application Server – A generalized platform which provides the services and capabilities to realize the server part of applications.

EJB: Enterprise Java Beans – Distributed Objects of J2EE platform.

ESB: Enterprise Service Bus – Acts as mediators between service provider and service consumer, decoupling and resolving the difference in protocols and format for simplified message exchange.

FpML: Financial Products Markup Language – FpML is an XML based financial message standard for the OTC derivatives industry, where financial products are specified in FpML format. Broad objective of FpML is to achieve the consistency and automation of back-office services at global level.

GIOP: General Inter-ORB Protocol – An abstract protocol of CORBA used by ORBs to communicate with each other. An implementation of GIOP is IIOP.

HTTP: Hypertext Transfer Protocol- An application protocol used by web explorer to connect with world wide web.

HTTPS: Hypertext Transfer Protocol Secure- Communication protocol for secure communication over a computer network. Technically HTTPS is simply layering the HTTP over SSL/TLS protocol.

IIOP: Internet Inter-ORB Protocol – CORBA 2.0 defines a network protocol called IIOP that allows CORBA client to communicate with CORBA objects where complete communication between client and server is handled by ORB. IIOP works cross the internet or more precisely, across any TCP/IP implementation.

J2EE: Java Platform Enterprise Edition – Full-fledged Java platform which natively integrates enterprise framework and platform together.

JAF: JavaBeans Activation Framework – Identifying the type of data and its operations and dynamically instantiating the appropriate bean to perform the required operations.

JDBC: Java Database Connectivity – J2EE client connects and reads/writes data from/to relational databases.

JMS: Java Message Service – Java API for accessing a MOM messaging system including the event capabilities.

JNDI: Java Naming and Directory Interface – Directory service to discover and look up objects.

JSP & Servlets – UI for J2EE platform is normally JSPs which are compiled as servlets. Servlet in J2EE platform acts as view-controller supported with servlet engine and interacts directly with JSPs and Models.

JTA: Java Transaction API – J2EE API which enables the distributed transaction across X/Open XA resources.

MOM: Message Oriented Middleware – Most elegant technology for supporting the distributed application to exchange message with sophisticated techniques.

OOM: Object Oriented Middleware – OOM facilitates distributed objects accessed by distributed applications to achieve process and functional level interoperability and enterprise integration.

ORB: Object Request Broker – ORB is an agent that mediates the isolated client and server and promotes the interoperability in distributed computing. Essentially ORBs handle the communication and marshaling (serialization) of data.

RMI: Remote Method Invocation – Object oriented distributed computing in J2EE domain equivalent to RPC. RMI over IIOP integrates J2EE resources with CORBA objects.

RPC: Remote Procedure Call – An inter-process communication that allows a computer program to invoke routine of remote computer without coding the communication software.

SSL/TLS: Secure Sockets Layer / Transport Layer Security – Cryptographic protocols to provide communication security over the internet.

UI: User Interface– An output displayed to user in text or graphical form. The graphical form of user interface is GUI.

H_EA: Enterprise Architecture (IT) wing of Haloedscape.

In this chapter, we will elaborate the development of Platform and Technology Architecture based on our IT Strategy, Business Architecture, Information System Architecture, Data & Application Architecture as discussed in previous chapters.

To illustrate the platform & technology architecture with examples, we use investment banking business functions like Private Equity, Venture Capital, Mergers and Acquisitions etc., wherever business examples are required.

4.1 Executive Summary

To compute the business function, the applications and services must be running on a platform empowered with required technology.

Platform enabling SOA based applications fulfills the strategic requirements, lowers down the risks & costs and delivers a new level of effectiveness. The business services are transformed into IT services which are supported by platform to achieve service based IT solution.

Our application architecture developed in previous chapter is primarily motivated from J2EE based solution which natively integrates with event based object-oriented and message-oriented middleware.

Many components of our investment banking functionalities like pricing engine, simulations, stress test and scenario analysis are made available as distributed objects programmed in C++ enabled by object-oriented middleware (OOM). OOM like CORBA provides this capability of high performance distributed computing environment.

Services provided for business functionalities are language and platform independent being accessed by any standard application thus achieving a high level of functional integration.

The platform needs to support the applications with session and transaction services so that application could maintain its state in interactive session and also the critical operations are guaranteed maintaining the state of consistent data and synchronized process.

Application also needs a platform where a component could subscribe to receive notification from server for required events which is achieved with events based message oriented middleware.

Application needs to be secured, for that security server is needed from platform to configure, enable and extend authentication, authorization and encryption.

Platform supporting events framework is required to automate workflow and execute the heavy computation in parallel, split & synchronize pattern.

The services are implemented on distributed computing platform supported with events based object and message oriented middleware.

Various platform components with different capabilities are elaborated here so that the business platform is equipped with these capabilities to realize innovative and sophisticated solution.

4.2 Overview of Platform and Technology Architecture

Platform is the heart of complete IT system which supports specific technology and allows software of specific business functions to run successfully and fulfill the defined objectives. Technology is scientific techniques, organization and methods to solve the problem efficiently and effectively.

As mentioned, focused enterprise architecture derived from business and aligned with IT strategy is a key to achieve effective-IT with low costs & risks fulfilling the strategic objectives. In previous chapters, we have consolidated our business-services, capabilities, IT services of business function and linked them with each other. In this chapter, we need to decide upon innovative, sophisticated and optimal platform featured with required technology which supports the information system and applications to enable the automation of business and fulfills the strategic requirements to achieve enterprise architecture.

The framework of TOGAF for "Architecture Development Method" guides that Technology Architecture gets its input from Information Systems Architecture to identify the platform requirements, decide upon platform and technology and enable the automation of data, services and applications.

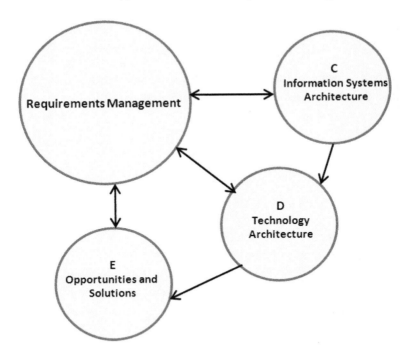

Figure 4.1: Copyright © The Open Group, TOGAF® 9.1, Architecture Development Cycle

The Technology Architecture sends the outputs to "Opportunities and Solutions" to assess the requirements, opportunities and improve the solutions. All of these phases of architecture (Information Systems, Technology, Opportunities and Solutions) interact in bidirectional way with "Requirements Management" so that each phase of architecture development keeps its essence of fulfilling the requirements as its top objective. *"Opportunities and Solutions" phase is beyond the scope of this book.*

In this chapter, we will analyze and identify the innovative technology platforms to support our information systems and applications as elaborated in previous chapter.

> *As per our business and information system architecture, we require the software platform which supports the following:-*
>
> - *Service platform to enable SOA based information system*
> - *Services for session, transaction and security management*
> - *Functionality exposed as enterprise distributed object*
> - *Data management and Integration*
> - *Distributed computing environment enabled by integrated Procedure, Object and Message based middleware*
> - *Enterprise Service Bus (ESB) for enterprise application integration at service level*
> - *Patterns based implementation like easy separation of components with architectural pattern MVC*
> - *Standardized thin client for UI*
> - *Events framework for workflow automation and real-time computation*
> - *Messaging system for guaranteed message delivery supporting sync/async mode of communication*
> - *Protocols support like RPC, IIOP, SSL, SNMP, HTTP etc.*

The focus of this chapter is to depict the technology platform to support information system, data and applications discussed earlier.

4.3   Platform, Technology & Infrastructure Principles

The strategic principles for platform, technology and infrastructure are elaborated herewith.

Platform & Technology Principles

Name	Business-aligned Agile IT
Description / Statement	The technology must support the agile feature of applications to adapt to changing customer

	requirement and market conditions. The business services are transformed into IT services with SOA approach supported by suitable platform and technology to achieve business aligned IT.
Rationale	Business aligned IT maximizes ROI and achieves strategic benefits. IT must have sufficient agility to adapt the changes in market conditions or customer requirements. Technology supporting SOA achieves agile IT solution aligned with business.
Implications	• The applications are developed from IT services directly transformed from business services. The IT services are enabled and executed by suitable technological platform to achieve business aligned IT. • IT services should be enabled by platform. SOA principles are primarily fulfilled by technological platform which enables the applications designed as services and enhances agility.

Name	Distributed Computing Environment
Description / Statement	The platform must facilitate sophisticated distributed computing environment to manage computing in client-server model on a system of distributed computers.
Rationale	Benefits of distributed systems include improving performance and availability, maintaining

	autonomy, reducing cost, and improving integration.
Implications	• The business functionalities are exposed as distributed objects which can be accessed by enterprise wide applications. • Users of a distributed system perceive a single, integrated computing facility even though it may be implemented by many computers in different locations. • Distributed computing environment delivers services like directory, security, transaction services to manage the distributed computation. • Distributed computing is state-of-the-art technology which is most important aspects of platform to attain sophisticated IT automation.

Name	Events Framework
Description / Statement	Platform must provide the events framework to achieve higher level of automation, real-time computation and computational efficiency. Events distribution, subscription, notification and handling should be facilitated as part of events framework.
Rationale	To achieve efficient and real-time computing, occurrence of events must be handled in real-time,

	which makes the system more responsive and intelligent.
Implications	• Event driven execution are typically used when there is some asynchronous external activity that needs to be handled by a program to accomplish real-time efficient computation. • Event notification is managed by events distribution server where message is dispatched on occurrence of events to all subscribed modules. • Event handler as a callback function is triggered based on notification from events distribution server.

Name	Enterprise Application Integration
Description / Statement	Platform must deliver integration framework composed of a collection of technologies and services to enable integration of systems and applications across the enterprise.
Rationale	Enterprise application integration links isolated applications together without extra investment in order to simplify and automate business processes to the greatest extent possible.
Implications	• Platform provides enterprise service bus which supports the integration with interoperability and communication for

	SOA based applications.
	• Enterprise services bus provides an abstraction layer over messaging system provided by platform to achieve enterprise application integration.
	• Integration is achieved in an enterprise at platform, data, services, application and presentation level, which is core basis to achieve SOA architecture. Most efficient and optimal integration is addressed in SOA based solution.

Name	Security and Availability with Technology
Description / Statement	The technology guarantees the secured process and data. Enterprise business operations are continued in spite of system interruptions due to guaranteed availability provided by technology.
Rationale	For mission-critical computation, it is essential that security and availability be guaranteed with technology. Mission-critical application (like e-banking, flight control etc.) must be guaranteed to be available and should never fail during computation. The process and data must be secured with technology.
Implications	• Acquire capability of authentication, authorization and data encryption for secure computing environment. Users must be authenticated to get access into system.

	User-authorization controls the accessibility of resources with specific control. • Develop Public-Key-Infrastructure (PKI) to manage digital certificates. • Secure the resources with demilitarized zone. • Improve the scalability to protect the resource-hogging. • Increase computing availability with cloning, clustering and load-balancing. Fail-over, fault tolerance should be in place to ensure automated availability. • Acquire distributed computing environment to enhance availability with cost-optimization.

Name	Technological Independence and Interoperability
Description / Statement	Applications should be independent of specific technology. Open standard technology gives the freedom of driving the technology with user's preferences and business requirements.
Rationale	Applications running on vendor specific platform makes maintenance, operation, migration, upgradation etc dependent on vendor, so it is required that applications are supported on open standard technology. The applications running on different platforms need to be interoperable, so

	open standards are required for interoperability in platform for applications to be integrated.
Implications	<ul><li>Applications should be transited to open standard technology.</li><li>Vendor dependence should be minimized.</li><li>Business drives the technology where business operation is improved with sophisticated technology.</li><li>Technology independence improves the development, operation, maintenance and upgradation.</li><li>The technology should be interoperable so that applications supported on it could be naturally integrated without much effort.</li></ul>

Name	Best of Breed Technology Platform
Description / Statement	Innovative and sophisticated Technology provides competitive advantage to deliver better capabilities for business functions.
Rationale	Applications deliver the best capabilities only if supported on best of breed technology platform. The best of breed technology evolves from requirements of market and customer and hence IT services are better aligned to business.
Implications	<ul><li>Most sophisticated & latest technology should be in place to support the</li></ul>

	applications.
	• Continual improvement in technology.
	• Do not rely on single technology to complete all tasks rather select mix of technology that best suits and supports different applications. The mix of technology should be interoperable and based on open standard to increase the interoperability and integration ensuring reduced costs and dependency.

Infrastructure Principles

Name	Cloud Computing
Description / Statement	The IT infrastructure should be available & accessible on business demand.
Rationale	Efficient and scalable use of resources as service based on business demand.
Implications	• Acquire capability for cloud computing. Resources should be used as services.
	• Resources should be scalable and optimally used.
	• Optimal resource utilization as business demands.

Name	Automated Maintenance
Description / Statement	The maintenance of infrastructure should be automated to large extent.
Rationale	Automated maintenance ensures the availability and optimal usage of infrastructure.
Implications	• Develop the automated process for maintenance of infrastructure. • Extension, upgrade, exchange etc. should be process based to avoid error-prone manual handling. • The infrastructure should be intelligent enough for events based maintenance handling.

4.4 Middleware Platform and Technology

Middleware is most important software component of platform which provides common programming abstraction, infrastructure and computing environment for distributed computing.

Common services and facilities provided by middleware to distributed application are:

- Naming, Location, Service discovery & Directory
- Protocol Handling, Communication
- Events Framework
- Messaging System and Enterprise Service Bus
- Distributed Objects

- Synchronization, Concurrency, Transactions, Storage
- Security like Access control, Authentication and Encryption

The characteristics of enterprise solution supported with advanced middleware are reliability, availability, security, scalability, quality, performance and maintainability.

Transaction oriented Middleware (TOM)

The initial middleware which successfully revolutionized the world were transaction oriented middleware (IBM'S DCE based DCICS, Encina, Tuxedo). TOM supports transactions using two-phase commit protocol across different distributed systems. TOM is a tight coupling request-reply interaction between client and server.

> *The legacy systems developed decades back were using TOM to manage their distributed computing. Newly developed system may need to be integrated with legacy systems for which the proper adapter needs to be developed to communicate on TOM specific proprietary protocol.*

Object oriented Middleware (OOM)

OOM like CORBA provides object features for distributed components and several services for managing the distributed computing. OOM provides object oriented programming model for distributed resources.

OOM is built on top of transport layer and implements the session and presentation layer. Session layer includes the object adapter, object activation, client and server object synchronization. Presentation layer resolves data incompatibility to provide common platform for heterogeneous distributed environment.

The remote objects have visible remote interfaces and are masked as being local using proxy objects. Object references are mapped to hosts and object activation policies are implemented in object adapter.

The most important component of CORBA is Object Request Broker (ORB) which interconnects the client (stub) and server (skeleton) using General Inter-ORB protocol (GIOP) implemented as IIOP. The Interoperable Object References (IOR) containing object location and Dynamic Method Invocation (DMI) for asynchronous communication are managed by ORB.

Important services of OOM are:

- Naming service provides the names of remote object references.

- Trading service provides attributes of remote object via references.

- Persistent object service provides implementation of persistent CORBA objects.

- Transaction service achieves object invocation as part of transactions.

- Event and Notification services fulfill the requirements of asynchronous communication with push & pull options built over synchronous communications.

Disadvantage of OOM are:

- Implementations of servants may not be loosely coupled.

- Automatics garbage collections are limited only to some type of data like Sequences.

- Static and heavy weight middleware.

- Messaging services are not so strong as compared to MOM.

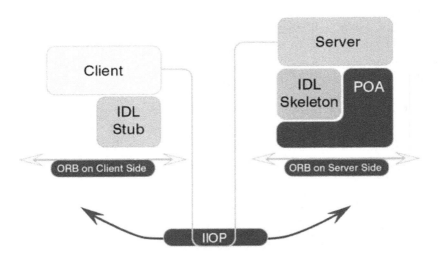

Figure 4.2: © HBS, Object Oriented Middleware Architecture

OOM is utilized for applications requiring high performance computation. The pricing engine and simulation of business functions need efficient and high performance middleware, so these modules are implemented on the OOM platform. The events service of CORBA support the distributed computing for modules requiring high performance.

OOM are inter-operable and integrated with message-oriented middleware (MOM).

Message oriented Middleware (MOM)

MOM like IBM-MQ support communication between distributed systems by facilitating message exchange. It supports multi-casting and asynchronous message delivery. MOM achieves service orientation by completely decoupling the client and server.

Communications takes place using common messages which are stored in message queues. Message servers perfectly decouple client and server applications.

JMS is full-fledged API specification accessing MOM implementations like IBM-MQ. Two modes of operations are provided: point-to-point (one to one communication using queue) and publish-subscribe for event based messaging.

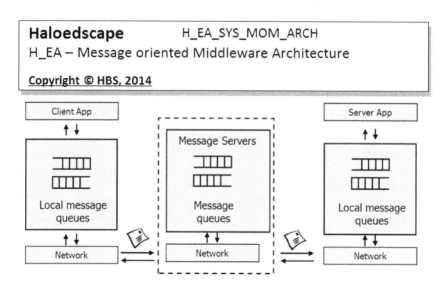

Figure 4.3: © HBS, Message Oriented Middleware- Message Queues

The Advanced Message Queuing Protocol (AMQP) is an emerging standard that defines the protocol and formats used in the messaging server and client, so implementations are interoperable. AMQP is defined to provide flexible routing, including common messaging paradigms like point-to-point, publish/subscribe, and request-response. It also supports transaction management, queuing, distribution, security, management, clustering, federation and heterogeneous multi-platform support. Java applications that use AMQP are typically written in Java JMS.

Advantages of MOM are:
- Asynchronous communication is powerful mode of communication in MOM designed using message provider.
- Messages are queued and designed for reliable delivery service.

Disadvantages of MOM are:
- Extra implementation required to develop applications.
- Computational performance is not so high like OOM.
- Dominant message capabilities with no object support.

MOM is utilized for applications requiring guaranteed delivery, asynchronous communication and perfectly loosely coupled client and server.

The isolated modules of business like portfolio management, risk management and fund administration which need the notification for the events of deal execution need to be automated through STP workflow where MOM is the best platform to achieve the required capabilities.

Essentially MOM is the platform which helps achieve front-office, middle-office and back-office integration with STP workflow implementation.

SOA based Web-Services

Web services are pragmatic well-known web standards for distributed computing. The messages are expressed in generic message language protocol XML bundled as message header and body accessed via Simple Object Access Protocol (SOAP).

SOAP is lightweight protocol for sync/async services consumption. Web Services Description Language (WSDL) provides description of interfaces to access web services. Universal Description Discovery and Integration (UDDI) provides directory with web services description in WSDL which helps find the right web services.

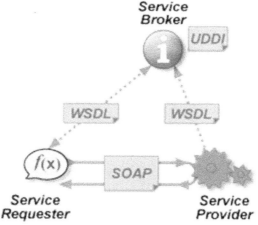

Figure 4.4: © HBS, Web Services Architecture

The sync/async web service is elegant implementation of SOA over the world wide web. For a part of our implementation which requires J2EE domain, web services are the best possibility to implement services. Web services are meant mainly for stateless session but stateful session can also be maintained with servlet or EJB linked inside web services.

Middleware Services

There is variety of services provided by middleware platform to support realization of information system and applications. These services are:

Directory services – The directory services are provided to discover and lookup the data and objects via logical name.

Database services – It provides connectivity with several databases for data persistency.

Session Services – The session is maintained between client and server so that the stateful or stateless session can be managed for interactive process of applications.

Transaction Services - Some of the process requires the transaction services where data are committed only if complete process succeeds or it completely rollbacks if failure occurs.

There are some mechanisms embedded in EAS to support the security and availability for critical applications:

Security Services- EAS provides the security services for authentication, authorization and encryption. SSL protocol is enabled to support the communication over HTTPS. The EAS should be placed inside DMZ so that open ports can be controlled and the system is protected from hacking.

Availability - The EAS delivers a feature to clone the complete enterprise application so that it could be available even if one of the clones dies and lost abruptly due to internal or external interruptions. The complete session of lost clone is shifted to another clone without any inconsistency in data or process. Besides cloning, availability is achieved with many factors like performance, robustness, exception handling, security, fail-over, fault tolerance.

Tracing and Monitoring – The complete process running on EAS can be traced and the computing resources can be monitored online.

As discussed earlier, we need a platform that delivers framework for services, event based message, and acts as advanced middleware for the business applications. We will analyze the features and capabilities of different middleware to innovate a sophisticated platform that supports our approach of business functions automation.

SOA based Service Platform

As discussed earlier, the service orientation is a revolutionary architecture style to align the IT to business. The agile design of SOA guarantees efficient time to market (TTM). The SOA based platform is compliant to IT principles and fulfills the strategic requirements.

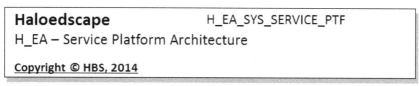

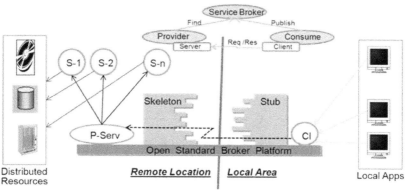

Figure 4.5: © HBS, Service Platform Architecture

The service provider crates a web service and publishes its interface to the service registry. The service consumer locates entries in the broker registry and then binds to the service provider in order to invoke the exposed services.

The enterprise resources to be accessed are treated as enterprise distributed components supported on broker agent.

The platform takes care of handling and managing the distributed component as service fulfilling SOA principles.

Security Server

The information systems must be properly secured from external and internal threats. There should be adequate security mechanism incorporated so that business continuity is guaranteed. The platform must support security and availability requirements of information system services and applications.

The security platform provides features like cryptography, authentication, authorization, secured communications and public key infrastructure.

Platform provides the fail-over feature with cloning which ensures availability even in the case of failure and interruptions.

Performance monitoring and tuning is also provided by platform so that timely computation of request is done and resources are prevented from hogging to keep the system available.

The platform provides the authentication mechanism which is configured and extended appropriately as per requirement to authenticate the users of application.

- The platform should extend the authentication data (Used-ID and Passwords) with random chars before being hashed and stored.

- The authentication data are persisted with transaction services to preserver the atomicity.

The platform provides the authorization patterns like Access Control List (ACL), attributes, policies etc. which are configured and parameterized by application to authorize its users.

- ACLs contain the user's identity and the highest allowed level for usage of information resources.
- Federation (Identity) service provides federated identity assertions for users or resources.
- Attributes are bound to users or resources that can be used for authorization decision.
- Policies are evaluated to decide if requests are permitted or not.
- Authorization decides on access rights for requests based on attributes and policies applied to the requests.
- Trust management aids the automated verification of actions against security policies. In this concept, actions are allowed if users demonstrate sufficient credentials, irrespective of their actual identity, separating symbolic representation of trust from the actual person.

The platform supports the SSL protocol to encrypt the application data in transmission. The communication of critical data takes place over https protocol enabled by SSL. The platform manages the keys and digital certificates. For mission critical solution like e-commerce, the keys management and distribution are handled by PKI infrastructure.

The platform providing security services to applications needs to be configured, extended and used as per requirement. Application security is achieved in following steps:

1- Configuration of security server
   a- Business roles are defined
   b- Security constraints for the web resources are created
   c- Web component authentication for the web modules are defined

      d- Security constraints are defined and roles are assigned to them

      e- Delegation role policy are defined

      f- Roles to users are assigned

2- Valid digital certificates are presented by the client in order to assess the integrity, non-repudiation and confidentiality.

3- The SSL protocol is enabled for data encryption accessed over HTTPS protocol

4- User registry of client's operating system is also used to authenticate the users/groups contained in system repository.

5- The security cache timeout is set generally to several minutes.

6- The security application attached with business application takes care of authenticating the user for first time and placing the single sign on (SSO) token in cookie.

7- The business validation components guarantee that business components are compliant to principles, guidelines, rules and laws.

The core system must reside in Demilitarized Zone (DMZ), where the open ports must be controlled with firewalls. The security software like anti-virus, anti-spyware etc. should protect the system. The system must be prevented from hacking, cracking or any kind of intrusion.

The business must be able to continue its operations even after normal foreseen external and internal hindrance to system. The system must provide the mechanism like fail-over, fault tolerance etc. The efficiency of system should be kept optimal even at heavy business activities. The core system must be cloned and supported with multiple servers to provide fail-over and ensure 100% availability in case of interruptions. The critical data are supported with clusters and guaranteed persistence.

System should have proper workload management (WLM) features so that the request for computation is dispatched only to healthy clone. The efficiency, reliability and health of server are assessed by WLM by checking the resources like CPU, memory, network etc.

The infrastructure should be available as service in form of cloud to be effectively used by process to optimize the usage of resources and ensure timely delivery of service to users.

4.5 Data Management System

Data management services makes the enterprise data set secured, accessible, shared, consistent, fault tolerant, persisted and essentially delivers interface of service to clients. Besides achieving logical unification, singularity, centralization, it is required to deliver the core data, transformed functional data in a uniform secured way across the organization.

Enterprise Repository (ER) is an enterprise data container which logically centralizes the core data of enterprise fulfilling the data principles and provides the accessibility of data through data service to valid user and application.

The guiding design principle of ER is to identify and implement a basic smallest granular unit of data service fulfilling the service-orientation principles.

Data management includes an intelligent background agent which administrates ER with predefined logic. The ER is equipped with sophisticated service & message broker supported with event based processing which makes it intelligent and efficient.

The services of ER interact through efficient service-broker to constitute a complex service to be consumed by client. The availability of broker with service architecture makes it possible to provide accessibility to the entity, contained in ER physically or logically. The metadata of entity provides the information of type and structure of entity.

The enterprise service bus (ESB) is used for designing and implementing the interaction and communication between mutually interacting application and services in SOA environment. ESB assures the enterprise application integration and service integration though a common interface to all available services.

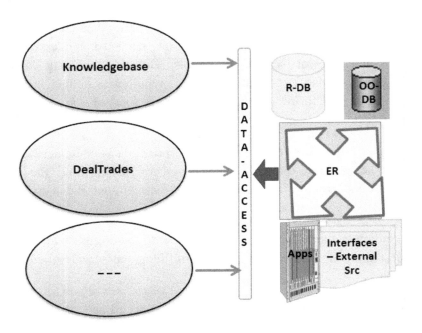

Figure 4.6: © HBS, Enterprise Repository

The services of ER could be implemented in any technology using Web-Services, CORBA, DCOM, etc. but the open specification of services should be fulfilled. The service broker could be implemented or used from third-party in any technology so that service interaction is automated and event based processing makes the resources efficient.

4.6 Enterprise Integration

Enterprise Service Bus

Enterprise Service Bus (ESB) acts as mediators between service provider and service consumer, decoupling and resolving the difference in protocols and format for simplified message exchange. ESB generally provides an abstraction layer on top of enterprise messaging system. The main task of ESB is to monitor, control and facilitate the routing of message exchange between services. In our approach, application is designed as choreographed service which is built by invoking many granular or other choreographed services via ESB.

The service broker of ESB provides a methodology to integrate the services and make them interoperable to be used in applications. Service broker provides the directory services to help locate the published service to be consumed by the client.

The consolidated services of business functionalities and data are accessed through a single point of contact provided by ESB. The Enterprise Application Integration (EAI) is also simplified by ESB where the interoperable and autonomous services are used across internal and external applications accessed through ESB.

In our approach, application is designed as choreographed service which is built by invoking many granular or other choreographed services via ESB.

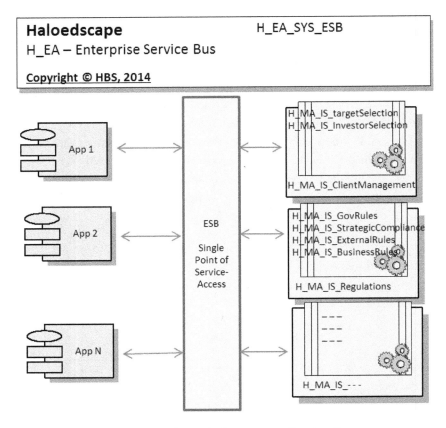

Figure 4.7: © HBS, Enterprise Service Bus

Enterprise Application Integration

Enterprise Application Integration (EAI) is achieved at various levels as follows:

Data integration – Core data in form of enterprise data services accessed from enterprise repository through enterprise service bus achieves the enterprise wide data integration.

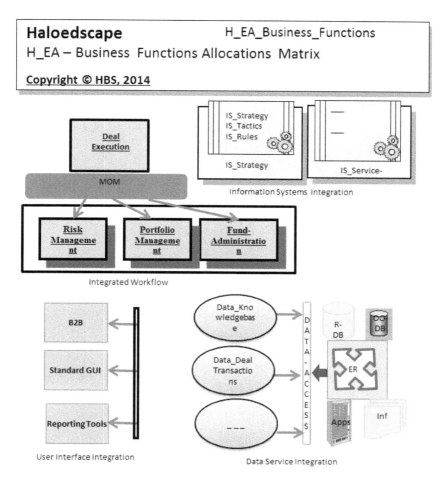

Figure 4.8: © HBS, Levels of Enterprise Integration

Functional Integration – The business functionalities transformed into IT services are accessible from any valid client (user or system).

UI Integration – The user interface could be integrated to any standard client where the send and receive (get and post) operations are available. Access to application can be facilitated to standard client or directly to external application for further processing.

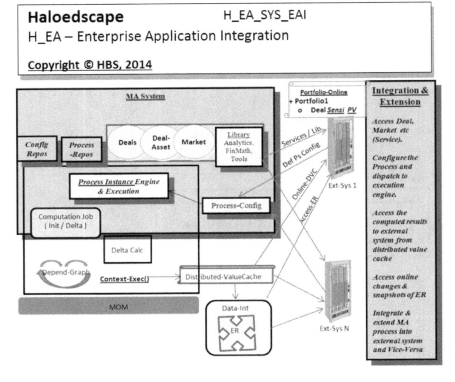

Figure 4.9: © HBS, Enterprise Application Integration

Workflow automation – The isolated modules of middle-office and back-office like risk-management and fund administration respectively are integrated with front-office activities like deal-execution with straight through processing.

System integration: Different systems are integrated with each other to use mutual capabilities. The strongest level of integration is the system integration which makes the platform interoperable. The system integration is only possible, if bottom-level system protocol is interoperable like J2EE based system accessing CORBA objects using RMI over IIOP.

Process of system integration could be viewed like - an external authorized system configures the process and sends the requests directly to computation engine of internal system. The computed results are accessed online via distributed value-cache or the snapshots are accessed from enterprise-repository for further processing.

> *External system, if authorized can access complete information system services and enterprise repository to achieve system integration. In similar way, an external system possessing information system services can be accessed from systems. This way, an integrated information system combining various IT-systems can be achieved.*
>
> *The components of system should be supported with right platform so that components remain interoperable on various systems.*
>
> *Information system and applications of system should be supported with technology like service platform, ESB, events framework, messaging system and distributed computing environment delivered by platform to achieve strongest level of enterprise integration.*

4.7   Platform for Real-Time Computation

As discussed earlier, business needs that application possesses the real-time delta computation capability.

The real-time computation is a mechanism to trigger a process when an event occurs. Real-time process   is an efficient way to compute only for the required changes in functionality dependent on events but the whole functionality is not processed again which is already computed earlier.

Real-time delta calculation is revolutionary capability of sophisticated middleware which achieves computational efficiency and effectiveness avoiding the redundant (repeated) computation.

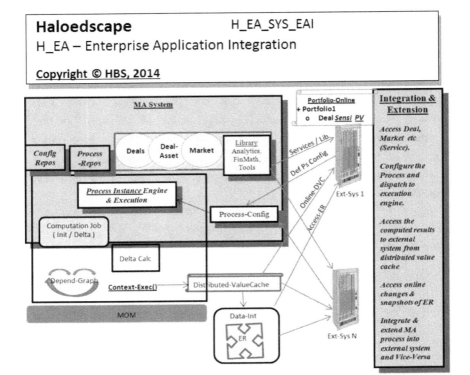

Figure 4.10: © HBS, Real-time Computational Architecture

Delta computation is transaction based, either whole process succeeds to be committed or whole process is rolled back if failure occurs, that ensures the consistent data and synchronized process. The delta computation of application is supported with event based message/object oriented middleware so that proper subscription and notification for event could be handled with calculation graph of process.

Real-time computation requires transaction services from platform. Platform should also provide event based message and object oriented middleware to the applications to implement the delta computation so that subscription and notification for event could be implemented.

4.8 STP Workflow

Straight through processing (STP) enables automation of different dependent processes belonging to separated business functions which are executed in sequential order. The functionalities like deal-execution, risk-management and performance-management are integrated together using straight through processing workflow.

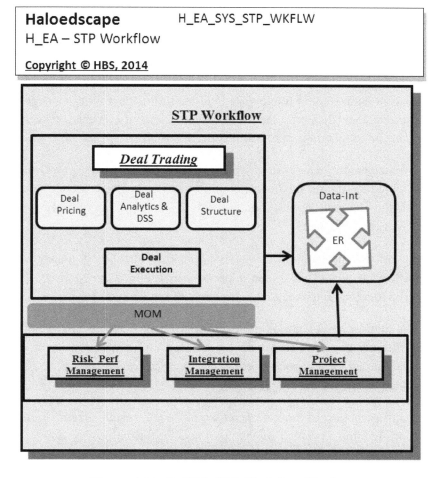

Figure 4.11: © HBS, STP Workflow Platform

Workflow patterns, parallel split and synchronization are used to implement the straight through processing for optimal efficiency.

> *The automation of workflow is achieved through event based message oriented middleware where the middle and back office functionalities subscribe to the event manager to get the notifications for the event like new/changed deal.*

Event Management Framework

The event management framework facilitates a logical tool to manage the events in four different layers - business activity events, workflow events, communication events and system events.

The management of workflow is handled at top level where workflow is configured to support the business activities. The business activity events are identified and appropriately used to manage the workflow for different functionalities.

The workflow automation of isolated business functions is managed by workflow events. The business process and interactive activities are ordered together and executed in the form of workflow.

At the platform and technology level, the workflow events are managed. The filtered messages sent with topic-based and content-based models are facilitated. The process collaboration and orchestration are also provided to integrate the interaction.

The infrastructure at bottom level handles the system events besides supporting the events of technology, information systems and applications. The events are physically managed by infrastructure which provides the complete physical computational resources for the events management.

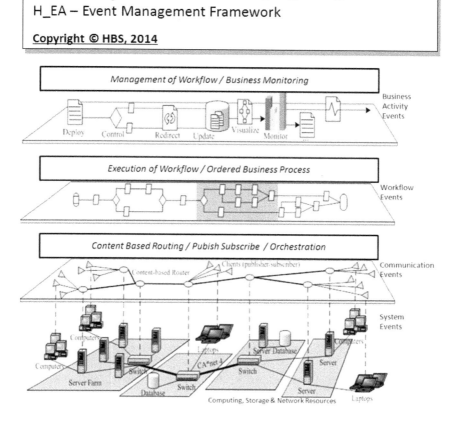

Figure 4.12: © HBS, Events Management Framework

The business activity events are the events which affect the dependent business function and require some action. The change of events like market-prices and new transaction affect the pricing and valuation which is automated with delta computation.

The business activity events like execution of new deal or change in deal are workflow events because these events are used to integrate the isolated business functions of back-office like risk management and compliance.

4.9 Enterprise Application Server

Enterprise Application Server (EAS) provides a platform to implement the server side application which serves the clients. The application server acts as a set of components accessible to developers to implement the required application through API defined by platform.

The application server should be capable of exposing the remote resource as distributed enterprise components in form of service accessible across the enterprise.

EAS should provide the support for protocol RPC, IIOP and HTTP so that the components could communicate together on various platforms for enterprise integration. The user interface could be designed in thick client mode or standardized thin client. The model-view-controller architecture pattern for their separation is also supported by platform.

There is variety of services provided by EAS to support realization of information system and applications. These services are:

Security Services- EAS provides the security services for authentication, authorization and encryption. SSL protocol is enabled to support the communication over HTTPS.

Directory services – The directory services are provided to discover and lookup the data and objects via logical name.

Database services – It provides connectivity with several databases for data persistency.

Session Services – The session is maintained between client and server so that the stateful or stateless session can be managed for interactive process of applications.

Transaction Services - Some of the process requires the transaction services where complete process succeeds or it completely rollbacks if failure occurs.

There are some mechanisms embedded in EAS to support the security and availability for critical applications.

Availability - The EAS delivers a feature to clone the complete enterprise application so that it could be available even if one of the clones dies and lost abruptly due to internal or external interruptions. The complete session of lost clone is shifted to another clone without any inconsistency in data or process.

Security – The EAS could be placed inside DMZ so that open ports can be controlled and the system is protected from hacking.

Tracing and Monitoring – The complete process running on EAS can be traced and the computing resources can be monitored online.

An instance of EAS mentioned above, is J2EE application server which provides the services and support for the required applications.

J2EE Application Server

J2EE application server is most sophisticated application server used for development of enterprise applications world-wide.

In J2EE application server, EJB container provides an entity (Java Bean) as distributed enterprise object whereas web container is used as controller with servlets and for generating the user interface with JSP.

The Model-View-Controller (MVC) architecture pattern could easily be implemented by separating the JSPs, servlets and EJBs. J2EE EAS provides servlet engine to compile JSPs and present the UI on standardized thin client. The server application could also be connected using thick client.

J2EE application server supports the communication protocol like RMI, IIOP, HTTP.

Some of important services provided by J2EE application server are:-

JMS – Java Message Service (JMS) provides message service which integrates the message oriented middleware with the system.

JNDI – The JNDI API provides the naming and directory services. JNDI discovers and lookup objects with a name which acts as object reference.

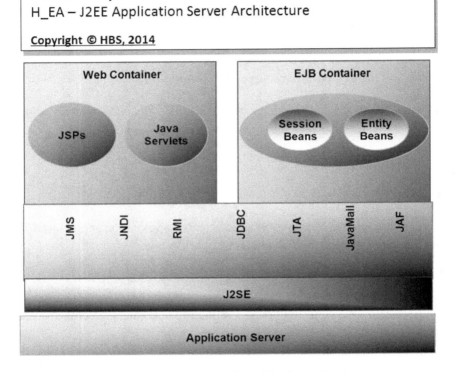

Figure 4.13: © HBS, J2EE Platform Services

RMI – Java API that provides the object-oriented distributed computing equivalent to Remote Procedure Call (RPC). RMI over IIOP supports integration with CORBA implementation.

JDBC – Java API to connect to relational databases for querying and updating the data.

JTA – Java Transaction API that facilitates transactions across multiple

X/Open XA resources in distributed computing.

JavaMail – Java API to send and receive email via SMTP, POP3 and IMAP.

JAF – JavaBeans Activation Framework is a dynamic framework to determine the type of data and operations permitted on it which leads to instantiation of appropriate bean to perform required operation.

J2EE provides the complete security with Java security technology using Java Cryptography Architecture (JCA), Java Security Architecture (JSA), Java Authentication and Authorization Service (JAAS), Java Secure Socket Extension (JSSE), Java SASL etc.

The features like cloning for availability, monitoring for performance tuning, tracing for troubleshooting etc. are also provided in J2EE application server.

4.10 Enterprise System Architecture

Architecture of System

At the bottom level, a broker ORB supports the communication and information exchange between client and server, communicating over IIOP protocol, which is an implementation of abstract GIOP. IIOP is a CORBA network protocol residing in ORB that makes CORBA client interact with CORBA distributed objects.

Above IT protocol layer, there is financial protocol which makes the financial product and events consistent across the industry. One of instances of financial protocol is Financial Products Markup Language (FpML) which is an XML based financial message standard for the OTC derivatives industry in domain of investment banking. FpML standardizes financial product content and its structure besides simplifying and integrating the complete workflow for downstream processing system by making the financial product enterprise-wide and externally consistent.

Server side platform possesses enterprise application servers where enterprise applications are deployed.

Our innovative platform possesses the mix of CORBA and J2EE to fulfill the requirement and achieve the business objective in efficient and effective manner. The pricing engine, simulations, decision support and analytics are supported with CORBA platform whereas portfolio management, risk reports etc. are supported with J2EE platform.

The enterprise applications for J2EE platform is essentially an Enterprise Application Archive (EAR) file which contains JSP, servlets and EJBs providing the UI, distributed objects, controller and web-services. The server implementation of CORBA for pricing, analytics and decision-support are programmed in C++ to achieve high performance. J2EE and CORBA components are interoperable due to accessibility of RMI over IIOP.

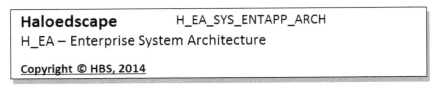

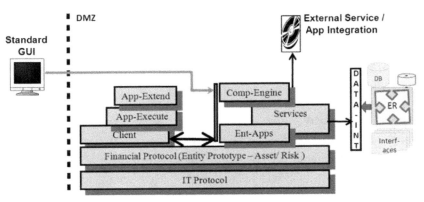

Figure 4.14: © HBS, Enterprise System Architecture

Information system is constituted of functional services and enterprise data services. Enterprise repository facilitates the core data required by information systems services. The ESB provides a central point to access different services from information system.

Enterprise-application configures and parameterizes, accesses the information system services and extends it with individual business-unit specific requirements. The platform provides the computational engine to compute the enterprise application in an efficient manner.

To keep up with high performance, analytical requirement and wide access of application, both modes of client - thick and thin are supported.

Thick clients can execute the complete enterprise application locally and extend or change the application for analytical purpose locally. This is Extend-App-Locally (EAL) feature of our approach which we find necessary in investment banking for complex analysis and testing which reduces the Time-To-Market (TTM).

Note that the client extended-application (EAL) is not an enterprise application and is not deployed in production; that means extended-application (EAL) is not supported with our platform capabilities of security, availability, integration etc. Client extended-application (EAL) is only for complex analysis and testing purpose which is essential in automation of financial industry like investment banking to sustain the dynamic requirements of customer and market.

There is also a support of thin client which can interface with enterprise application where whole application is accessed on web based browser. The web server delivers the web content that can be accessed by HTTP client through internet. The web server is configured to link with J2EE based application server so that whole application is transformed into web based solution allowing users to access the application from anywhere.

Our innovative platform possesses the capabilities of CORBA, MQ and J2EE to fulfill the strategic requirements of high performance IT solution to enable the business objectives in efficient and effective manner.

Our platform empowered with sophisticated technology supports and enables the required information system and applications.

Our system architecture shows that there is support for both thick and thin clients. Thick clients are provided for running the application locally and extending/changing it for complex analysis and testing. HTTP based thin client provide the accessibility of enterprise application from anywhere.

Business Platform Services

An enterprise platform is one which provides the services to fulfill the requirements of whole enterprise for its automation.

An enterprise platform is infrastructure resources delivering the computational technology to support the automation of whole enterprise in an efficient, effective and sophisticated manner which achieves highest ROI on medium and long run.

Some important services provided by platform are as follows:

Vertical Services to Applications & Information Systems:

- Communication services: The communication required by applications and information system should be supported by platform. The interoperability of business process is achieved with support of different protocols like RMI, IIOP, SOAP, HTTP etc.
- Connectivity services: The application and information system services need technical services to connect to databases, message queues, services, distributed objects etc.

- Security Services: The application and information system needs the security services to implement the authentication, authorization and encryption. The sophisticated public-private key cryptography and PKI are also provided by platform.

Workflow Services:

- Content Management Services (CMS): Application manages the contents from central interface besides managing the workflow in collaborative environment with the help of CMS.
- Collaboration Services: Application needs the collaboration support that enables group of isolated activities work together such as social networking, messaging, team space, web sharing etc.
- Orchestration of Services: These services are automated arrangement, coordination and management of business processes, services and computing platform. There are different levels of orchestration. Orchestration of inter-company business process is effectiveness of business process whereas cloud computing orchestration achieves effectiveness of infrastructure.

Application's User Interface Services:

- Enterprise Information Portal (EIP): EIP is a framework for integrating the information, processes across organizational boundaries which are accessed by valid users with simplified and centralized access point. EIP also aggregates and personalizes information for specific user and application.
- User Interface Integration: Application should support any client that fulfills the basic operation (like get & post). User interface should be loosely-coupled so that user gets the freedom to decide upon any appropriate client. One application can integrate another application by implementing basic get & put operation inside a component without any visualization which is named as Business-2-Business integration.

Platform Services for Information Systems & Applications:

- Transaction Services: Execution of different statements which needs to be processed as indivisible atomic operation is transaction. The deal execution and notification to subscribers are implemented with transaction services so that either whole operation succeeds or whole operation is rolled back in case of failure.

- Messaging Services: Business automation is heavily dependent upon messaging services to implement delta computation and automated workflow.

- Distributed Component Services: Platform provides distributed environment where distributed entity is exposed as an enterprise object to be used in different applications. The Object oriented middleware facilitates this capability to applications. Distributed objects are computational representation of business functionality.

- Events management Framework: Innovative hybrid model of messaging based on events is required by business functions to implement an efficient implementation.

- Directory: Organizing and providing access to directory acts as naming service provided by platform which is used by application to locate the distributed objects and access it.

- Service Platform: Platform provides the capabilities to applications and information system to expose the enterprise functional and data entity as service.

- Enterprise Service Bus (ESB): A broker provided by platform facilitates central access point to consolidated services and manages the service interoperability and communication. ESB is important component to achieve enterprise application integration.

- Distributed Computing Environment: Platform provides the distributed computing environment which manages the communication and distributed objects and services to support applications.

Infrastructure Services:

- Scheduling: The process threads, data flows are given access to system resources by scheduling method provided by platform. Scheduling optimizes the usage of system in order to increase the availability of system.

- Pooling: A set of initialized resources that are kept ready for use so that performance of system could be increased. Optimal performance is achieved when client receives an object from pool, performs operations that it needs and returns the object back to pool rather than destroying it. Platform provides pooling mechanism to achieve better performance. Resource caching is commonly used like connection pool, thread pool, memory pool etc.

- Clustering and Cloning: Clusters are a set of loosely coupled computers which act as logically single system to achieve fail-over and availability in distributed computing of mission-critical applications. Cloning is supported by platform to replicate the whole application so that if a session dies at one system due to some interruption, the complete session is shifted to another clone to complete the processing successfully. Cloning achieves fail-over to increase availability of mission-critical applications.

- Cloud Services: Infrastructure is logically accessed as service by the applications so that optimal usage of infrastructure is accomplished.

J2EE – An ideal Enterprise Platform

An instance of enterprise platform is J2EE platform which provides the services to automate the functionalities of whole enterprise in effective and sophisticated manner.

The vertical communication services of J2EE platform support several protocols (like HTTP, SOAP, RMI, IIOP etc.) for communication and interoperability.

The vertical connectivity services of J2EE for information system and application are JDBC, Web-Services client, Message bridges etc.

At the top level, J2EE provides the business intelligence, personal information management to application.

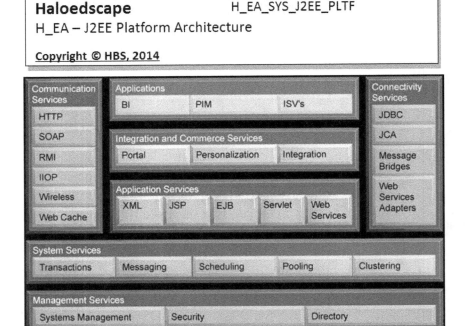

Figure 4.15: © HBS, J2EE Platform Components Architecture

The application's client services of J2EE are portal and personalization. The client could be JSP, servlet, standalone swing or any other bean of application which sends the request and receives the response, which is used for further processing in external application, as in case of B2B integration.

Platform provides the XML technology for inter-platform message services, JSP for client development, EJB container for distributed objects, servlet-engine for controller/user-interface and web services platform.

The system services provided to applications are transaction, messaging, security and directory services.

The infrastructural services are scheduling, pooling, clustering and cloning.

> *Most sophisticated enterprise platform is J2EE which provides full-fledged services, technology and support for automation of different business functions of whole enterprise effectively.*

4.11 Conclusion - Platform and Technology Architecture

To develop the platform and technology architecture, TOGAF's framework is extended to combine the various frameworks and technologies to acquire sophisticated IT Platform which could support IT solution for business.

Technology and infrastructural principles provide the directions and guidelines for selecting and acquiring a suitable platform.

As next, middleware platform is discussed in detail which delivers service platform for SOA, most important aspects of enterprise architecture. SOA is revolutionary architecture style ensuring business aligned agile IT leading to most effective enterprise IT solution. Service platform architecture shows provider publishing loosely-coupled, distributed services for consumers mediated through service broker. Security service delivered by middleware makes the applications and whole enterprise secured from internal and external threat. Selected platform delivers authentication, authorization, cryptography, and secured communication. Platform also provides availability with fail-over and tuned resources for efficiency.

Core enterprise data stored logically in enterprise repository are supported with service bus to fetch the data from central access point in form of data-services, where ESB based service broker acts as mediator between provider and consumer.

Enterprise Application Integration was described which addresses different levels of integration.

- The enterprise data accessed from enterprise repository through enterprise services achieves the enterprise wide data integration.
- The business functions transformed into IT services residing in information system are accessible from any enterprise wide applications achieving functional integration.
- Access to application can be facilitated to standard client or directly to external application (B2B) for further processing.
- The isolated functions of middle-office and back-office like risk-management and project-administration respectively are integrated with front-office activities like deal-execution with straight through processing
- Enterprise Service Bus (ESB) provides an abstraction layer on top of messaging system. Different applications access the different services through central point of access managed by ESB. Application is designed as choreographed service which invokes other information system based services via ESB.

Real-time computation is a mechanism to trigger a process when an event occurs, which achieves computational non-redundancy. Real-time computation capability of business is supported with event based message/object oriented middleware so that proper subscription and notification for event could be handled with calculation graph of process.

Platform Architecture is presented in this chapter which mentions the consolidated technical services and capabilities delivered to IT solution.

Platform should deliver distributed computing environment, ESB, EAI, STP and service oriented capabilities to applications.

Client/server based distributed architecture is supported on IT and financial protocol. Applications access functional services from information system which fetches data from enterprise repository in form of service through service-bus. An innovative approach of Extend-App-Locally (EAL) feature is also described which is required in investment banking for complex analysis and testing leading to significant reduction of time to market (TTM).

Enterprise platform delivers the services and support for communication, connectivity, security, workflow, user-interface, transaction, messaging, events, directory and distributed computing. The infrastructure services include scheduling, pooling, clustering, cloning and cloud services. J2EE platform is open-standard, most successful enterprise platform which delivers all of enterprise services and capabilities to support the information system and applications.

Information system and applications are supported with platform possessing required technology, so that IT solution acquires the enterprise characteristics and strategic capabilities.

With this much in this book, we have specified, and illustrated "focused Enterprise Architecture" aligned with "Business & IT Strategy" leading to an efficient, effective, and sophisticated IT-Solution for enabling business services to achieve business objectives.

5 Appendix - UML

Unified Modeling Language (UML) is a standardized (ISO/IEC 19501:2005), general-purpose modeling language for specifying, constructing, and documenting the artifacts of systems in the field of software engineering. The Unified Modeling Language includes a set of graphic notation techniques to create visual models of object-oriented software-intensive systems for all application domains and implementation platforms.

UML Relationships

UML relationships are grouped into the following categories:

Category	Function
Activity edges	Represent the flow between activities
Associations	Indicate that instances of one model element are connected to instances of another model element
Dependencies	Indicate that a change to one model element can affect another model element
Generalizations	Indicate that one model element is a specialization of another model element
Realizations	Indicate that one model element provides a specification that another model element implements
Transitions	Represent changes in state

Generalization

The Generalization relationship ("is a") indicates that one of the two related classes (the subclass) is considered to be a specialized form of the other (the super type) and superclass is considered as 'Generalization' of subclass. In practice, this means that any instance of the subtype is also an instance of the superclass.

Here in diagram above, B as a child inherits from parent A. B is sub class and A is super class. Generalization is also called inheritance.

Association

In UML models, an association is a relationship between two classifiers, such as classes or use cases, that describes the reasons for the relationship and the rules that govern the relationship.

An association represents a family of links. Binary associations (with two ends) are normally represented as a line. An association can be named, and the ends of an association can be adorned with role names, ownership indicators, multiplicity, visibility, and other properties.

There are four different types of association: bi-directional, uni-directional, Aggregation (includes Composition aggregation) and Reflexive. Bi-directional and uni-directional associations are the most common ones.

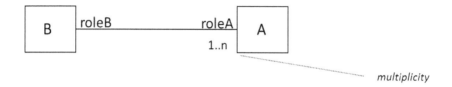

The association relationship indicates that (at least) one of the two related classes makes reference to the other. In contrast with the generalization relationship, this is most easily understood through the phrase ' A has a B' (a mother cat has kittens, kittens have a mother cat). In the diagram depicted above can be explained as one or many As have 0 or 1 B.

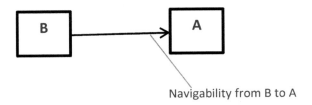

Navigability from B to A

In the diagram above, A is navigable from B – that means, if we are at instance B then we can reach to instance A. In terms of entity-relatinship, it is correspoding to say that account entity (class B) finds its customer (class A) using foreign key of customer embedded in account. The navigability from A to B is not specified. If at B, we attach a cross instead of arrow then it is corresponding to say that B is not navigable from A.

The UML representation of an association is a line with an optional arrowhead indicating the role of the object(s) in the relationship, and an optional notation at each end indicating the multiplicity of instances of that entity (the number of objects that participate in the association). A directed association indicates that control flows from one classifier to another; for example an actor to a use case. This flow of control means that only one of the association ends specifies navigability.

Aggregation

In UML, an aggregation relationship shows a classifier as a part of or subordinate to another classifier attached with unfilled diamond diagram.

Aggregation is a variant of the "has a" association relationship; aggregation is more specific than association. It is an association that represents a part-whole or part-of relationship. As a type of association, an aggregation can be named and have the same adornments that an association can. However, an aggregation may not involve more than two classes.

Here in diagram above, B is the the aggregate i.e. acts as parent class for child class A.

As an exmaple, B can be thought of as a class Company and A as class Department implying that company has embedded inside one or many department/s. That is, A (Department) is a part of B (Company). In other words, B has A. Here class B (Company) represents the aggregate which is a single point of control for subordinate class A (department).

Aggregation can occur when a class is a collection or container of other classes, but where the contained classes do not have a strong life cycle dependency on the container—essentially, if the container is destroyed, its contents are not.

Composition

A composition association relationship represents a whole–part relationship and is a form of aggregation. A composition association relationship specifies that the lifetime of the part classifier is dependent on the lifetime of the whole classifier.

Composition usually has a strong life cycle dependency between instances of the container class and instances of the contained class(es): If the container is destroyed, normally every instance that it contains is destroyed as well. (Note that, where allowed, a part can be removed from a composite before the composite is deleted, and thus not be deleted as part of the composite.)

Here in diagram, A is a subordinate class contained in conatiner class B. As an example, B can be though of class Book which has one or many class Chapters (class A). Lifespan of instance of Chapters is dependent upon instnace of Book.

Composition is a stronger variant of the "owns a" association relationship; composition is more specific than aggregation.

Dependency or Instantiation

In UML, a dependency relationship is a relationship in which one element, the client, uses or depends on another element, the supplier. Dependency is a weaker form of relationship which indicates that one class depends on another because it uses it at some point in time.

One class depends on another if the independent class is a parameter variable or local variable of a method of the dependent class. This is different from an association, where an attribute of the dependent class is an instance of the independent class.

In the above diagram, instantiation relatinship indicates that B instatiates A whereas dependency diagram shows that B depends on A.

Reference:

Object Management Group: http://www.omg.org/spec/UML/2.0/; http://www.omg.org/spec/UML/2.4.1/Superstructure/PDF/ IBM: http://www-01.ibm.com/software/rational/uml/

6 Appendix - BPMM

Refer the original source of Object Management Group (OMG) for details:

The Business Motivation Model (BMM) in enterprise architecture provides a scheme and structure for developing, communicating, and managing business plans in an organized manner. Specifically, the Business Motivation Model does all of the following:

i)   identifies factors that motivate the establishing of business plans;

ii)   identifies and defines the elements of business plans; and

iii)   indicates how all these factors and elements inter-relate.

BMM captures business requirements across different dimensions to rigorously capture and justify why the business wants to do something, what it is aiming to achieve, how it plans to get there, and how it assesses the result.

The main elements of BMM are:

- Ends: What (as oppose to how) the business wants to accomplish
- Means: How the business intends to accomplish its ends
- Directives: The rules and policies that constrain or govern the available means
- Influencers: Can cause changes that affect the organization in its employment of its Means or achievement of its Ends. Influencers are neutral by definition.
- Assessment: A judgment of an Influencer that affects the organization's ability to achieve its Ends or use its Means.

Refer Business Motivation Model V 1.1- Object Management Group (OMG)

Elements of Business Motivation Model

1- End

An End is something that business sells to accomplish. This will be categorized into Vision, Goal and Objectives.

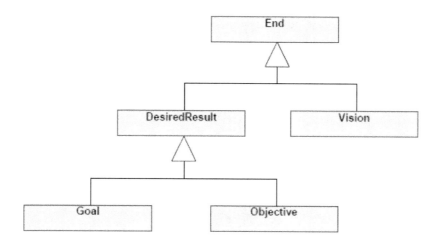

End concepts in BMM (OMG)

Vision / Ends: Vision describes future state of enterprise without regard to how it is achieved. Vision or End is the ultimate state the enterprise would like to achieve.

Goal: A Goal is state or condition of enterprise to be brought about or sustained through appropriate Means. A Goal amplifies the Vision. In contrast to objectives, goals are of longer term, qualitative, general and continuous concept. A Goal is narrow-focused vision quantified by Objectives.

Objectives: Objectives are more specific, time-targeted, attainable and measurable statements in order to achieve Goals.

Means:

A Means represents any device, capability, regime, technique, restriction, agency, instrument, or method that may be called upon, activated, or enforced to achieve Ends. Remember that a Means does not indicate either the steps (business processes and workflow) necessary to exploit it, nor responsibility for such tasks, but rather only the capabilities that can be exploited to achieve the desired Ends.

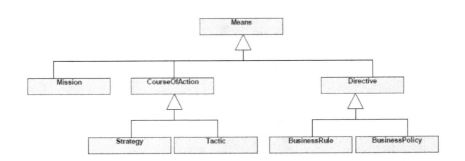

Means of BMM - OMG

Course of Actions:

A Course of Action is an approach or plan for configuring some aspect of the enterprise involving things, processes, locations, people, timing, or motivation undertaken to achieve Desired Results. In other words, a Course of Action channels efforts towards Desired Results. To help ensure success in this regard, Courses of Action are governed by Directives.

One Course of Action can include other Courses of Action. One Course of Action can be enabled by another Course of Action.

Strategy:

A Strategy represents the essential Course of Action to achieve Ends (Goals in particular). A Strategy usually channels efforts towards those Goals.

A Strategy is more than simply a resource, skill, or competency that the enterprise can call upon; rather, a Strategy is accepted by the enterprise as the right approach to achieve its Goals, given the environmental constraints and risks.

Tactic:

A Tactic is a Course of Action that represents part of the detailing of Strategies. A Tactic implements Strategies.

Directive:

Directive governs Courses of Action. It defines or constrains or liberates some aspects of enterprise. Directives are categorized into Business Policies and Business Rule.

Asset & Liability:

Some Fixed Assets provide Resources in the form of capacity over time (for example, production equipment, storage buildings, skills possessed by people). The Resources they provide are either consumed, or are dissipated as time passes without their being used.

Offerings (specifications of products and services) may use intangible Fixed Assets, such as designs, licenses, patents, and brands. An Offering requires Resources (materials, equipment capacity, people's time) for production of things that meet the specification.

A Liability claims Resources (it reserves resources needed to meet commitments), which means that the resources cannot be used for other purposes.

Figure 8.22 illustrates connection of Asset and Liability to the rest of the Model.

Courses of Action (COA):

• COA deploys Assets: determine how Assets will be assigned and used in realizing the Courses of Action.

• COA defines Offerings, the products and services that can be supplied by the enterprise.

• COA discharges Liabilities: ensure that commitments are met.

A Directive may govern use of Assets, regardless of which Courses of Action deploy them.

Other placeholders may be associated with Assets and Liabilities. Business Processes may

• COA delivers Offerings

• COA manages Assets

An Organization Unit may be responsible for Assets and/or Liabilities

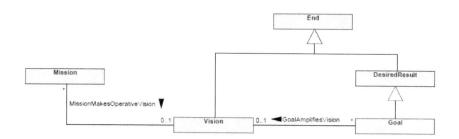

End – Vision - Goal

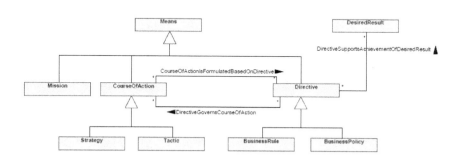

Interrelating Directives with Courses of Actions and Ends

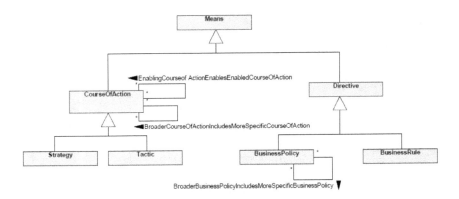

Means: Course of action & Directives of BMM

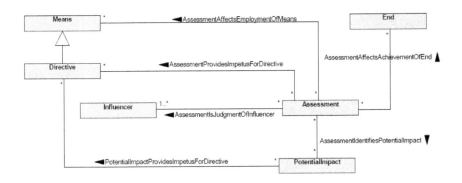

Assessment & Directive of BMM

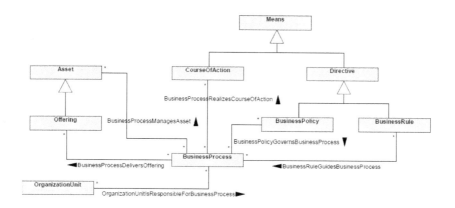

BMM association with Business Process

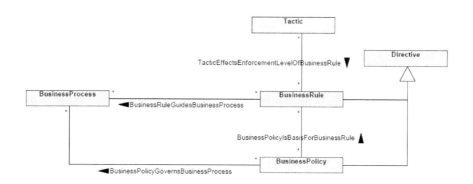

Business Rule of BMM

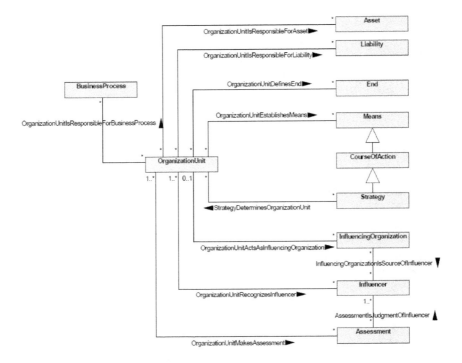

Organizational unit of BMM

References:

- Object Management Group www.bpmn.org

- Business Rules Group: http://www.businessrulesgroup.org/

- http://www.ibm.com/developerworks/rational/library/08/040 1_amsden/

- Documents Associated with Business Process Motivation Model (BPMM) Version 1.1 : http://www.omg.org/spec/BMM/1.1/

7 Appendix - BPMN

Refer the original source of Object Management Group (OMG) for details:

Business Process Modeling Notation (BPMN) provides the capability of defining and understanding the internal and external business procedures through a Business Process Diagram (BPD). Business Process Model (BPM) is used to describe business process, workflow, orchestration of services, collaboration, choreography etc.

The goal of the BPMN effort is to provide a notation that is readily understandable by all business users that create the initial drafts of the processes to the technical developers responsible for implementing the technology that will perform those processes.

BPMN defines a Business Process Diagram (BPD), which is based on a flowcharting technique meant for creating graphical models of business process operations. A Business Process Model (BPM) is a network of graphical objects, which are activities and the flow controls that define their conditional order of performance.

The Business Process Management Initiative (BPMI) has developed a standard Business Process Modeling Notation (BPMN). The ontology used in BPM is vendor-neutral, globally accepted based on open standards and global interoperability.

The five basic categories of elements to describe process are:

   i)   Flow objects

    o   Events, Activities , Gateways

ii) Data

    o   Data objects, Inputs, outputs & stores

iii) Connecting Objects (4 ways of connecting the flow objects)

    o   Sequence flows, Message flows, Associations, Data Associations

iv) Swimlanes

    o   Pools, Lanes

v) Artifacts

    o   Group, Text annotation

Flow Objects

A BPD has a three core elements as the Flow Objects.

| Event | An Event is represented by a circle which affects the flow of the process and usually has a cause (trigger) or an impact (result). Events are circles with open centers to allow internal markers to differentiate different triggers or results. There are three types of basic events:

Start, Intermediate, and End as shown in the figures to the | ◯ ◎ ⬤ |

	right, respectively.	
Activity	An Activity is represented by a rounded-corner rectangle and is a generic term for work that company performs. An Activity can be atomic or non-atomic (compound). The types of Activities are: Task and Sub-Process.	
Gateway	A Gateway is represented by the familiar diamond shape and is used to control the divergence and convergence of sequence flow. Thus, it determines traditional decisions, as well as the forking, merging, and joining of paths. Internal Markers indicate the type of behavior control.	

Data Object

BPD has core elements for data object used to represent data objects, input / output.

Data	Data Objects provide	

Object	information about what activities require to be performed and/or what they produce. Data Objects can represent a singular object or a collection of objects. Data Input and Data Output provide the same information for Processes.	Data

Connecting Objects

The Flow Objects are connected together in a diagram to create the basic skeletal structure of a business process. There are three basic connecting objects that provide this function.

Sequence Flow	A sequence flow is represented by a solid line with a solid arrowhead and is used to show the order (the sequence) that activities will be performed in a process.	⎯⎯⎯⎯⎯▶

Message Flow	A message flow is represented by a dashed line with an open arrowhead and is used to show the flow of messages between two separate process participants (business entities or business roles) that send and receive them.	◦- - - - - - - - - - - - -▷
Association	An association is represented by a dotted line with a line arrowhead and is used to associate data, text, and other artifacts with flow objects. Associations are used to show the inputs and outputs of activities.	·················>

Swimlanes

Swimlanes are used to organize activities into separate categories in order to illustrate different functional capabilities or responsibilities. BPMN supports swimlanes with two main elements as follows:

Pool	A pool represents a participant in a process	

	from a context distinguished from other shown in different pool. Pool also acts as a graphical container for partitioning a set of activities.	Name
Lane	A lane is a sub-partition within a pool and extends the entire length of the pool. Lanes are used to organize and categorize activities.	Name Name / Name Name

Artifacts

BPMN allows modelers and tools some flexibility in extending the basic notation and in providing the ability to additional context appropriate to a specific modeling situation, such as for a vertical market (e.g., insurance or banking). Any number of Artifacts can be added to a diagram as appropriate for the context of the business processes being modeled.

Data Object	Data objects are a mechanism to show how data is required or produced by activities. They are connected to activities through associations.	Name [State]

Group	A group is represented by a rounded corner rectangle drawn with a dashed line. The grouping can be used for documentation or analysis purposes, but does not affect the sequence flow.	
Annotation	Annotations are a mechanism for a modeler to provide additional text information to the reader of a BPM diagram.	Text Annotation Allows a Modeler to provide additional Information

Extended Elements

Events: An Event is something that happens during the course of a business process. Events affect the flow of the process and usually have a trigger or a result. Events can start, interrupt, or end the flow. An extended sets of events are as folows:-

Events

Start	Intermediate	End
◯	◎	⬤

Event Types

	Start	Intermediate	End
Message	✉	✉	✉
Timer	🕐	🕐	
Exception		N	N
Cancel		✕	✕
Compensation		⏪	⏪
Rule	▤	▤	
Link	➡	➡	➡
Terminate			●
Multiple	✶	✶	✶

Activity

An activity is work that is performed within a business process. An activity can be atomic or non-atomic (compound). Process, sub-process, and task are the types of activities and a part of a process model.

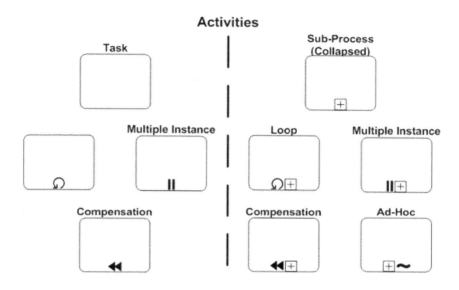

Sub-Process can be in an expanded form that shows the process details of the a lower-level set of activities.

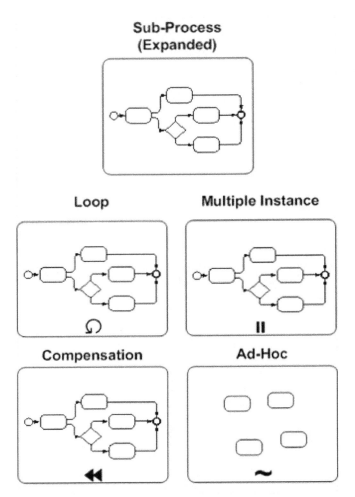

Gateways

Gateways are modeling elements that are used to control the sequence flows interaction as and when they converge and diverge within a process.

Gateways

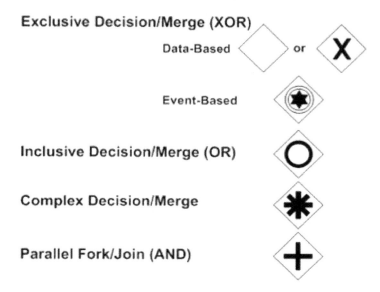

Exclusive Decision/Merge (XOR)

Data-Based ⬦ or ◇ X

Event-Based

Inclusive Decision/Merge (OR)

Complex Decision/Merge

Parallel Fork/Join (AND)

Modeling of business process by BPM - Examples

Example-1

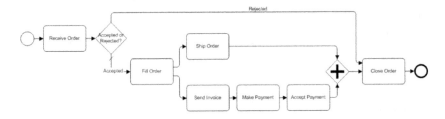

Example-2

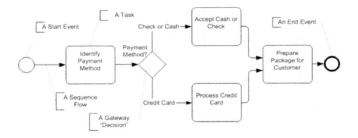

Reference

- BPMI : www.bpmi.org

- Object Management Group/Business Process Management Initiative: www.bpmn.org

- Documents Associated with Business Process Model and Notation (BPMN) Version 2.0 :
  http://www.omg.org/spec/BPMN/2.0/

8 List of Figures

Chapter 1: Strategy & Foundation of Enterprise Architecture

Chapter 3: Information System, Data & Application Architecture

Chapter 4: Platform & Technology Architecture

9 Index

Haloedscape Series – HBS

Company Overview

- **Solution Provider, Consulting, Offshore Development and Advisory Company**

- **Mission is to be global leader in strategic automation of financial industry and empower our clients to achieve competitive edge in market**

- **Provider of our own developed next-generation sophisticated and innovative financial solutions and automation frameworks supported with our own strategic middleware**

- **Our Services at all major financial locations of world. Our Significant work achievement at New York, London, Frankfurt, Singapore and Patna.**

Values Addition

- Analysis of client's requirements, design and development of solutions, consulting onsite or directly from offshore team.

- Cost savings for clients with offshore development model

- Analysis and development of Business and IT strategy to achieve Enterprise Architecture

- SOA based agile solutions to lower down the cost & risk; increase adaptability of change in customer's requirements and market condition.

- Business driven efficient and effective IT services completely aligned with business.

- End-to-end advanced and innovative solution provider right from scratch or at any phase of business function based on sophisticated frameworks and platforms.

Achieved Milestone

- Corporate & IT Strategy development framework for optimized & effective IT Foundation

- Development of next gen strategic operating model and comprehensive capability model

- Precise and Comprehensive Business Architecture development for whole Investment Banking

- **Development of simplified SOA framework for business aligned effective and efficient IT**

- **End-to-end Investment Banking Solution with Decision support & Analytics supporting the managerial actions and decision.**

- **Strategic Middleware Implementation having object, message and events based capabilities to support distributed computing for effective financial solutions**

- **Any many others …**

We deliver sophisticated and innovative solution with highest quality to cost ratio.

For any further enquiries, contact HAVES services group at: <
< haves<A~T>harappanet.com >

www.harappanet.com